ARK ENCOUNTER

# Ark Encounter

*The Making of a Creationist Theme Park*

James S. Bielo

NEW YORK UNIVERSITY PRESS

New York

NEW YORK UNIVERSITY PRESS
New York
www.nyupress.org

Library of Congress Cataloging-in-Publication Data
Names: Bielo, James S., author.
Title: Ark encounter : the making of a creationist theme park / James S. Bielo.
Description: New York : NYU Press, 2018. | Includes bibliographical references and index.
Identifiers: LCCN 2017034135 | ISBN 978-1-4798-4324-4 (cl : alk. paper) |
ISBN 978-1-4798-4279-7 (pb : alk. paper)
Subjects: LCSH: Ark Encounter (Amusement park) | Creationism—Miscellanea. |
Noah's ark—Miscellanea.
Classification: LCC BS651 .B487 2018 | DDC 222/.11093—dc23
LC record available at https://lccn.loc.gov/2017034135

New York University Press books are printed on acid-free paper, and their binding materials are chosen for strength and durability. We strive to use environmentally responsible suppliers and materials to the greatest extent possible in publishing our books.

Manufactured in the United States of America

10 9 8 7 6 5 4 3 2 1

Also available as an ebook

*For Judith S. Bielo, my mother, and her unflinching love*

# CONTENTS

LIST OF FIGURES

# Introduction

We spoke to Noah about [the Dinosaur] . . . he confessed
that in the matter of stocking the Ark the stipulations had
not been carried out with absolute strictness—that is, in minor details, unessentials. He said the boys were to blame for
this—the boys mainly, his own fatherly indulgence partly.
They were in the giddy heyday of their youth at the time, the
happy springtime of life, their hundred years sat upon them
lightly, and—well, he had been a boy himself, and he had not
the heart to be too exacting with them.[1]
—Mark Twain, "Adam's Soliloquy"

Even Mark Twain, in signature style, grappled with the Genesis story
of Noah, the Flood, the ark, and the animals. Is this a story of righteous
faith or sinful judgment, revelation or delusion? What is at stake in reading Genesis 6 through 9 as allegorical myth or literal history? Whatever
your answer, there is no mistaking that this biblical story captivates the
modern imagination.

Artistic renderings of Noah's ark date to as early as the fourth century
on the walls of Saint Peter's tomb in Italy, instigating a long tradition "in
paintings and sculpture."[2] These images have thrived alongside imaginings of plausibility. As early as the fifteenth century, a Spanish bishop
sought to explain how Noah and family accomplished the unenviable
task of disposing with all the animal waste.[3] German polymath Athana-
sius Kircher elaborated on this inquiry in the seventeenth century, cal-
culating "in exhaustive detail" the number of stalls, beasts, snakes, and
birds and "the logistics of stabling, feeding, and cleaning the animals."[4]
Such exercises in scriptural historicity helped birth modern geologic science in the eighteenth century, as some defended and others refuted why
a universal flood explains everything, anything, or nothing about the
empirical realities of our natural world.[5]

The details and imagery of the Genesis story are equally pervasive in popular culture. They are fodder for lyricists, from John Prine ("I got kicked off Noah's ark / I turn my cheek to unkind remarks / There was two of everything but one of me") to Talib Kweli ("Without the smoke in my lungs I started dreaming again / I dreamed of candy-coated cars and panties that go with bras / Hurricanes named Sandy, I'm floating on Noah's ark").[6] It is the basis for narrative films, from the romantic melodrama *Noah's Ark* (1928) to the comedy *Evan Almighty* (2007) and the dramatic blockbuster *Noah* (2014). It is the namesake for "America's largest water park" in the Wisconsin Dells and for countless animal shelters and hospitals, as well as a staple inspiration for school and church-yard play sets. Since at least the 1700s, ark-themed toy sets for children have been popular both in commercial contexts and in Sunday school classrooms.

Historians and archaeologists regularly revisit debates about local and global flood legends.[7] Compelled by the quest for historical evidence, pious and curious adventurers launch expeditions to discover physical remains of the ark in Turkey's Mount Ararat region. This activity was sparked in the 1940s, when a Seventh-Day Adventist periodical published the first story reporting an ark sighting.[8] *In Search of Noah's Ark*, a fundamentalist Christian documentary claiming to track the ark's discovery, was among the highest-grossing films of 1976. Other discoveries were claimed in subsequent years. The Wyatt Archaeological Museum—a three-room exhibit hall located sixty miles south of Nashville, Tennessee—details an expedition and displays replicas of ark artifacts. No actual ark discovery has been widely accepted (even among fundamentalists), but the search continues. In 2012 former *Baywatch* star Donna D'Errico launched a Kickstarter campaign to fund her own Ararat expedition.[9]

Thanks to Kircher, Twain, D'Errico, and countless others, the Genesis account of Noah's ark is among the most recognizable scriptural stories in our cultural repertoire. The historicity of Noah's ark has been especially important in the development of modern creationism. In 1902 a Seventh-Day Adventist teacher, George McReady Price, began popularizing the idea that only a literal reading of Genesis could explain the world's geologic facts and mysteries.[10] *The Genesis Flood* (1961), a book that launched the creationist movement that continues today, fused

Price's arguments with fundamentalist Protestant theology. Creationists seized on Noah's ark as a key symbol for their biblical literalism and the key event for their hermeneutic of "flood geology." In doing so, they invoked not an obscure tale with no public resonance but a story that has enchanted for millennia.

This book is an anthropological study of a dramatic new addition to the lore of Noah's ark, with its centerpiece the to-scale re-creation of the ark as a creationist theme park in the U.S. state of Kentucky. The primary concern is how this form of religious publicity mobilizes the strategies and imperatives of modern entertainment to claim cultural legitimacy and authority.

\*\*\*

On May 28, 2007, the Creation Museum opened in northern Kentucky, about twenty miles southwest of downtown Cincinnati, Ohio. It was created by Answers in Genesis, a fundamentalist Christian ministry that teaches a literalist view of scripture and a wholesale rejection of evolutionary science. Kentucky's Creation Museum is not the first of its kind. There are dozens of others in the United States and other nations, but most—like the Wyatt Archaeology Museum—have been small, low-budget attractions that generate little public attention. At a cost of $30 million, the Creation Museum has sought to play in a different league. By mid-2015 more than 2 million visitors had been to the museum, establishing it as the public face of contemporary creationism.[11]

Fundamentalists have been vying for cultural authority in American public life for more than a century. They have done so in part by charging evolutionary science as incongruent with a biblical literalist worldview, and therefore morally and spiritually destructive. By 1899, mainstream science was celebrating Darwinian evolution, and a few years later, in 1904, William Jennings Bryan made his first public anti-evolution speech.[12] In 1925, the famous revivalist preacher Billy Sunday equated evolution with Nazism during a Memphis, Tennessee campaign that attracted more than 200,000 people. Later that year, the Scopes Trial in Dayton, Tennessee, generated a record-setting 2 million telegraph words of media chatter.[13] Six decades later, in 1981, twenty state legislatures introduced education bills requiring "equal time" for evolutionary science and creationism in public school science classrooms. In 2005, split state decisions marked a continuing social and ideological division. The Kansas school board voted that teaching evolution in public schools required an "only a theory" disclaimer, while a U.S. district court in Pennsylvania ruled that teaching "intelligent design" in public schools was unconstitutional.

From state and federal court rulings to national magazine covers, presidential stump speeches, prime-time cable news debates, documentary films, and best-selling books, fundamentalist controversies occupy a fixed place in our public sphere. Kentucky's Creation Museum is a fundamentalist victory, a brick-and-mortar claim to public legitimacy, and a refusal to be dismissed as a religious sideshow.

On December 1, 2010, Answers in Genesis announced its next major project—more expensive, more ambitious. Ark Encounter was announced as a "full-scale Noah's Ark tourist attraction," a creationist theme park with a price tag exceeding $150 million.[14] Set on 800 acres of Kentucky rolling hills—directly off Interstate 75 halfway between Cincinnati, Ohio, and Lexington, Kentucky—Ark Encounter opened to the public on July 7, 2016. The centerpiece of the park is a re-creation of Noah's ark, built to creationist specification from the text of Genesis 6 through 9. The ark stands 51 feet tall, 85 feet wide, and 510 feet long, contains nearly 4 million board feet of timber, and features more than 100,000 square feet of themed exhibit space. Ark Encounter expands the cultural and political work of the Creation Museum: to edify and embolden committed creationists, to convert non-Christians to Christianity and noncreationists to creationism, and to advance fundamentalism's legitimacy in the public sphere.

This book examines Ark Encounter as a form of fundamentalist Christian public culture. In the chapters to come, I will explore how a creationist theme park exemplifies the global phenomenon of materializing the Bible (i.e., transforming written scripture into an experiential, choreographed environment), the creative labor that produced the park, and the experiential possibilities afforded on board the re-created ark. The organizing argument is that Ark Encounter's ambitions of religious education, conversion, and publicity are structured by the strategies and imperatives of modern entertainment. This book is not a study of creationism per se; excellent histories and ethnographies already do that work.[15] But, especially for uninitiated readers, a brief primer will help contextualize the analysis of Ark Encounter as fundamentalist public culture.

## Creationism: A Primer

### Defining

The term "creationist" is used by and for an assortment of cultural identities, from intelligent design advocates who have no stake in biblical literalism to liberal Protestants who believe in a divinely orchestrated evolutionary process.[16] This book uses "creationist" and "creationism" more narrowly, referencing a Protestant fundamentalist movement defined by four commitments:[17]

1. The Bible is the perfect, inerrant "Word of God," wholly authoritative over any other source on all matters—moral, cosmological, historical, scientific, and theological. Creationists promote "biblical literalism," a textual ideology and interpretive style that prizes the historicity of scripture.[18]

2. A literal reading of Genesis is theologically pivotal for the veracity of Christianity. Read literally, Genesis teaches that human beings are a special creation "made in God's image," foreclosing any possibility that humans evolved from a primate ancestor. God created the universe in its current form roughly 6,000 years ago, including the Earth, human beings, and the basic skeleton of earth's biodiversity. In turn, humans must have coexisted with every animal for which there is fossil evidence, including dinosaurs.

3. A universal flood killing all but eight people, detailed in Genesis 6 through 9, was a real historical event with geologic and biological implications. This literal Flood explains natural formations throughout the world (e.g., Arizona's Grand Canyon formed rapidly as a result of floodwaters receding in the days of Noah, not gradually over time) and archaeological discoveries (e.g., the global distribution of fossils). Biologically, the ethnic and linguistic diversity of our global human population can be traced to the ark's eight passengers: Noah, his wife, their three sons, and their wives.

4. Darwinian evolution instigated a total attack on the Bible's absolute authority. Evolutionary theory is inherently corrupting to

individuals and society, the root cause of numerous civic, spiritual, and moral problems. The destructive agenda of evolution operates conspiratorially, and creationists are especially equipped to discern the real truth.[19] While waiting for the Second Coming of Christ, fundamentalists must heal the world by defeating evolution and teaching creationism.

These commitments make clear that creationism exceeds a set of doctrinal beliefs. Like all religious systems, creationism must be lived: "embedded in wider conceptions and social relations of the believing subject—a subject whose commitment to the faith is an ongoing process."[20] Public projects like the Creation Museum and Ark Encounter enliven and bolster this ongoing process. They do so by mobilizing the power of the material and mediated nature of believing. As the religion scholar David Morgan writes, belief "is not simply assent to dogmatic principles or creedal positions, but also the embodied or material practices that enact belonging to the group."[21] One aim of this book is to rescue categories such as *literalism* from a purely textual understanding and to explore how ideologies of scripture are re-created through material processes, such as the choreography of religious space and the testimony of the senses.

*Counting Creationists*

How many Americans adhere to creationism?[22] This is an empirical question, but its asking is politically charged. Communities with opposing ideologies (both pro-creationist and anticreationist) seize on whatever answer emerges as baffling or promising, dangerous or hopeful, proof of scientific illiteracy or proof of God moving in the world.

National Gallup polls are a widely cited source for answering this question. On eleven occasions between 1982 and 2012, Gallup collected survey data from a representative sample of Americans regarding their beliefs about human origins.[23] The question reads as follows:

> Which of the following statements comes closest to your views on the origin and development of human beings? 1) Human beings have developed over millions of years from less advanced forms of life, but God

guided this process; 2) Human beings have developed over millions of years from less advanced forms of life, but God had no part in this process; 3) God created human beings pretty much in their present form at one time within the last 10,000 years or so.

In 1982, 44 percent of respondents chose the third option. This option peaked at 47 percent twice, in 1993 and 1999, and reached as low as 40 percent in 2011, rising back to 46 percent in 2012. These results are often treated as a measure for Answers in Genesis–style creationism, but this association is misleading. Gallup's question focuses only on the human species as a special creation of God, which is only one of creationism's interlaced commitments.

A far more accurate measure was detailed by the National Study of Religion and Human Origins (2014). Using a more sophisticated survey instrument, this study found that roughly 8 percent of Americans definitively identify themselves as Answers in Genesis–style creationists.[24] This number grows to 22 percent if we count respondents who affirm with certainty a literal Genesis but are uncertain about the timeline of creation.[25] Put differently, roughly 26 million Americans might visit the Creation Museum and Ark Encounter as committed adherents looking to be educated and edified, while an additional 45 million might visit to earnestly examine their commitments.

*History*

The biblical chronology that anchors creationism dates to 1650 and James Ussher, a bishop in the Anglican Church of Ireland. But the modern creationist movement's more direct roots trace to Seventh-Day Adventism.[26] In 1864, Ellen White, the denomination's founding prophetess, published a literalist account of the six days of creation and Noah's Flood, claiming her account was directly revealed from God. George McCready Price, one of White's disciples, popularized her literal revelation in several books beginning in 1902. In the 1930s and 1940s, several national organizations formed to debate the scientific and theological bases of creationist claims, but a public creation-evolution controversy "had lapsed into near silence."[27] Still, the public ambitions of creationists were not completely lost during this time. For example, the Moody

Institute of Science, a project of Chicago's Moody Bible Institute, was founded in 1945. Based in Los Angeles, the Institute of Science produced science education films from a "biblical" standpoint. Perhaps the institute's crowning achievement was when the U.S. Air Force required mandatory viewing of several of its films in 1949.[28]

The space race and America's structural investment in scientific progress helped to galvanize the creationist movement that thrives today. After the Sputnik launch in 1957, the U.S. Congress authorized "millions of federal dollars to support scientific research and training," including a $100 million National Science Foundation program in 1958 to reform the public school science curriculum.[29] This sharpened a double-edged sword in American public life. It "marked a high point in the prestige of science considered as a social model and a delivery system of social betterment" but also a peak in populist "suspicion, mistrust, and misunderstanding" of scientific authority.[30]

In this milieu of populist suspicion two men—John Whitcomb (a conservative Protestant theologian) and Henry Morris (a hydraulic engineer with a doctorate from the University of Minnesota)—published *The Genesis Flood* in 1961. This book launched the modern creationist movement and the moniker of "creation science." A series of landmark U.S. Supreme Court decisions in the 1960s (e.g., outlawing prayer in public schools; barring compulsory Bible reading in public school classrooms; authorizing the teaching of evolutionary science in public schools) further galvanized creationists. They viewed these decisions as evidence of a "secular" conspiracy to spread the moral and spiritual plague of evolution.

In 1972, Henry Morris founded the Institute for Creation Research (ICR) in a northeast suburb of San Diego. ICR was a creation science epicenter, designed to employ researchers, produce publications, host conferences, and build a creation museum.[31] Answers in Genesis (AiG) was founded in 1994, the vision of three former ICR employees. One of the founders explained to me at the outset of my research that AiG began as "a populist ministry," designed to complement ICR's more "technical" character.[32] The founders chose Kentucky with a populist, pragmatic logic of proximity: "almost 2/3 of America's population lives within 650 miles" of the Creation Museum.[33] This same explanation was marshaled at the December 2010 press conference announcing Ark Encounter. Reprising the spirit of the Moody science films, AiG's ambition is to reach the broadest possible public with its religious publicity.

## Controversy

Ark Encounter sparked immediate controversy upon its announcement. The debate began with the project's application for a tax incentive program under the Kentucky Board of Tourism. The program is a performance-based rebate of the park's sales tax. If the park generates a state-declared minimum of revenue in its opening years, it will receive a state-declared percentage of already-paid taxes. This amount was initially estimated to be $18 million over the first ten years.

The application for the tax rebate was given preliminary approval, resulting in charges that this approval was unconstitutional. Americans United for Separation of Church and State and the Freedom from Religion Foundation both outlined plans to prosecute the State of Kentucky for violating the First Amendment establishment clause if the application received final approval. Their reasoning was that any for-profit entity that successfully applies for this tax incentive program is subject to all state regulations, including legal prohibitions on discriminatory employment. In June 2015, the State of Kentucky denied Ark Encounter's application because the park was using an Answers in Genesis–authored hiring statement that required employees to sign a fundamentalist statement of faith. In response, Ark Encounter officials sued the state for violating their First Amendment rights of free exercise. By January 2016, the court had ruled that AiG's hiring policy was constitutional, and Ark Encounter was once again approved for the rebate. Following its first year of operation, Ark Encounter received $1.8 million in tax rebates.

Eighteen million dollars over ten years is a substantial amount of money to gain or lose, but it was never the financial mechanism that would enable Ark Encounter to open or prevent it from doing so. Grant County, the location of the park, helped by approving subsidies and incentives. The capital to purchase the 800 acres, secure the necessary building permits, and construct the park was privately generated by Ark Encounter and Answers in Genesis. When the project was announced in December 2010, the advertised opening date was "spring 2014."[34] But fund-raising proceeded much slower than the ministry anticipated.

By early 2012, the ministry had stopped advertising an opening date and had decided to open the park in multiple phases, scaling back the planned exhibits for the initial phase.

On February 27, 2014, Ark Encounter announced that it had secured the necessary funding to proceed with construction. Two years of uncertainty about when (and sometimes *if*) this creationist theme park would successfully open finally ended. The fund-raising mechanism that moved the project forward was a bond program in which individuals and organizations could purchase Ark Encounter investment shares. If the project does well financially, then investors will increase their money; if not, they will lose whatever they purchased. Newspaper and magazine articles, op-ed columns, and popular blogs speculated about whether a highly publicized and widely viewed debate in early February 2014 between Ken Ham (Answers in Genesis cofounder and Bill Nye (evolutionary science celebrity and public educator) jump-started creationists to assume the financial risk of investment.[35]

The official groundbreaking for Ark Encounter occurred six months later, in August 2014. The timing of construction was always closely managed by the ministry due to building permit regulations. Once ground was officially broken, Ark Encounter was on a two-year clock. If not completed in this time, construction would be legally halted until all permits could be renewed (an expensive and lengthy process). Starting construction without all the finances in order would be bad business, but the decision to wait also made sense in terms of religious publicity. An indefinite delay midconstruction would not just be embarrassing; it would delegitimize AiG's ongoing effort to bolster the reputation of creationism. Once Ark Encounter's future became more certain, the debates about tax incentives were revived. With every legal challenge, Answers in Genesis fed its publicity machine, voicing established fundamentalist narratives about "biblical authority" being under siege by "secular evolutionists."

## Conclusion

From state tourism incentives to legal challenges, widely circulated debates, and international media coverage, Ark Encounter emboldens and enlivens creationism. This book approaches the creationist theme park as a form of public culture seeking to bolster fundamentalism's cultural legitimacy. Throughout this book, I explore how Ark Encounter engages this process of vying for public trust.

Scholarly treatments of creationism range from sympathetic to polemical, but almost without exception they keep creationism fixed within one analytical frame: religion-science. No doubt, this is an important frame. There are significant consequences of cultivating an ever-refined anthropological understanding of how fundamentalist Christians appropriate the symbolic and material infrastructures of science. But it is not the only frame available to us and not the only kind of work we can do.

The chapters to come recalibrate the analytical focus by placing creationism within a different frame: religion-entertainment. For some this approach will be revealing; for others it will be frustrating. To noncreationist readers: consider who else creationists might be other than people who fail to reckon with the authoritative facts of modern science. Participate in what anthropology does best: rip a hole in the fabric of what you know, or suppose you know, about this religious movement. What can we learn from the figure of the creative creationist that we cannot learn from the creation scientist? To creationist readers: be reflexive. Consider how your theology and your use of scripture are wedded to other cultural systems. How do these ties bind you to other Christians and to the power of modern entertainment? To all readers: my wager as an anthropologist is that creationism and fundamentalist public culture will become more legible if we can nurture multiple frames of analysis.

1

# The Power of Entertainment

## The Trailer

*September 2012.* I had visited the Answers in Genesis Creation Museum numerous times. But today was different. Instead of moving methodically through the teaching exhibits to make careful observations and absorb the museum's many dimensions, we hurried with a singular purpose. We walked against the current of visitors reading signage and managing children. Five of us—myself and the four core members of Ark Encounter's creative team—snaked through exhibits on the fastest route out of the building and into the parking lot.

We were there to preview a sixty-second video trailer for Ark Encounter (Figure 1.1).[1] The team had designed the physical set and written the script for the trailer, but the labor of filming and postproduction was completed by the ministry's audiovisual team. The trailer was an important product; it was used initially as a fund-raising tool and in subsequent years featured prominently in the park's publicity materials. The script was crafted to be exactly sixty seconds, which allowed for the trailer's potential future use in television advertising. The team members devoted a month of overtime summer days to building the set, the filming was completed in a single overtime day in August, and today was their first chance to see a rough cut.

Seeing the trailer on this particular day was a surprise for all of us. The members of the creative team had not been given a firm date for when the first cut would be ready, and they were waiting to see the fruits of their creative labor: patient, but eager. When I arrived at the design studio in the morning, the team was disassembling the set. The creative director, Roger, was in his office working, while Tyler, Kevin, and Emily (the three lead artists) took the set apart piece by piece.[2]

Figure 1.1. Scene from the Ark Encounter trailer.

Everyone was excited about the look and feel they had created with the set. Emily, who had trained in theater design at the California Institute of Arts, was especially pleased; this project was close to her heart. Spatial design was her primary area of expertise, and she described working on the trailer as "being back in my element." Her primary design inspiration was a weeklong research trip the creative team had taken to Morocco in 2010. Roger wanted the team to see the region, in particular its architecture, to stoke its imagining of a re-created biblical village at Ark Encounter. The trailer's main setting is a small house: Noah sits, drawing schematics for the ark. Emily based her portrayal of the dwelling on her recollections and photographs of a particular Moroccan hallway that she had seen on the trip.

As Emily explained all this, Kevin added: "With the lights, you stepped in and were somewhere else. It was cool." Throughout the morning of disassembling the set and reflecting on the design process, the team members made repeated references to "Hollywood." This was not unusual. I had become accustomed to their citing Hollywood as a standard-bearer for quality, and particular films as creative exemplars. But the frequency of references that morning was notable. Creating the script, building the set, overseeing the filming—the team members rel-ished the sense that their creative labor was akin to that of working art-ists in the movie industry.

The news came just before lunch: the rough cut of the trailer was ready. The audiovisual team invited everyone to come over in the af-ternoon for a viewing in Legacy Hall, the museum's main auditorium, with theater-quality projection and sound. We took separate cars for the short drive from the design studio to the museum. Roger and I arrived at the same time, and we walked in together to meet the others. I noted how full the parking lot seemed for a random Friday in September. Roger agreed favorably, adding that the summer had been busy despite "the economy." I silently observed a few bumper stickers as we walked: "Don't Tread on Me," complete with a coiled, hissing snake, and "We're Taking Dinosaurs Back," an Answers in Genesis trademark.

Although I was familiar with the museum exhibits, garden, and pet-ting zoo, I had yet to attend an event in Legacy Hall. I noticed imme-diately how comfortable the cushioned seats were. I sat down without much care as to where, so long as I was near the team. The team mem-bers targeted seats more strategically, commenting on features like how far back you needed to sit so the stage podium did not block your view of the screen. They settled in, joking about obscuring one another's sight lines. Roger signaled upstairs to the audiovisual team that everything was ready, and the lights lowered. Sixty seconds later, without a com-ment from anyone, the team asked for a replay. Sixty seconds later, the lights rose, and a critique commenced.

It was all very polite, with no indication of resentment, anger, or frus-tration. The critique was brief, no more than five minutes, but it was re-lentless. Quick, back-and-forth observations were traded, with nods and exclamations of agreement. It was a collaborative cataloging of changes that needed to be made before the trailer could be released to the public.

Some comments were quite specific. Emily asked why the voice-over stopped at the words "found you righteous," even though scripture says Noah was "righteous in his generation." Roger disliked the sound edit-ing, saying it was "too loud at first, then too soft at the end, won't be good for an older crowd." Tyler rattled off a series of criticisms: the "cuts to the props, like the tools," were "all wrong"; the blur effect when Noah looks out to the ark construction happened too slowly; the ending cut to the Ark Encounter logo was too abrupt (it "doesn't stay on the ark long enough—if you didn't know the story you couldn't make the connection, you need a breath before the logo)"; and the voice at the start came in too quickly (it's "not mysterious enough"). Emily disliked the voice-over altogether, saying, "It's just too *BRAH*, you know what I mean?" (I wondered silently, if that is not the right voice, then what is? How should God's voice sound?)

The team's specific critiques were united by a general description of the whole thing being "off," including the "rhythm," "mix," "transitions," and "cuts." One moment was "not fluid," the next was "disjointed." With the exception of Emily's comment about ending the scripture reading too early, the entire critique scrutinized matters of aesthetics: the "feel" created by the postproduction editing of sound, color, and flow. Still, the discussion was all very calm, with no sense of overexcitement.

Roger mobilized us to go upstairs and share the team's notes with the audiovisual producer. We couldn't find him at first, and Emily joked that he was "probably hiding; they know us too well." After a few minutes a tall, handsome man in his early thirties emerged from an office full of AV equipment. His appearance contrasted sharply with that of the team members. They were casual as usual, with T-shirts and jeans, sweatshirts, and unfussy hair. The producer wore stylish dress slacks, a silvery dress shirt, and a narrow tie; his dark hair was slicked back. He was more *Mad Men* than disheveled artist.

He asked how everyone liked the trailer. After a polite and positive, but brief and generic, response, Roger, always the leader, said they had "notes" to share. "Oh, I'm sure it's a mile long," the producer teased. For several minutes the team repeated, nearly verbatim, the exchange from downstairs. The producer nodded along but did not appear to be listening very keenly. He promised to take a second look at the sound but said that "everything else is pretty set." In a tone that was almost dismissive, he said, "It is a teaser, after all," in response to the suggestion that the trailer should linger on the ark construction scene longer before cutting to the Ark Encounter logo. Roger asked why the words "in his generation" had been left off from the scripture reading, explaining why the absent qualifier conjures a different meaning. The producer responded that "Ken approved the final script, so there shouldn't be any theological issues." (He was referring to Ken Ham, cofounder of Answers in Genesis and a creationist celebrity.) In response to a comment that the voice-over was too jarring, he noted with visible delight that the ministry had recruited one of Hollywood's most popular voice actors for the reading.

Abruptly, the vibe changed. The producer informed the team that the trailer had already been released and was being shown that afternoon at a fund-raising event. Emily was standing to my right, so I missed her facial expression, but it must have registered unambiguous disapproval. The producer blurted out a stunned "uh-oh," and the mood transformed from polite and constructive to assertive and corrective. Soon after this revelation, Roger concluded the discussion, thanked the producer for his time, and led us on a beeline into the parking lot. Moving briskly, I asked Tyler if he was disappointed. He confirmed in a decidedly serious tone that he was, about both the "quality" of the trailer and not being consulted before its release for public viewing. Emily and Roger walked ahead of us, out of earshot but talking in obvious displeasure.

When we reached Tyler's car, the team members resumed their critique, with all politeness drained, having been replaced by frustration. They repeated much of what had already been said, looping in a few new observations. Roger mocked the round pegs that were visible in the scene with workers building the ark, saying that "they look straight from Lowes," with no attempt to fashion a "handmade" look. Kevin thought the "color wash" was "way off"; it was too dark and needed bright contrasts. Emily admonished herself: "I should have been more insistent about the hallway." She had been suspicious throughout the process of construction and filming that the dimensions were too wide and too tall to re-create her Moroccan inspiration. Kevin wondered if the voice could be dropped altogether, citing the latest *Batman* trailer as a bird's-eye view of Gotham's cityscape with no dialogue. Tyler and Emily spoke to Roger in unison, in an uncommon tone of forcefulness, telling him, "You have to put your foot down," referring to their getting bypassed on final cut approval. Roger did not respond, returning instead to the critique. The whole thing was "too linear," he said. "It's not interesting or fun. Noah looks like a mannequin." He was not convinced by the "teaser" response for this same reason: teasers should be "immensely interesting." Tyler attempted a constructive conclusion: "All the right pieces are there; it just needs some love." Unmistakably strident, Roger summarized what had animated their entire critique: the trailer was "just not Hollywood quality."

\*\*\*

This scene from September 2012 occurred about a year into my research with the Ark Encounter creative team and was a revealing fieldwork moment. It was the first time I had been with all the team members outside the design studio and the first time I saw them galvanized as a collaborative unit. I had observed numerous moments of tension in that first year, but this was an especially candid moment. Even more, their creative labor of building the set and performing the critique crystallizes the major themes of this book.

There is the prizing of immersion. The team members' frustration owed partly to the fact that they wanted the trailer to transport viewers "somewhere else." At its core, this book is about how entertainment strategies and imperatives structure the production and consumption of Ark Encounter. Related to this, team members were concerned with how historical plausibility was treated. The round pegs Roger criticized are visible for only one second on-screen, but the failure of authenticity exceeds the moment. For the team, small artistic details could make or break the immersive effect and the demonstration of scripture's historicity. We also see the pivotal role of materiality in the team's aesthetically driven critique. Sensory elements of sound, color, light, physicality, and "feel" were decisive for generating an affective response for viewers. We see the team's commitment to professionalism; only "Hollywood quality" has the potential to convert a skeptical public. Anything less threatened to undermine the ambition to bolster creationism's public legitimacy. Finally, this vignette provides a glimpse of the team's collaborative dynamic. The team members' mutual frustration was a moment of artistic-bureaucratic clash; demands of financial need had usurped creative control.

In subsequent weeks, a few adjustments were made to the trailer. It was nothing close to the extensive revision the team members wanted, but their anxiety about a fundamentally flawed product circulating in public was quieted. They moved on to other projects, other creative dilemmas. After all, this was a sixty-second trailer; they had an entire theme park to design.

## A Different Set of Questions

When I began this project, my anthropological curiosity was captivated by the promise of getting behind the scenes and capturing unique moments like the viewing of the trailer. Ultimately, the team generously granted me unprecedented access to the making of a creationist theme park. This experience taught me a great deal about the creative labor of a small team and the imperatives that organize its work. By the end of this project, it was not the team alone that fascinated me. I discovered Ark Encounter to be expressive of a global phenomenon with a long history—materializing the Bible—in which the written words of scripture are transformed into physical, experiential, and choreographed environments. And I learned how the team's creative ambitions shape a visitor experience that integrates immersive entertainment and fundamentalist Christianity.

Ark Encounter was announced to the public in December 2010 at a press conference that included the governor of Kentucky on stage with Ark personnel and local politicians. During the question-and-answer session, one journalist commented, "Some Christians have expressed concern with things like this . . . that this kind of money should be used to help folks in need as opposed to these, you know, overstated or large symbols of the Bible and Christianity. What do you say to that criticism?"[3]

Throughout my fieldwork I never once heard the creative team voice any doubt or hesitation about the necessity of Ark Encounter. Likewise, I heard no such misgivings from creationists I interviewed about the park. Still, for many people the project is strange, surprising, or disturbing. This reporter voiced a widely shared sentiment among the noncreationist public. Is re-creating Noah's ark the best way to spend $150 million? Why not use those funds for humanitarian projects, directly effecting positive change in the lives of poor, marginalized, and underserved people?

The answer from Ark Encounter personnel during the press conference was one they would repeat in countless publicity forums leading up to the park's opening: the public message of the park and the ministerial work enabled by its profits will do more good than any other use of the funds. Of course, that answer does not satisfy religious and secular critics who see Ark Encounter as, at best, silly and, at worst, dangerous for its corrosive effect on the public's scientific literacy.

When listening to the details of this research, my noncreationist friends, students, and colleagues (that is to say, nearly all of them) expressed genuine bafflement at the reality of a creationist theme park. This book aims to make clear why Ark Encounter makes sense not only to committed creationists but also within multiple historical and cultural contexts: American fundamentalism, materializing the Bible, modern entertainment, and other widespread patterns. I will not resolve how best to use $150 million, but I will address a different set of questions that render a $150 million creationist theme park more legible. Where does Ark Encounter fit within the global phenomenon of materializing the Bible? What kinds of creative labor define the production of fundamentalist public culture? How does Ark Encounter integrate the religious imperatives of creationism with the entertainment imperatives of creativity, immersion, and fun? How might committed creationists interact with Ark Encounter as a religious attraction? And what does producing and consuming a creationist theme park say about modern fundamentalism?

The answers to these questions will show how Ark Encounter's goals of religious education, conversion, and legitimacy are pursued. To orient the analysis, I introduce here a set of key concepts used throughout the chapters to come: devotional consumption, entertainment as play, and religious publicity.

## Devotional Consumption

"Commerce and pious entertainment were not regarded as antithetical in principle by most nineteenth-century Americans, who had at least as much P. T. Barnum in their souls as they did Emerson or Thoreau."[4] With this observation, religion scholar David Morgan captures an essential truth about American piety. Christians, in particular, have sought to sacralize their consumption of cultural goods, transforming purely economic or functional activity into something integrated into the moral and spiritual fabric of life. They use these transformed goods for religious education and sociality, devotional praise, prayer, witnessing, everyday reminders of faith, and a host of other purposes.[5] In doing so, they refuse any strict sacred-profane division, instead engaging the whole of life in religious commitment.[6] Ark Encounter joins this prolific, if not always fully comfortable, entanglement among religion, consumer capitalism, and recreational leisure.

Devotional consumption is prone to accusations that the purity of religious life has been corrupted by the forces of capitalism. Arguments about "the growing worldliness of religion" may bolster secular critiques and advance theological agendas, but they offer no advantage to historical or anthropological accounts.[7] I follow the lead of many scholars in the critical study of religion in arguing that devotional consumption reveals more about the creativity of religious actors (and the force of capitalist conditions) than it does categorical contamination.[8]

The use of commerce and recreation to enhance religious ambitions has a long history. It is exemplified in the lives of faith-wise entrepreneurs who have shaped America's spiritual and cultural landscapes. We might highlight George Whitefield's use of dramatic theater to attract and compel audiences during the First Great Awakening; Aimee Semple McPherson's stadium spectacles to advance Pentecostalism; Billy Sunday's rousing urban revivals; Oral Roberts's strategic use of mass communication technology to build a charismatic healing empire; the proliferation of televangelism in the 1970s and 1980s; or Oprah Winfrey's consumption-fueled message of ecumenical spirituality.[9]

Devotional consumption has also shaped the routes of religious travel. Numerous Methodist attractions became widely popular in the late 1800s, such as western New York's Chautauqua Institution, which was founded in 1873. In *Holy Leisure*, historian Troy Messenger details how vacationing, escape from the city, and spiritual regeneration melded together at the Holiness camp meeting of Ocean Grove, New Jersey. There, "recreation was an essential means of grace," and devotion merged with play.[10] Grafting family and congregational leisure onto religious life continues in the modern industry of religious tourism. Entire cities—such as Branson, Missouri—market themselves as family-friendly, faith-friendly destinations.[11] While Ark Encounter breaks the mold in terms of financial cost and technological sophistication, it is merely the latest iteration of a long-standing cultural pattern of attractions created for religious leisure.

Making capitalism and recreation a religious practice is guided by an imperative to fill the consumer marketplace with faith-based alternatives. Whether it's tuning in to the radio, listening to music, reading books, watching television and film, surfing the Internet, downloading a podcast, or picking a vacation destination, the fundamentalist marketplace pulses with alternatives. As a familiar question asks, "Why should *the Devil* have all the good music?" For modern fundamentalism, creating alternatives has extended from politics (e.g., the Moral Majority) to mass media (e.g., Trinity Broadcasting Network) and the intimacies of selfhood (e.g., biblical counseling).

This fundamentalist production of alternatives has also included an enduring search for "secular" cultural goods corrupting the public. Part of the ideological and political work of modern fundamentalism was the invention of a durable cultural antagonist, "secular humanism," conceived as a moral and spiritual threat responsible for pornography, drug addiction, abortion rights, rising divorce rates, and evolutionary science.[12] "Secular" became a portable label that could be placed on any cultural good that fundamentalists deemed incongruent with proper faith. Fundamentalists led a "moral panic" in the 1980s to condemn the fantasy role-playing game Dungeons & Dragons, and they did the same with the *Harry Potter* franchise two decades later.[13] Producing fundamentalist-friendly alternatives is not limited to the lives of individual consumers; it is about transforming public life. Creating spiritually nourishing goods and eliminating spiritually destructive ones is central to fundamentalism's claim for cultural authority.[14]

Ark Encounter expands the ambition to bolster creationism's public legitimacy by adding a "theme park" to the fundamentalist marketplace. The fundamentalist ambition is not simply to create alternatives but to create alternatives that rival or surpass the quality of secular counterparts (again, "Why should the Devil have all the *good* music?"). For many creationists, the opening of the Creation Museum in 2007 advanced this feat because it boasted a sophistication on a par with that of evolutionary natural science and history museums. Standards of quality and imperatives of devotional consumption were always present in the creative team's labor. A hand-drawn reminder remained pinned on one cubicle wall throughout my fieldwork. Written in black Sharpie ink, it read:

Entertainment – (minus) truth = Bad. Empty fun. Vanity.
Entertainment + (plus) truth = Teaching. Thinking.

Disney is SAFE. Reputation.
Disney has $.
I'm just a witness of truth.

The second line was circled, and to the right of the text was a sketch of a compass with the caption "Where is your North?" Much like a posted verse of scripture, this sign functioned as a daily reminder. Composed in poetic form, it visually inscribed the sharp contrast between "bad" and good entertainment onto the design studio work space.

### Entertainment as Play

So far I have used the word "entertainment" rather loosely. Many readers might assume it simply references a general realm of leisure that aims to provide pleasure. Not so. Here, "entertainment" carries a more exact meaning. I adopt anthropologist Peter Stromberg's definition of entertainment as an activity that allows consumers to become physically, emotionally, and/or cognitively "caught up" in a frame of role playing that transports them away from the frame of everyday reality.[15] In short, entertainment is about creating and participating in immersive environments. As the opening vignette suggests, immersion is integral for how the success of Ark Encounter as a form of public culture is envisioned.

Stromberg argues that our modern culture of entertainment has become "the most influential ideological system on the planet."[16] As modern consumers, we prioritize and gravitate toward forms of leisure, gaming, and education that are interactive, participatory, and experientially compelling, not passively consumptive. This observation echoes what some scholars have termed the "Disneyization of society," in which Disney-style strategies colonize other forms of consumer experience.[17] Religion scholar David Chidester observes how Disney's influence has created a widespread imperative to "create imaginary worlds that evoke a thematic coherence through architecture, landscaping, costuming, and other theatrical effects to establish a focused, integrated experience."[18]

Modern entertainment is not just more dominant than other cultural forms; the strategies and imperatives of entertainment have actually infused other cultural forms. Stromberg writes, "As Darwin argued for the survival of the fittest, we now have survival of the most entertaining. . . .

The entertaining politician gets elected, the entertaining class gets the enrollment, the entertaining car is the one that sells, and over time a competition emerges to enhance entertainment value wherever possible."[19] This infusion is realized in examples as diverse as urban planning and restaurant dining.[20]

Immersive entertainment has proved especially influential for the field of museum education.[21] While Ark Encounter seeks to immerse visitors in a literalist biblical past, other places conjure other pasts. Theater studies scholar Scott Magelssen argues that "simming," or participating in simulations of past conditions, is now a dominant trend in heritage tourism.[22] For example, he describes an Indiana living history museum where visitors role-play as 1830s fugitive slaves seeking freedom on the Underground Railroad. Visitors are immersed through a range of sensory and theatrical practices: they are forced to kneel by angry slave hunters, flee from their captors on foot, and hide silently in safe houses.

Another prominent example of entertainment as play is the U.S. Holocaust Memorial Museum in Washington, DC, a site that thoroughly enacts an immersive imperative. The museum's designers insisted that the architecture, not only the teaching exhibits, contribute to a particular affective experience: "It would have to communicate through raw materials and organization of space the feel of inexorable, forced movement: disruption, alienation, constriction, observation, selection."[23] Numerous spatial and sensory strategies are choreographed toward this end: the use of "closed, blind windows"; objects historically associated with the Holocaust, such as canisters of Zyklon B, a poison that was used in Nazi gas chambers; "intentionally ugly, dark-gray metal elevators"; narrow and crowded spaces; and distribution of a biographical card when visitors first enter the museum to transform the Holocaust from a mass, anonymous event to an individual, intimate experience.[24]

I participated in a striking example of museum immersion at the National Center for Civil and Human Rights in Atlanta, Georgia.[25] The center's first-floor permanent exhibition, *Rolls Down Like Water*, uses multimedia displays to tell the history of the American civil rights movement in the 1950s and 1960s. Publicity materials promise that "visitors will be immersed in a visceral experience of sights, sounds and interactive displays depicting the courageous struggles of individuals working to transform the United States from Jim Crow laws to equal rights for all."[26] The most memorable display was a re-created 1950s lunch counter. As a visitor, you are invited to sit down, put on a pair of headphones, place your hands on a pair of motion sensors, and close your eyes. The headphone audio track plays a barrage of increasingly violent yells and insults that demand that you leave the diner immediately. The sensors alert you if your hands flinch. Although I managed to keep my hands in place for the duration of the recording, I opened my eyes feeling shocked and unsettled.[27]

Creating immersive environments requires significant investments of time, space, money, labor, and creativity. Why go to all this trouble? One answer is that immersion excels at generating affective attachments to the past. Conjuring, mobilizing, and circulating affective bonds is increasingly understood as a vital resource in the making and remaking of culture.[28] Choreographed spaces like museums and theme parks testify to the power of affect, as material and sensory channels register effects on and through the bodies of visitors. In turn, visitors are drawn into the "affectively rich worlds" orchestrated by cultural producers.[29] This argument echoes historian Vanessa Agnew's depiction of reenactment as a form of "affective history," in which the past is imagined through the "physical and psychological experience" of individuals.[30] Ark Encounter teaches creationism viscerally and experientially, using immersion to induce an affective response. For the creative team, achieving this response meant successfully setting the conditions for converting noncreationists.

Ark Encounter exemplifies how religious cultural producers are not exempt from the new Darwinian contest of survival of the most entertaining. Arguably, Answers in Genesis has embraced it as enthusiastically as anyone else. Through the team's creative labor, we see a religious system that is organized by an "aesthetics of persuasion" originating from another cultural orbit.[31] A central question of this book is this: How does Ark Encounter use material and sensory channels to create relations between play and piety, fun and faith, leisure and devotion, imagination and morality, affect and education?

As Ark Encounter embraces the immersive imperative forged by modern entertainment, it also prizes an intrinsic quality of being human—the capacity for play.[32] As *Homo ludens*, we experience rewarding pleasure from activities that are voluntary, distinct from the flow of everyday life, and utterly absorbing.[33] Johan Huizinga, an influential theorist of play, described play as "not serious," by which he meant that play has "no material interest" as a means to some other end.[34] The play of religion resists this nonserious characteristic because it has distinct material interests, whether intensifying the intimacy of one's relationship to tradition or spiritual transformation.

Religious life is replete with ludic performance. Rituals, for example, are often designed as a space where adherents can exist entirely within their religious worlds. Special locations, buildings, clothes, objects, music, and languages all work as techniques to immerse adherents in a sacred space-time. An example that intentionally capitalizes on our human penchant for play is the use of religious toys and games. Such objects of playful devotion have been commercially produced in America since at least the 1840s.[35] As forms of religious materiality, their fun is always meaningful: "In the context of games played to educate, proselytize, or instill moral values, they instead take on a utilitarian function and become a kind of work."[36] Religious toys and games continue the work of devotional consumption, highlight the "hegemony of fun" in American life, and scratch the human itch to get caught up in play.[37]

Cultivating playful capacities may be especially resonant for religious commitment in late modern America. Anthropologist Tanya Luhrmann argues that in the context of a "pluralistic, science-oriented" society, in which a biblical worldview cannot be taken for granted even among devoted believers, the "as-if imagination" becomes a vital resource.[38] In response to an awareness that their biblical worldview conflicts with other—socially legitimized and authorized—worldviews, the charismatic Christians in her ethnography cultivate "a deliberatively playful, imaginative, fantasy-filled experience of God."[39] They encourage multiple ritual activities toward this end, such as pouring a second cup of coffee for God to make the experience of prayer more intimate. Just as play can heighten the intimacy of personal spirituality, it is a mechanism that enables Ark Encounter to work affectively through re-creating a literalist biblical past.

The creative team hoped to ignite the as-if imagination of visitors. As Roger explained to me in an interview, the team's job was to create an immersive experience so successfully that visitors say to themselves: " 'Wow! Maybe that was possible. Maybe that did happen.' That's all we can do. The rest is up to the Holy Spirit. Call people to the church. All we can do is open the door and give them something to think about, and then the rest is up to God to save them." The wager is that if members of the noncreationist public will allow themselves to get caught up in a literalist biblical past, the conditions for conversion will be set.

I never heard the team members consider the potential that play might trigger reactions contrary to their ambitions. For example, they never expressed any worry that playing in the creationist past would produce ironic reflection among visitors or doubt about scriptural veracity. By not recognizing this potential, a basic characteristic of play is elided: "It is free and therefore unpredictable. Fun may lead to both questioning and questionable behavior that challenges institutions of power as well as social mores. It may produce creative thinking, laughter, or even derision and mockery."[40]

## Religious Publicity

The final organizing concept that orients my analysis concerns the role of religion in America's public sphere. Sociologist Jose Casanova coined the term "public religion" to mark the fact that secularization theories predicting either the decline of religion in modernity or its increasing confinement to private life have lost the bet. Casanova argues that religions throughout the world have asserted themselves in very public ways, vying for authority and legitimacy in fields such as governmental politics, humanitarianism, global mass media, and the law.[41] In the U.S. context, we have excellent scholarship on phenomena like the rise of the Religious Right in American politics, the urban activism of suburban megachurches, the popularity of black televangelists, and defenses and challenges of the First Amendment's free exercise clause.[42] Projects like Ark Encounter remind us that publics do more than vote, fund-raise, volunteer, tune in, and engage jurisprudence. Publics also want to have fun, and it is even better if fun can foster loftier ambitions, like faith.

This book joins anthropologist Matthew Engelke's critique that "when we talk about 'public religion' today we are often actually talking about 'religious publicity.'"[43] By this he means that the status of being public should not be taken for granted. Instead, "public" should be understood as an achievement that is actively pursued, promoted, and managed by

socially positioned religious actors who are possessed by particular strategic aims. In response, Engelke offers the concept of "religious publicity," which captures the process of producing and circulating religious
material in the public sphere.

This concept emerges from Engelke's ethnographic research on the
British Bible Society, in which he traces the work of the Bible Advocacy
Team in English cities. Through various campaigns, from holiday displays to billboards, this team sought to "counteract the idea that religion
ought to be, or even must be, a private affair" by "trying to promote and
in many cases improve the image, relevance, and uptake of the Bible."[44]
Recalibrating from public religion to religious publicity enables a more
refined understanding of how religious actors seek to shape and occupy
public life.

Akin to the Bible Society, Ark Encounter desires both to mobilize a
constituent public and to transform a diverse mass public. Social theorist Michael Warner's work on "publics and counterpublics" provides
a useful vocabulary here.[45] On one hand, Ark Encounter engages the
creationist public. This is the same public that celebrates the Creation
Museum, consumes Answers in Genesis media, and attends AiG conferences. This is the public that homeschools their children, sends them to
private fundamentalist schools, or teaches them to reject the science and
history education of public schools.[46]

On the other hand, the creationist public in America operates as a
counterpublic, "defined by their tension with a larger public . . . making
different assumptions about what can be said or what goes without saying" in the public sphere.[47] These individuals are "not merely a subset
of the public but [are] constituted through a conflictual relation to the
dominant public."[48] In this case, the dominant public celebrates basic
tenets of evolutionary science, does not read the Bible as literal history,
does not support ministries like Answers in Genesis, and does not support using $150 million to build a religious theme park as an ethical use
of money.

As we saw earlier, the National Study of Religion and Human Origins estimated that roughly 8 percent of Americans (approximately
26 million people) are committed Answers in Genesis–style creationists.[49] This is a significant number of people, but the dominance of the
noncreationist public is about more than counting heads. Dominance

is about social and symbolic capital.[50] It is about what successfully earns research funding from the National Science Foundation and the National Institutes of Health; what is aired by National Public Radio; what adorns magazine covers like *Scientific American* that fill kiosks on city streets and in airports; what is displayed at world-renowned museums such as the Smithsonian in Washington, DC, or the Field Museum in Chicago; and what earns a grade of A at America's premier universities. Creationists are a counterpublic in American society because they exist at ideological, institutional, and everyday odds with a dominant public.

Given creationists' counterpublic identity, their religious publicity is always ultimately about vying for authority. Cultural authority is an ever-contingent product of ongoing social processes. It is exerted and challenged, obeyed and critiqued, internalized and rejected. Counterpublics continually seek to wrest authority away from dominant publics and claim it for themselves. Through forms of religious publicity like the Creation Museum and Ark Encounter, creationists work to sow suspicion about the cultural legitimacy of evolutionary science and bolster the status of fundamentalist Christianity.

Religious studies scholar Bruce Lincoln's conception is helpful here because he understands authority as a relational achievement between cultural producers and audiences. As he notes, "Authority depends on nothing so much as the trust of the audience."[51] Ark Encounter is fundamentally about trust. It asks all publics to trust its version of history, science, and scripture over other accounts. For the creative team, any chance of winning this game of trust requires the team to successfully perform the imperatives of immersive entertainment—that is, to be "Hollywood quality." A central question of this book is this: How does Ark Encounter seek to mobilize and solidify the creationist public, convert the noncreationist public, and claim legitimacy and authority for creationism through its work of religious publicity?

*Chapter Organization*

The concepts outlined here—devotional consumption, entertainment as play, and religious publicity—orient the analyses in the chapters to come. Chapter 2 zooms out from my fieldwork on the production and consumption of Ark Encounter to ask how this park expresses a global, historical phenomenon. Around the world, more than 400 attractions materialize the Bible; that is, they create a choreographed place in which the written words of scripture are transformed into a physical, experiential environment. I explore how these attractions promise visitors greater intimacy with scripture, seek to foster affective access to the biblical past, and reproduce commitments to biblical authority through aesthetic strategies.

Chapters 3, 4, and 5 return to the context of the opening vignette, zooming back in to focus on the creative team. Chapter 3 explores the team's creative labor and process, arguing that these dynamics are critical for understanding Ark Encounter's ultimate ambitions of religious publicity. Chapter 4 closely analyzes the team's creative labor to understand how its model of conversion integrates biblical literalism with entertainment strategies and imperatives. Chapter 5 illustrates how Ark Encounter extends the work of history-making already established by the Creation Museum. We see how the team mobilizes the power of entertainment to construct a creationist past that exists in ideological opposition to the past of evolutionary science.

Chapter 6 shifts the focus to Ark Encounter as a realized project. Integrating observations from the park's publicity materials, repeated visits to the park, and interviews among prospective creationist visitors, I analyze the material, embodied elements of the park. On board, I argue, Ark Encounter requires a walking poetics of faith in which visitors move between two frames of immersive experience: the creationist past and the creationist present.

The conclusion returns to the core themes introduced here and analyzed throughout the book and considers their implications for the future of fundamentalism.

Finally, the methodological appendix details the research journey of this project, highlighting key moments, decisions, and challenges.

This book aims to provide distinctive insight into the significance of fundamentalist public culture and the broader phenomenon of materializing the Bible. In making Ark Encounter legible as a religious project, I hope to achieve a different portrait of a counterpublic that is often reviled by both religious and secular communities. I hope readers will discover what I did: creative people who are fully engaged in cultural patterns that orchestrate American public life. Further, I hope this book will be read not only as the story of a creationist theme park in Kentucky but also as a comparative anthropological account of religious creativity and the material life of scriptures. Through these interlaced themes, I hope to demonstrate anew the power of entertainment in modern life.

2

Materializing the Bible

When Ark Encounter opened in July 2016, it became the largest, most expensive, and most elaborate example of its kind. In the chapters to come, we go behind the scenes to explore the design team's creative labor and learn how the team united the imperatives of immersive entertainment with those of fundamentalism. We also go inside the ark to explore its experiential possibilities. Here, we zoom out from Ark Encounter to ask what kind of place a creationist theme park is.

Re-creating Noah's ark expresses a form of religious replication that I term "materializing the Bible": transforming the written words of scripture into a physical, experiential, and choreographed environment. To materialize the Bible is to perform two interlaced religious desires: building an intimate relationship with sacred scripture and gaining access to the biblical past. While creationist theme parks and museums emerge from these desires, they did not invent them. There is a long history—in the United States and globally—of not just reading a material text but interacting with scriptural replications in embodied, experiential ways.

Consider the biblical panoramas that began in the 1800s. Panorama technology consisted of a painted canvas—hundreds of yards long and several meters high—that was slowly unfurled for audiences. The optical experience often included auditory annotations of spoken narration and dramatic music. The result was a multisensory spectacle that toured urban and rural churches in mid-nineteenth-century America. Arthur Butt, a Pennsylvania art student and amateur preacher, developed a popular panorama in 1880 that toured for several years. His re-creation of the book of Revelation, stretching across twenty-two painted scenes, each measuring fifteen by twenty feet, sold out shows in opera houses, schools, churches, and theaters throughout the southern United States. Audiences described the experience as "overwhelming," "stupefying," "sublime," and "exalted." One man's reaction to the show captured the potential of this aural-visual experience to shape how adherents were engaging scripture: "A person can learn more of the Book of Revelation in one evening than he would from reading it in a life-time."[1]

The success of touring panoramas illustrates the "aesthetic education" of modern Christianity.[2] Visual experience has been endowed with the authority to teach theology, and visuality is enhanced by mobilizing other senses. This aesthetic education unites biblical panoramas and the mass consumption of religious commodities, from portraits of Jesus to the paintings of Thomas Kinkade and Mel Gibson's theatrical blockbuster *The Passion of the Christ* (2004). Materializing the Bible extends this education to the multisensory worlds created by religious attractions.

Exploring how scripture is materialized across multiple genres of place, from museums to gardens, contextualizes Ark Encounter as a form of public culture. A comparative analysis of global attractions helps to address two central questions: How do material forms of body, technology, object, and place intersect to shape visitor experience? And how do these choreographed material performances reflect and re-create ideological relations with scripture?

## The Material Life of Scriptures

Anthropologists developed "the social life of scriptures" as a framework to understand how sacred texts are not just read but put to creative use in culturally important ways. John Bowen, the originator of the phrase, analyzed how Gayo Muslims in Indonesia circulate stories of Cain and Abel, using them to explain lifeworld processes like birth and subsistence.[3] Susan Harding explored the discourse of an American fundamentalist empire, examining the verbal art of Religious Right leaders through their strategic play with biblical tropes.[4] Jonathan Boyarin advocated for detailed ethnographies of reading based on his work with Orthodox Jews who collectively interpret midrashic texts in yeshiva settings.[5] Brian Malley and I developed this framework further, exploring how local congregations are sites for hermeneutic training and play among evangelical Bible readers.[6]

For both everyday readers and virtuosic leaders, the social life of scriptures has illustrated how cultural commitments to textual authority and intimacy are authorized, reproduced, and negotiated. Recognizing this contribution, it is also true that the social life of scriptures has largely focused on issues of language and discourse. What role might materiality play in the social life of scriptures?

We can pose this question with clarity thanks to the media turn in the study of religion, which highlights how processes of religious mediation work.[7] A central issue for this turn has been how religious actors use different material forms (e.g., body, technology, object, place) to mediate religious experience, communication, and learning. The primary theoretical conceit is that mediation is actually constitutive of religious worlds, not simply an incidental by-product or practical necessity.[8] Religious actors use material forms to address the fundamental problems that animate their traditions, such as authority, belonging, and presence. The media turn has put to rest tired ideologies that doubt or dismiss the fact that religious life is centrally entangled with life's gritty and polished materialities.[9]

Themes of material mediation in the social life of scriptures are ripe for elaboration. For example, religious studies scholars highlight examples of textual physicality shaping biblical use. The heft and decoration of family Bibles heightened their display in Victorian homes.[10] Changes in children's illustrated Bibles between 1950 and the present mark a modern sensory hierarchy in which visual capacities are elevated.[11] Similarly, the optical experience of the Wordless Book offered readers a Bible transformed.[12] The written text of verses, chapters, and books became a volume of four-color pages: black communicated the fallen condition of human sinfulness; red the sacrificial blood of Jesus; white the promised righteousness of a life devoted to Christ; and gold the glory of heaven and life everlasting. Core theological commitments were taught through visual contrast and Western color symbolism. Made famous by Charles Spurgeon in the 1860s, the Wordless Book was adopted by D. L. Moody soon after for use in orphanages, Sunday schools, and urban missions and with global missionaries.

The material life of scriptures extends beyond bounded texts, illustrations, and popular commodities to cultivated spaces. In the southern United States, some African Americans recontextualize biblical texts as yard displays in the front of homes.[13] The Bible has also been materialized through replicating biblical scenes and stories. A glimpse of this practice's longevity is visible with the tradition of Holy Land re-creations. American Methodists built Palestine Park at Chautauqua in 1874, a 400-foot topographic model of biblical geography, and a scale model of nineteenth-century Jerusalem at the Ocean Grove camp meeting in 1879.[14] The evangelical esprit for Holy Land replications did not wane with a new century. To name just a few examples, it reappeared as a temporary exhibit at the 1904 St. Louis World's Fair; a 245-acre "nature sanctuary" in southwestern Virginia from 1972 to 2009; and an Orlando theme park that opened in 2001, combining scale models, "exact" replicas, and Passion play reenactments.[15]

Attractions that materialize the Bible make a promise to visitors: that the power and meaning of scripture will be revealed or rediscovered. They invite visitors to "experience," "encounter," "engage," "interact with," "see," and "step into" the Bible. Rhetorically, they seek to persuade visitors that they should be intimate with scripture, and the choreography of their physical, experiential environment promises to bolster that intimacy.

This promised intimacy is inseparable from the task of reaching across space-time. Materializing the Bible is also about constructing a sense of direct access to the past. Sites that materialize the Bible promise to collapse the distance that separates the here and now from the scriptural there and then. They do so through a series of devotional and pedagogical strategies, all of which resonate deeply with the imperatives of immersive entertainment. They use objects, technology, and the human body as channels for contacting the world of scripture. Some rely on natural elements, such as biblical gardens, while others rely on the art and architecture of themed environments, like Ark Encounter. While the range of channels that are used varies widely, the aim endures: to create a direct experience of scripture by engaging a visitor's sensorium and imagination. Of course, as select biblical pasts are imagined, others are elided and obscured. As this book unfolds, we see how the Creation Museum and Ark Encounter conjure a distinctively creationist past.

Creationist or not, commitments to scriptural intimacy and accessing the biblical past ultimately accomplish a broader kind of religious work. Materializing the Bible is a strategy for actualizing a virtual problem that animates any and every lived expression of Christianity.

The terms "virtual," "actualize," and "problem" carry precise theoretical meanings. They derive from anthropologist Jon Bialecki's framework to account for the dizzying plurality of global Christianities without conceding a coherent and comparative sense of a shared Christianity.[16] Bialecki uses philosopher Gilles Deleuze's concept of "the virtual": a state of potential that is not yet actualized but nonetheless real. Virtual fields are not defined by formations like belief, ritual, or institution. These personal and social realities are already actualized; that is, they are limited realizations of the diverse potential that is possible within a particular sociohistorical context. As a virtual field, Christianity is composed of problems that require realization. Problems are not like jigsaw puzzles that are solvable once and for all. They are more like steadily churning engines, keeping the tradition in motion by continually producing new formations. In turn, the dizzying plurality of global Christianities (and their range of beliefs, practices, and institutions) are all attempts to resolve a shared bundle of virtual problems.

What virtual problem does materializing the Bible actualize? It is the problem of Christian authenticity. All Christians must reckon with an irreducible fact: they are separated from the origins of their faith—all of them temporally, and most of them geographically, linguistically, ethnically, and culturally. This problem is accentuated with each schism. The historian Paul Conkin captures this fact when writing about the rise of new Christian movements in America: "In some sense, almost all new Christian movements have advertised their return to an early or pure New Testament church."[17] One way to address the problem of authenticity is to construct historical continuity, bolstering a bond with a past that is long gone and mediated many times over. Sites that materialize the Bible mobilize promises of intimacy to perform this temporal collapse.

## A Global Genre

With media cameras from around the world recording, Ark Encounter added itself to the list of American attractions that materialize the Bible. With more than 200 sites, the United States boasts more such attractions than any other nation. However, it is certainly not the only nation that hosts them. There are more than 200 further sites operating in forty-one nations: Argentina, Australia, Austria, the Bahamas, Bosnia, Brazil, Canada, China, Croatia, the Czech Republic, Denmark, England, France, Germany, Hungary, India, Ireland, Israel, Italy, Japan, Kenya,

Latvia, Lithuania, Malta, Mexico, New Zealand, the Netherlands, Northern Ireland, Pakistan, the Philippines, Poland, Portugal, Russia, Scotland, Slovakia, South Africa, South Korea, Switzerland, Taiwan, Ukraine, and Wales.[18] This global reach testifies to this chapter's organizing argument, namely, that materializing the Bible addresses a core problem that animates Christianity as a religious tradition.

Selected sites have attracted significant scholarly attention. The Holy Land Experience in Orlando, for example, has been variously interpreted as heritage entertainment detached from archaeological evidence;[19] as a spectacle past eliding the presence of Catholics, Orthodox Christians, and Muslims in Jerusalem's history in favor of a "purist apostolic form";[20] and as a spatial performance of Christian Zionism.[21] Several scholars have analyzed sites in comparative perspective. Religion scholar Burke Long's *Imagining the Holy Land* explores how biblical Palestine has been replicated numerous times throughout American history, typically remade in the theological and sociological image of its re-creators.[22] In her book *Sensational Devotion*, theater arts scholar Jill Stevenson explores how "evangelical dramaturgy" works to affectively instill core religious commitments.[23]

Long and Stevenson integrate observations from sites that materialize the Bible with other Christian cultural spaces and forms, but the most dedicated comparative analysis of the genre is Timothy Beal's *Roadside Religion*.[24] Beal's research reveals how these sites can be read as extensions of religious selves and ambitions. Through their creations, designers and builders of these attractions publicly display their stance toward scripture and their unique version of spirituality. Beal shows how sites that materialize the Bible exist as theological, biographical, and aesthetic imprints on local landscapes.

Sara Patterson presents a similar argument in *Middle of Nowhere*, which explores the life of Leonard Knight, creator of Salvation Mountain in the southern California desert.[25] The mountain, which is several stories high, is a 100-yard-long heap of adobe bricks (straw, water, clay), discarded car tires, and other scavenged and donated desert finds, all covered with thousands of gallons of paint. Knight began the project in 1984 after a born-again conversion experience, watched five years of work wash away in a massive rainstorm, and began again, working continuously until his death in 2014. A Sea of Galilee is the only direct biblical replication; the remainder materializes a singular biblical interpretation: "God is love." Through his creative labor, Knight built a sacred space, an emplaced mirror of his theological conviction, and a popular destination for ecumenically minded Christians, interfaith activists, outsider artists, and others seeking "weird" America.[26]

Scholars have expertly demonstrated how individual attractions have fascinating histories and how idiosyncratic projects still speak clearly to core issues in the study of religion (from embodied belief to sacred space). What remains to be written, and what I provide here, is a genre-wide appraisal, a global comparative analysis of the material, ideological, and experiential forms that unite seemingly disparate sites. Ultimately, it is the promises of intimacy and direct access to the biblical past that address the problem of authenticity.

## Of Gardens and Theme Parks: Four Subgenres

Looking across the world's sites that materialize the Bible, we find tremendous diversity. Sites fashion themselves quite differently, from art collections to educational museums, historically accurate replicas, devotional spots for prayer, and family-friendly, fun-filled spaces. While some attractions concentrate on a singular installation, such as Salvation Mountain, most are a choreographed jumble of different spaces, objects, and activities. The Fields of the Wood Bible Park in North Carolina's far southwestern corner is a good example.[27]

This "biblical outdoor theme park" takes its name from the King James translation of Psalm 132:4–6: "I will not give sleep to mine eyes, or slumber to mine eyelids until I find out a place for the Lord, an habitation for the Mighty God of Jacob; Lo, we heard of it at Ephrathah, we found it in the fields of the wood." Its history is coupled with the origins of the Church of God of Prophecy, a Holiness Pentecostal denomination born out of a nearby charismatic revival in 1896. An early convert, A. J. Tomlinson, received a prophetic word from God while praying at the site on June 13, 1903. Four decades later, he began constructing the place that still welcomes visitors.

Imagine turning right off a two-lane road and passing through an entry gate into a valley. The landscape is gorgeous, with rolling hilltops densely covered with tall trees and steeply ascending hillsides. There is no guided route through the park. Wandering around, you discover two Holy Land replicas: the Garden Tomb (with the stone rolled back to reveal an empty tomb) and Golgotha (complete with three wooden crosses). Numerous monuments recontextualize scriptural verses, including sections from Psalms and the New Testament Lord's Prayer. Written out across one of the steep hillsides are "the world's largest Ten Commandments." If you are able and inclined, you ascend 358 steps through the middle of the Commandments to reach a large monument displaying the text of Matthew 22:37–40. Ascending another hill takes you up 321 steps to Prayer Mountain and the spot where Tomlinson prayed in 1903; twenty-nine monuments spell out charismatic doctrine along the pathway up this hill.

Back in the valley, a gated baptismal pool with a bilingual (English-Spanish) sign announces that entry is by appointment only. Nearby there is an old two-engine plane, a retired part of the "White Angel Fleet." Signage explains that this plane was dispatched by the denomination for several years in the 1950s, "mainly within the United States and the Caribbean holding meetings, flyovers, and dropping tracts on cities and towns." The sign also observes that the Wright brothers' pioneering flight on the Atlantic coast occurred just three years after Tomlinson's prophecy, evidence that God used flight technology to advance evangelism.

Finally, a small restaurant and shop features gifts and souvenirs for purchase, such as a T-shirt that reads, "I climbed 11 Commandment Mountain"; the number 10 is also visible, but it is crossed out and replaced by the number 11, which refers to Jesus as the only "road to eternity." Fields of the Wood does not promise visitors a precisely re-created world but an immersive biblical destination. It is less about being transported to a particular moment in the biblical past (e.g., Noah and the Flood) and more about being in a biblically saturated environment that ties the present to the sacred past.

Given the diversity within and between sites that materialize the Bible, one wonders what unites them. All these sites create a space in which the written words of scripture are transformed into a physical, experiential, and choreographed environment. They offer visitors a place to travel to, visit, move through, interact with, and dwell in. (To learn the history? Pray? Read scripture? Walk alone? Walk with others? Picnic? Meet for business?) Though the world's more than 400 sites all create this kind of space, trying to view the collection as a single mass is challenging. While many attractions combine multiple elements, it is useful to divide them into four subgenres: biblical gardens, creation museums, biblical history museums, and re-creations.

### Biblical Gardens

The basic idea of a biblical garden is rather simple: select a space, create a boundary around it, and use yours hands and tools to fill the soil with herbs, flowers, shrubs, and trees named in the Bible. Perhaps olive and fig trees, rosemary and coriander, oleander and onion. Altogether, these gardens name more than 100 botanical varieties known from scripture, though they vary in how many varieties are said to exist and how many are planted. This subgenre is the most pervasive form of materializing the Bible, constituting about 40 percent of all sites.

How do the garden sites characterize themselves? Caretakers, tour guides, guidebooks, brochures, and websites consistently foreground devotional possibilities. Biblical gardens are places for prayer, meditation, silent reflection, and contemplation. In Paradise Valley, Arizona—an affluent Phoenix municipality—a United Methodist Church started its garden in the 1960s when the congregation was founded (Figure 2.1).

The site is variously described as a "sacred place of healing and beauty," "a place of [God's] presence," a place "for a quiet stroll, a time of meditation or a picnic," and "a place of prayer, healing, and celebration."[28] The devotional promise of gardens is accentuated by the presence of other prayer-centered spaces, most commonly a seven-circuit walking labyrinth. Biblical gardens testify to critiques of theology and theory that sever the history of prayer from physical channels of place and materiality.[29]

Biblical gardens are also designed to teach, promising unique access to the stories, places, and figures of scripture. An Evangelical Lutheran Church of America garden in rural Circleville, Ohio, integrates devotional possibilities ("rest and meditate") with the space's potential to work as a teaching aid to "show what some of the plants mentioned in the Bible look like [and] remind us of lessons taught by Jesus."[30] The Germantown Jewish Centre in northwest Philadelphia, an Orthodox Jewish synagogue and social hub, uses a brief story to highlight its gar-

Figure 2.1. Gated entryway to the biblical garden at Paradise Valley United Methodist Church. Photo by author.

den's pedagogical potential: "One of our gardeners, reading in Psalms about the wicked, who are 'like chaff that wind blows away,' realized from her experience gathering wheat in the Israel Garden that the chaff does not separate from the grain without human intervention. The image in the Psalm became for her not vaguely agricultural but specifically, and richly, about harvest."[31]

The pedagogy of the garden is fundamentally experiential. It calls to visitors, inviting them to learn the text of scripture better through a physical encounter with cultivated nature. Mass pilgrimage-tourism to Palestine made a similar call when it began in the mid-1800s, attracting travelers through the promised revelation of scriptural geography. Historian Stephanie Stidham Rogers neatly captures this promise in her study of Protestant travel narratives: "The 'fifth gospel' (i.e., the Holy Land) became a way to skip centuries of ecclesiastical corruption and excess . . . to return to the basic, original, and undeniable truths of the Gospel."[32] Biblical gardens—like their close cousin, Holy Land replications—invoke this tradition of the fifth gospel. The Rodef Shalom Biblical Botanical Garden, a Reformed Jewish site in downtown Pittsburgh, does so in the welcome text of its website home page: "Enter the Holy Land, a replica of ancient Israel in our Biblical Botanical Garden with more than 100 temperate and tropical plants. See the land of the Bible, the Holy Land—ancient Israel, in a setting of a cascading waterfall, a desert, a bubbling stream, the Jordan, which meanders through the garden from Lake Kineret to the Dead Sea."[33]

Biblical gardens aim to immerse visitors in the natural world of scripture. Direct access to the biblical past is promised through the human sensorium. Feel the branches, rub the leaves between your fingers, smell the flowers, taste the fruit and herbs, appreciate the vibrant colors. If Holy Land pilgrimage promises travelers the opportunity to walk where Jesus walked, gardens promise visitors they can smell what Moses and Jesus smelled. At the biblical garden, the quality of the Bible as a printed book is sidelined, at least temporarily; while it may be the Book for the devout, it is by no means only a book.

## Creation Museums

If gardens are united by botanical and sensorial immersion, creation museums are united by their unrelenting performance of a particular biblical hermeneutic. These museums, which constitute about 10 percent of all sites that materialize the Bible, are found in the United States, Canada, Germany, Australia, England, Northern Ireland, and Portugal. This subgenre is defined by five traits: (1) Creation museums promote the creationist worldview, including the belief that the earth is approximately 6,000 years old; that human beings are a special creation of God (not the result of biological evolution); that humans and dinosaurs coexisted because God created all living things in successive days as recorded in the book of Genesis; and that the Flood of Noah was a literal historical event that killed all but the eight people on board the ark. (2) These museums re-create biblical scenes to illustrate the textual ideology that the Christian Bible is God's inerrant and authoritative revelation to humanity and should be read as literal history. (3) They reject the legitimacy of evolutionary science, often in vehemently antagonistic terms. (4) They argue for the legitimacy of "creation science," which is the appropriation of selected scientific theory and method to support creationist tenets. (5) They present an evangelical theological message of born-again salvation.

What do producers and supporters hope to accomplish in a creation museum? The genre of "museum" is in itself revealing because it marks the creationist movement's public ambition to wrest cultural authority away from mainstream science by producing its own version of the natural history museum. A significant aim for creation museums is the edification and training of committed creationists, to better equip adherents as witnesses for creationism. Of course, there are also hopes for the religious transformation of visitors, converting noncreationists to creationism and non-Christians to Christianity.

A few creation museums are designed to travel (i.e., they can be put up and taken down in a day), but most are brick-and-mortar attractions. Ranging widely in size and technological quality, all are affiliated with either a ministry, a congregation, or a youth camp. For a closer portrait, consider two museums that teach nearly identical creationist content but pursue the task with different resource capacities.

Just west of Akron, Ohio, is the Akron Fossils and Science Center.[34] Family owned, this 4,500-square-foot museum opened in 2005 after two years of construction. The building sits at an intersection of two-lane roads, and parking is available for about twenty cars. Outside on the property there is a small play area for children and a 200-foot zip line. The museum offers only guided tours with a staff member. The roughly one-hour experience moves through four spaces: a welcome room that poses creationist questions; a "geology and archaeology" room that combines physical evidence with negative biographic profiles of famous evolutionary scientists and an argument for why dragon legends explain human-dinosaur coexistence; a "biblical authority" room that asserts a literalist reading of Genesis; and a gift shop area with one bookshelf and small trinkets (including dinosaur figurines). Fluorescent lighting, low ceilings, and a musty smell pervade the space.

Two hundred fifty miles to the south is the Answers in Genesis Creation Museum in northern Kentucky. Answers in Genesis broke ground on the facility in 2001, and six years later, the 75,000-square-foot, $30 million project opened to public controversy and media fanfare. Visiting the Creation Museum is at least an all-day experience, once you explore the petting zoo, the botanical gardens, the zip line course (twenty different lines, the longest stretching to 1,800 feet), the café, the planetarium, lectures by AiG staff, the large bookstore and gift shop, the lobby with exhibits, and the sixteen-room "Museum Experience Walk."

Creationist supporters, media journalists, and critical and sympathetic scholars all recognize that the Creation Museum is the world's most elaborate and technologically sophisticated creation museum. Indeed, places like the Akron Fossils and Science Center—deeply sincere as they are—force an appreciation of the scale, creative design, marketing savvy, and professionalism of the Kentucky attraction. If I was a creationist, and Akron was the going standard prior to 2007, then AiG's facility would be an undeniable source of celebratory pride.

### Biblical History Museums

The promise to make the Bible "come alive," to transport visitors "back in time," is also performed by the subgenre of biblical history museums. These attractions collect scriptural manuscripts and/or archaeological objects from the Levant and display them in narrated exhibits. Most of these sites are affiliated with Protestant denominations or organizations and reproduce a pervasive Protestant textual ideology: as "God's Word," the Bible has been divinely preserved, protected, and promoted throughout time. Such museums, which constitute about 15 percent of all sites that materialize the Bible, can be found in the United States, Australia, Brazil, Canada, the Czech Republic, Germany, Hungary, India, Ireland, Israel, Latvia, the Netherlands, Pakistan, the Philippines, and South Korea.

Biblical history museums concentrate on different curations. Some emphasize the history of Bible translation, globally or with a focus on a particular language, and feature a range of influential and unique manuscripts. You are likely to find historically significant items like copies of a Latin Vulgate, a Wycliffe New Testament, or Dead Sea scroll fragments. You are also likely to find more idiosyncratic inventions, like the Bible on microfilm (perhaps the world's smallest Ten Commandments) or the Holy Bible for Minecrafters. Other museums focus on lavishly illustrated versions of the Bible. For example, at Trinity College Dublin, the Book of Kells exhibition invites visitors to interact with the illustrated scriptural pages of this ninth-century iconic Irish book and early model of Anglo-Celtic Insular art.[35] Together, these two forms of biblical history museum perform a collaborative relationship between agentive Christians, missionaries and artists, and their divine inspiration.

Other museums focus on original artifacts and artifact replicas from archaeological excavations in biblical lands. Pottery, coins, and other discoveries are paired with biblical texts and narrated to show how they illuminate scriptural stories. These collections emphasize aspects of ancient quotidian and economic life, such as agricultural and domestic practices. For example, the Bade Museum of Biblical Archaeology (housed at the ecumenical Pacific School of Religion in Berkeley, California) displays finds from a Palestinian site, "most likely the biblical town of Mizpah", excavated in the 1920s and 1930s, that "provide graphic evidence of everyday activities in a provincial town of three thousand years ago."[36]

Like Fields of the Wood, many biblical history museums provide a jumble of experiences. Most feature some combination of translation, art, and archaeology, and many integrate other elements. You can find biblical replicas (an Ark of the Covenant, Herod's Temple, the Wilderness Tabernacle), floor models of Holy Land topography, model and working replicas of a Gutenberg press, replicas of archaeological dig sites, and various interactive activities (e.g., ones that allow you to make your own cuneiform tablet or operate a printing press).

Like the global set of creation museums, biblical history museums vary widely in ambition and financial backing. Just north of Dollywood and the Great Smoky Mountain National Park, one can visit the Treasuring the Word Rare Bible and Book Museum. In a rented one-room space in a strip mall next to an insurance office, visitors can view such items as a 1250 Hebrew scroll, a 1591 Geneva Bible, and a first-edition King James Bible, all housed in protective glass.

Then, there is the Museum of the Bible: a multistory, 430,000-square-foot attraction owned by the founders of Hobby Lobby and located two blocks from the U.S. Capitol in Washington, DC. The museum contains the Green Collection, the world's largest private assemblage of biblical antiquities, consisting of more than 40,000 pieces. It promises to "provide guests with an immersive and personalized experience as they explore the history, narrative, and impact of the Bible."[37] Although they emerge from vastly different resource capacities, Treasuring the Word and Museum of the Bible ensue from shared imperatives and are grounded by the same promise.

Whatever their composition or emphasis, biblical history museums exist primarily as educational institutions. Most of them have no admission charge, and most invite visitors to schedule group tours. Some are evangelically oriented, while others operate more as public institutions. No matter their affiliation, they place particular emphasis on the historicity of the Bible. While the Bible is recognized or revered as a sacred text, these museums promise visitors a "journey through history" using culturally significant objects from the past. If biblical gardens call attention away from the quality of the Bible as a book, these museums call exaggerated attention to the Bible as a book in history. Yet they also insist that the Bible is far more than a text to be read; it is a phenomenon of history, culture, creativity, and providence.

*Re-creations*

The fourth subgenre is the most diverse and accounts for about 30 percent of sites worldwide. Here, particular biblical scenes, stories, and characters are replicated across multiple media. Some attractions have a singular focus, such as re-creations of Noah's ark or the Wilderness Tabernacle. Historically, the most robust form of re-creation is the concentrated replication of Holy Land spots and geography. The oldest documented site is in the northern Italian province of Vercelli. Here, in the town of Varallo, a hilltop area is arranged as a re-creation of New Testament scenes in Jerusalem's Old City. The site was built by Franciscan monks in the 1490s to offer a surrogate pilgrimage experience, emerging from this monastic order's role as "custodians" of Jerusalem's sacred sites beginning in the thirteenth century.[38]

This subgenre has been especially popular in the United States, with nearly twenty different Holy Land replications. The first, Palestine Park, was sculpted from and into the earth by New York's Chautauqua Institution in 1874. This 400-foot landscape model included mountains, rivers, seas, and cities in miniature. Palestine Park was part of Chautauqua's broader Methodist project of training Sunday school teachers. Chautauqua Lake was transformed into the Mediterranean Sea, and visitors, taken to the model by boat, were encouraged to envision themselves stepping off the boat onto scriptural territory. Chautauquans often attended lectures at the model dressed in Middle Eastern cloaks and robes. By inviting audiences into a re-created landscape, Chautauqua capitalized on the immersive impact of role playing in a themed setting. Emplacement was the goal, and the material environment, natural and human-shaped, was the means. As described by religion scholar Burke Long, "Realism was the driving aim, fantasy the enabling impulse."[39]

Others sites have come and gone on the American landscape. For example, Holy Land USA in Waterbury, Connecticut, was an eighteen-acre park that operated from 1955 through 1984. A walking path among miniature replications of Jerusalem and Bethlehem, Holy Land USA was built during the post–World War II economic boom and welcomed 40,000 annual visitors during its peak years. It closed amid the deindustrialization that swept across America's northeastern Rust Belt, and today it sits dormant, corroding and overgrown. However, it may be poised for a comeback. Local business owners purchased the park from the city in June 2013 for $350,000 with the aim of restoring and reopening it. The newly re-formed Holy Land USA describes itself as a "historic, cultural, and educational landmark honoring religious and spiritual traditions."[40] When I visited in December 2015, it was closed to the public, but we ignored the "No Trespassing" sign and explored the grounds. Although it was mostly dreary, there were signs of life. In 2015, a local Boy Scout erected a two-meter-tall replica of the Tower of Babel for his Eagle Scout project, built from local gray stone with the words "Tower of Babel" freshly painted in red and white.

America's most (in)famous Holy Land replication is built on fifteen acres, eleven miles northeast of Walt Disney World. The Holy Land Experience (HLE) opened in 2001, struggled financially, and was purchased in 2007 for $37 million by Trinity Broadcasting Network, the thriving, transnational Pentecostal media corporation. Among the park's many exhibits is a floor model of Jerusalem circa 66 ce, which HLE claims as the world's largest indoor replica of Jerusalem. The room is painted purple from floor to ceiling, and the model is situated by cardinal direction, with a replica of the Wailing Wall to the east, complete with artificial weeds sprouting from crevices (Figure 2.2).[41] The floor on the east and west sides inclines slightly, enhancing the bird's-eye view

Figure 2.2. Jerusalem floor model at the Holy Land Experience. Photo by author.

when a viewer circles the model. The wooden floor creaks beneath the worn, yet plush, bright purple carpet.

Four guided presentations of the model, lasting thirty minutes, are performed every day at staggered intervals. When I visited in March 2014, Dr. Bill, a veteran pilgrimage guide to Israel-Palestine, stepped onto a tiny square of a speaking platform atop the model. He joked in a literalist register: "The Bible says there were giants in the land, and here I am." Speaking with a headset microphone, Dr. Bill used a flashlight to highlight spots of interest on the model. The crowd seemed to listen attentively, sitting in chairs and leaning against the model's sides, periodically snapping photos with their iPhones or their point-and-shoot or more sophisticated cameras. Dr. Bill's presentation mixed biblical events with Protestant-inflected anecdotes. For example, he explained that this was Jerusalem at its population peak before the Roman invasion; Herod was as architecturally gifted as he was morally corrupt; Satan tempted Jesus to jump from the Temple's highest point; and Peter and John healed a man on the Temple steps in the book of Acts. Visitors also learn that today's valley is forty-two feet higher than that represented in the model. This kind of narration mirrors evangelical Holy Land pilgrimages, in which other periods and lives (namely, Ottoman and Muslim) are erased as "oriental clutter" obscuring scriptural truth.[42] Dr. Bill closed his sweeping historical tour by proclaiming a modest ambition, "I hope the scriptures come a bit more alive with the model in your mind," and inviting us all to purchase a laminated map of the model to enhance our Bible study back home.

***

Through four subgenres—gardens, creation museums, history museums, and re-creations—the Bible is materialized around the world, and multiple kinds of cultural work are performed. In many cases, sites that materialize the Bible are about creating sacred space and expressing the spiritual and theological convictions of their founders.[43] Along with their devotional possibilities, many of these attractions are also pedagogical, working as a form of, and forum for, Bible study. Via various modes of replication, visitors can gain contact with the land of scripture without actually traveling to Israel-Palestine. This pedagogy mimics what religion scholar Hillary Kaell observes about the use of historical immersion tools in late nineteenth-century and early twentieth-century Sunday schools: "Students were taught to navigate the atlas's densely covered maps and memorize its practical guides to Bible life, [facilitating] imaginative journeys with Jesus in his own time."[44] Similarly, sites that materialize the Bible are designed to increase visitors' intimacy with scripture and afford more direct access to the scriptural past. Given this survey of attractions, we can pose a further question: How are select material forms used to organize the devotional and pedagogical promises of attractions?

## Performing Authenticity

Materializing the Bible is a response to the core Christian problem of authenticity. It is a means of reckoning with the irreducible fact of temporal and cultural separation, a way to construct and secure a continuity of faith. Consider three particular strategies used to increase intimacy with scripture and access the biblical past: architecture, land, and cultivated nature.

These strategies are best understood in semiotic terms, that is, embedded in processes of signifying meaning and action. I borrow the terms "indexicality" and "iconicity" from American philosopher Charles Sanders Peirce and his framework for how signs work.[45] Peircean semiotics rests on a distinction between three types of sign—"symbol," "index," and "icon"—which differ based on the relationship they construct between the object in the world being referenced and the linguistic or material item used to make the reference. Symbols function according to a relation based on social convention, whereas indexical and iconic signs function, respectively, via natural and mimetic relations. Smoke, for example, is indexical because it is naturally linked with its object, fire.

To construct an intimacy with scripture, and perform religious authenticity, sites that materialize the Bible appeal to ideologies of direct connection (indexicality) and resemblance (iconicity). As anthropologist Webb Keane has argued, indexical and iconic signs are particularly potent because they connect ideology with materiality. Their potency is aesthetic, registering via the body by mobilizing sensory experience.[46]

*Architecture*

One strategy for performing authenticity is to make architectural appeals. This strategy takes two forms. First, sites play on the indexical property that the replica they have created is not merely *like* the biblical original but is built according to the *exact* dimensions named in scripture. Ark Encounter is a premier example of this type of site. In the public press conference held in December 2010, and in nearly every piece of publicity for the next five and a half years, the ministry's re-created ark was described as "full-scale." Other examples include re-creations of the Garden Tomb and the Wilderness Tabernacle.

The second oldest Tabernacle replica in the United States is housed at the Mennonite Information Center in Lancaster, Pennsylvania. Created in 1948 by an evangelical pastor in St. Petersburg, Florida, and moved to Pennsylvania in 1970, the site features "a full-size, wax figure of the high priest," clothed in "authentic robes," surrounded by "made-to-scale" replicas of the Golden Candlestick and Table of Shew Bread, and "a fully researched design of the veil [that] separates the people from the presence of God just like in olden times." These replicas reside in a layout built according to the dimensions named in the book of Exodus.[47] The Pennsylvania replica is a permanent display, but there are also several "life-size" traveling Tabernacle exhibits. One California-based ministry describes its replica as "not a museum [and] not a theatre production. The Tabernacle Experience is an Encounter with the Living God! One step inside the Tabernacle Courtyard will transport you into Old Testament times."[48]

Life-size Noah's arks and Wilderness Tabernacles insist on accuracy, not approximation. They construct an indexical link between sign-vehicle (replication) and object (Bible). As sensory experiences, "exact" replicas promise a powerful form of embodied presence. When visitors are inside the Tabernacle, they are encouraged to recognize that the scale of everything around them is just as it was for Moses and others for 500 years: the height of the ceiling, the size of ritual items, the distance between items. Embodied presence is about the feel of being inside a biblical structure, not merely viewing it from a distance.

The experiential promise of Ark Encounter is anchored largely by this feeling of stepping into scripture. After all, the theological content being taught is no different from what creationists have circulated for decades in websites, books, and museums. Numerous explanatory placards on board the ark come directly from previous AiG publications. Just after the park opened in July 2016, the ministry released a one-hour video of a walking interview with the exhibits' lead "content manager." The detailed tour, which included camera close-ups of images and signage, poses no threat of spoiling the experience because the affective force is illegible unless the viewer is physically present inside the park. Roughly halfway through the tour, the interviewer observes to the viewing audience: "[Before being here] I was just seeing it on the live stream videos, like you guys are today. And, one thing that I noticed, when I came here, it was totally different, grander, very unique. You can only get a glimpse of what you're seeing in the live stream as when you actually come."

Alongside indexical sites that claim to be of actual biblical size, iconic sites claim to be "exact scale models." Among others, you can find scaled-down replicas of Noah's ark, the Tower of Babel, Solomon's Temple, Herod's Temple, and the Western Wall. The lure of Palestine Park was wedded to its claims of mathematical accuracy as a landscape replica. The same is true of the still-operating Palestine Gardens in

Lucedale, Mississippi. There, a Holy Land in miniature invites visitors to come and "cross the River Jordan, pass the ruins of Joshua's Jericho, see the New Testament Jericho, one of the palaces of Herod, continue on to Bethlehem, and Jerusalem."[49]

Five years after Chautauqua's debut, a scale model of nineteenth-century Jerusalem was added to the attractions at Ocean Grove, New Jersey, a Holiness Methodist camp meeting site that sought to meld leisure, urban escape, and spiritual regeneration.[50] Visitors were led on virtual tours, mimicking the Palestine tours that became immensely popular after the Civil War. A 1919 description by an Ocean Grove Camp Meeting Association trustee boasted that the model had 1,200 miniature trees, cost $2,500 to create (approximately $57,000 in contemporary dollars), and was "so accurate in the reproduction that scores of travelers who have visited Jerusalem have found keen delight in identifying its different sections and even individual buildings."[51] The primary sensory register for these iconic scale models is the visual. The historian Troy Messenger captures this well in his description of how Ocean Grove visitors consumed the model: "The experience of 'awe' at a visual representation of the holy sounds distinctly un-Protestant. But because the model was an 'exact' representation, to visit it was somehow to visit the real city, not just because it was the educational equivalent but because it was also the spiritual equivalent."[52]

## Land

In various ways, land is put to indexical and iconic uses. For example, natural materials from biblical lands are used to construct sites. In northwestern New Jersey, the Holy House of Loreto replica at the Our Lady's Blue Army Shrine includes "stones from the actual Holy House."[53] Holy Land USA in southwestern Virginia, which is now closed, included sand from the Negev Desert. And the Temple of Solomon replica in São Paulo, Brazil—headquarters for the Pentecostal Universal Church of the Kingdom of God since 2014—includes stones that cost $8 million and were flown directly from Israel. We could think of such landscape integrations as a kind of devotional relic, or we could think of them as bolstering the performance of authenticity. The latter aligns more closely with how similar practices work for modern Holy Land pilgrims. As

Kaell describes in *Walking Where Jesus Walked*, such pilgrims commonly bring home stones, sand, and olive wood as gifts and souvenirs, not for any magical properties they possess but for their indexical associations with the places of scripture.[54]

The Coming King Sculpture Prayer Garden in the Texas Hill Country uses an iconic link to land that is not present at other sites. This twenty-three-acre park, which opened in 2004, features a series of bronze Mary and Jesus statues, as well as *The Empty Cross*, a seven-story, seventy-ton steel sculpture designed to signify the Resurrection. The nondenominational, charismatic ministry that operates the site narrates its history as a series of "supernatural miracles." One such miracle is the plot of land that God "set aside" for purchase, "which looks just like the Biblical Holy Land . . . the site is 'high and lifted up,' 1,900 feet above sea level, halfway between the Atlantic and Pacific Oceans on Interstate 10, at the same exact latitude of Israel!"[55]

Landscape can also form an iconic link between a replica and the original. Timothy Beal's *Roadside Religion* takes readers to Virginia's Holy Land USA, just a few years before the park permanently closed. The effectiveness of this site was deeply reliant on its setting. Located in the foothills of the Blue Ridge Mountains, the local geology and geography could claim little indexical link with Israel-Palestine. Nevertheless, it set the conditions for "profound religious experiences" by immersing visitors in "a wilderness context." The setting invokes pivotal biblical events, in which figures ("think of Moses, Elijah, David, and Jesus") were transformed by a nature experience, separated from their everyday contexts.[56] Similarly, Sara Patterson argues in *Middle of Nowhere* that Leonard Knight's seeking of and settling in the desert have intense symbolic resonance with the biblical wanderings of Moses and Jesus.[57] It is not merely the literal landscape itself that signifies, but the sense of emplacement that can be generated. How far might these iconic associations extend?

In March 2016, I first visited the Garden of Hope in northern Kentucky, directly across the Ohio River from Cincinnati. Completed in 1958 by an evangelical pastor who traveled to the Holy Land in 1938, this small attraction sits on the backside of a working-class neighborhood. It is largely hidden, with little road signage; if you are not seeking it, you are not likely to find it. The main attraction is a replica of Jerusalem's Garden Tomb (Figure 2.3).

Figure 2.3. Garden Tomb replica at the Garden of Hope. Photo by author.

The hilltop location sits directly above I-75, and the constant sound of rushing freeway traffic directly below saturates the soundscape. When facing the tomb, you turn around to an unobstructed view of the Cincinnati skyline. Perhaps it was the founder's reason for choosing this particular spot, or perhaps it is a common visitor association or just a product of my comparative imagination, but I wonder if the city in the backdrop serves as a kind of Jerusalem. If Jesus left the tomb and encountered his city, perhaps visitors are encouraged to leave this tomb to encounter theirs.

## Cultivated Nature

One of the more sensorially engaging indexical strategies occurs through the cultivation of nature, which is exemplified by biblical gardens. Most gardens adhere closely to the aim of teaching how flora were used during the biblical past and how the botanical qualities of flora accent the meaning of scriptural content. To achieve this goal, biblical gardens aim to immerse visitors in the Bible's natural world. This immersive imperative is captured nicely by the opening text of a guiding pamphlet prepared by an American Baptist congregation in eastern Connecticut:

> Welcome members, friends and visitors to a special garden to *rest your senses* by the simplicity of *rewinding time*—to Biblical time! *Sit* under the Tamarix; let the *coolness* of its shade and gentle breeze *touch* your face *just as Jesus* and his disciples did during their travels. As you *watch* the bees bounce among the Hyssop, *imagine* the *taste* of honey they make for you *just as* they made honey for Jesus. *Enjoy the smell* of Juniper sage mint *as enjoyed by Jesus* as he visited many gardens. In the sunlit renewal of spring, *look upon* the colorful bulbs in bloom *just as Jesus* did when he spoke of the "lilies of the field." Do this and comfort and joy will come.[58] (emphasis added)

This framing text uses a familiar biblical poetic device, the parallelism of "just as," to perform an immersive imperative that is decidedly sensory: sit, touch, watch, imagine the taste, enjoy the smell.

Almost without exception, biblical gardens around the world include two features: pathways and benches. These features pose as mundane, but they are anything but because they work as experiential invitations. They insist that the garden is not designed to be gazed on from the outside or hastily hurried through. Biblical gardens are designed to be moved through, experienced from the inside, and lingered in. In this way, biblical gardens follow a principle of cultivated nature more broadly: "Gardens build in a mobile, participatory aesthetic that emphasizes movement and continuing hands-on engagement in all dimensions."[59]

As visitors move through and linger in biblical gardens, they are encouraged to get caught up in sensory immersion. Smell the fragrant lavender. Touch the gnarled trunk of an olive tree. Pick a bay leaf and rub it between your fingers. Pinch a small sample of herbs and taste. Appreciate the vibrant red skin of a ripened pomegranate. Hear the sound of grape leaves rustled by the breeze. Be surrounded by scripture via Holy Land botanicals.

The sensory immersion of the biblical garden rests on what Keane calls a semiotic ideology, a belief about what counts as a sign and how it signifies.[60] The ideology at work is about the fixed quality of human-nature engagements, a relation unaffected by time, history, or culture. The promise to visitors is that they are gaining unmediated access to the biblical past: lavender smells as it always has, olive trunks feel the same, rustling grape leaves sound the same. This promise has characterized the subgenre since its beginning. In one of the first how-to books published for a popular audience in 1941, *Bible Plants for American Gardens*, the author writes in her preface: "Plants mentioned in the Bible are the living link between us and the people of these hallowed and distant times. . . . We can reach back to Bible days, through two thousand springtimes, when we plant a garden."[61] You are linked to the biblical past because the human sensorium and the natural world have not changed. The ancient botanical world is your botanical world. Your embodied experience was their embodied experience. In short, a semiotic ideology of sensory indexicality organizes the garden experience.

Other rituals that materialize the Bible also rely on this bodily testimony. Consider the "biblical meal," a service that is offered at numerous re-creations, such as the Biblical History Center in western Georgia. Visitors eat a meal composed solely of foods native to Israel-Palestine, such as "fruits, dates, nuts [and] pita bread," all prepared according to "traditional" or "ancient" methods.[62] The indexical promise mirrors that of the biblical garden: experience the Bible directly through the evidence of your senses. The meal and the garden have, not surprisingly, been combined. A 1976 cookbook, *Biblical Garden Cookery*, details more than 300 recipes that use only biblical ingredients.[63] And, during a tour of the Paradise Valley United Methodist garden in April 2016, the caretaker explained that birds eat the figs before they can be harvested, but the pomegranates, dates, and edible herbs grown on site are regularly incorporated into church meals.

## Conclusion

"Any form of representation is gloriously presumptuous and deeply engaged in contention about truth."[64] David Morgan offers this reflection in the context of analyzing how religions mobilize visual culture. Around the world, more than 400 sites materialize the Bible; that is, they transform the written words of scripture into physical, experiential, and choreographed environments. They do so through diverse subgenres:

museums, theme parks, and gardens. Some are educational, some devotional, some evangelistic, and some designed to be fun. Some are all four. Some are elaborate and expensive, others rather basic. Some are controversial, others not. Some are playful, all are sincere. Variously flirting with and exemplifying Morgan's maxim of glorious presumption, all attractions that materialize the Bible are anchored by the promise to build an intimate, affective bond with scripture.

Some readers may question the potential gaps between the promises sites make to visitors and the historical facts that nag replication. The Garden Tomb is an example. Many Protestants believe this spot in Jerusalem, first unearthed in 1867, is the authentic site of Jesus's burial and Resurrection. They embrace this commitment in opposition to the Catholic-Orthodox tradition, dating back to at least the fourth century, that names the Church of the Holy Sepulcher as the authentic site. And they do so against a mass of historical and archaeological evidence that favors the Holy Sepulcher.[65]

Biblical gardens confront other gaps, such as the difficulty of equating scripture's botanical terminology with modern varietals. In July 2016, I took the audio tour of the Bible Path at the Jerusalem Botanical Gardens. The tour consisted of twenty-seven short segments, including discussions of twenty-two plants in the garden and five framing discussions. One framing discussion, "The Challenge of Identifying Biblical Plants," directly engages this gap. For example, the audio track asks what fruit the Tree of Knowledge bore. It dismisses the apple, identifying this image as a product of European art, and goes on to explain different rabbinical interpretations: fig, wheat, grape, and other possibilities that have been suggested. The track concludes with two short sentences: "So, what was it? We'll never know."

Although these and other gaps are quite real, they pose no fatal danger to the experiential promises of the attractions. The indexical and iconic strategies of these sites continue to operate because the significations at work are embedded in historical, social, and ideological processes.[66] That is, the strategies are not functioning on their own; they are functioning in an ecology with each other and vis-à-vis durable cultural patterns, such as textual ideologies about biblical authority and theologically specific gazes onto places like the Holy Land.[67]

At sites that materialize the Bible, the physical, sensory, and orchestrated channels of body, technology, object, and place intersect to promise direct access to the biblical past. Taken together, the strategies used to enhance intimacy and collapse temporal distance address the core problem of authenticity that animates Christianity. To close, I highlight a related scriptural quality performed by these sites.

Materializing the Bible highlights how the cultural reproduction of biblical commitments is intimately tied to creativity and imagination. We can appreciate these dynamics further when we recognize that the category "Bible" is transmedial.[68] To consider a cultural object as transmedial is to observe that it is mobile across multiple media genres, rather than being confined to a single genre. This observation resonates with the argument that "the Bible" cannot be reduced to simply being a book.[69] Rather, "the Bible" is an open category that can be variously actualized. A volume of sixty-six translated texts is one actualization, but so are other textual versions (such as children's Bibles, manga Bibles, illustrated Bibles, or Braille Bibles), stained glass art, films, television miniseries, live theater productions, board games, video games, the Wordless Book, biblical garden terrariums, virtual reality simulations, and so on.

Attractions that materialize the Bible—from nineteenth-century touring panoramas to Kentucky's Ark Encounter—continue to expand the transmedial boundaries of the category "Bible." The communications scholar Mark Wolf, in his study of fantasy world-making, argues that "trans-medial growth and adaptation enrich an imaginary world beyond what any single medium could present, and also make the world less tied to its medium of origin."[70] This works for fostering market consumption and for bolstering affective attachments to the transmedial object. If virtual reality simulations of biblical stories offer a digitized experiential layer, attractions that materialize the Bible offer an emplaced, embodied layer. Resonance expands with each transmedial addition. In this way, traditions of biblicism may have significant similarities with franchises like *The Lord of the Rings*, *Star Wars*, and countless others.

In later chapters, it will be helpful to recall the context outlined here regarding the aesthetic promises, affective ties to authority, and transmedial dynamics of materializing the Bible. From this global view, we next zoom in to Ark Encounter's creative team and its cultural production of a creationist theme park. How does the team's creative labor reflect its dual commitment to fundamentalism and to the strategies and imperatives of immersive entertainment?

# 3

# Cultural Producers

Cubicles and creativity. Are these words you typically hear spoken in the same breath? Not me. The former conjures images of boring, mindlessly repetitive, and unrewarding labor. Pop culture satires are the connotations that come to mind—the film *Office Space*, the sitcom *The Office*, the comic strip *Dilbert*—followed by corporate experiments with "open" office arrangements that promise to extract maximum productivity.[1]

Religion scholar Kathryn Lofton writes a different history of the most recognizable symbol in American office life. She discovers that the cubicle was conceived as a blank canvas on which individuality could emerge: "The limited territory of quiet the system provided was a staging area where the worker's ideas could be born."[2] This description is much closer to what I found in a warehouse-turned-design-studio in northern Kentucky, where the Ark Encounter creative team began renting space in January 2011. Here, the team erected basic cubicles in a large windowless area atop polished concrete floors (Figure 3.1). This was the team members' blank canvas for more than six years of creative labor in their effort to produce creationist religious publicity.

## Cultural Production

Ethnographies of cultural production promise a payoff: by studying processes of making, we will better understand what is made and how made things circulate socially. Production processes are obscured or hidden when we study only processes of circulation and consumption.[3] In turn, distinctive insight is generated about cultural content, aspiration, and identity. With Ark Encounter, getting backstage meant gaining access to creative labor, design decision making, collaborative artistry, project planning, and clashes of artistic vision. The value of capturing these processes is that they always point beyond themselves. Understanding the team's creative process and labor is pivotal for understanding its

Figure 3.1. The main room at the Ark Encounter design studio. Photo by author.

ambition to create public culture that would bolster the cultural legitimacy and authority of creationism.

Anthropology has a long history of studying cultural production, from the Hollywood film industry to public television, anime studios, and advertising agencies.[4] Much of this work can be called "studying up" because it shifts the ethnographic focus from poor, marginalized, disempowered, and subaltern communities to people "who shape attitudes and control institutional structures."[5] Such research typically reveals that the process of production is replete with creativity and fraught with contingencies, complicated social relationships, and often competing agendas. Further, cultural producers are not exempt from the patterns of culture; they themselves are shaped by those patterns. The Ark Encounter team was shaped primarily by modern entertainment and Protestant fundamentalism. Producers are not puppeteers pulling the marionette strings of consumers, but their work is influential. It plays a structuring role in establishing the potential range of consumptive practices.

Ethnographies of producing Christian public culture informed my fieldwork with the Ark Encounter team—works such as Matthew Engelke's study of the British Bible Society and Katrien Pype's study of Pentecostal melodramatic TV fictions in Kinshasha, the capital of the Democratic Republic of the Congo. Pype focuses on the television actors, from their work in the studio to their everyday lives at home and in the city, and finds that the production of these serials is both contested and collaborative. Actors argue over directorial and performative decisions, but they work together from the shared imperative that the Congolese public sphere should be populated with a Pentecostal presence. Much like Ark Encounter, these melodramatic serials seek "to trigger the emotions of awe and amazement that might push viewers to [convert]."[6] Engelke, Pype, and others have demonstrated that we can better understand Christian public culture when we understand contexts of production.

My fieldwork with the Ark Encounter creative team instilled in me a deep appreciation for how forms of public culture emerge from years of preparation and planning, and the work of countless decisions both large and small. It also engendered a deep appreciation for how cultural producers will invest significant time, energy, and creativity in even the smallest of details, some of which are efforts that never make it past an initial concept stage. Studies of cultural production enable the discarded draft and the unrealized idea to join the ethnographic record.

How do the backstage processes of producing Ark Encounter inform the park's ambitions of religious publicity? I use the concept of "dialogic creativity" to address this question. The qualifier "dialogic" comes from the literary critic Mikhail Bakhtin and references the fact that any cultural product (e.g., a creationist theme park) is not defined by a singular voice but emerges from networks of existing ideology and discourse.[7] The team's creativity is best characterized as dialogic because it is inflected with the voices of multiple networks: the relationships among team members; references to their past work together (namely, the Creation Museum); antagonism with "secular culture" and "evolutionism"; and enthusiastic engagements with Disney and Hollywood. Because the creative labor discussed here centers on the Ark Encounter team, this analysis begins by introducing the team members.

*The Team*

Talking with colleagues, family, friends, students, and strangers through-out the research process, I was frequently asked whether or not the artists themselves are creationists. Yes, they are. Still, this is an instructive question. Those who ask it wonder whether a creationist theme park could be dreamed up only by true believers or if any hired hand could do the job. It is a question about sincerity and professionalism, about the relation between creative labor and religious commitment.

All Answers in Genesis employees and volunteers are required to af-firm a "statement of faith," which combines biblical fundamentalism, Religious Right culture wars, and young earth creationism. The twenty-nine-point statement includes declarations such as the following: "The 66 books of the Bible are the written Word of God. . . . Its authority is not limited to spiritual, religious, or redemptive themes but includes its assertions in such fields as history and science"; "The only legitimate marriage sanctioned by God is the joining of one man and one woman in a single, exclusive union, as delineated in Scripture"; and "Scripture teaches a recent origin for man and the whole creation, spanning ap-proximately 4,000 years from creation to Christ."[8]

Although I interacted with numerous AiG employees during my fieldwork, the core creative team consisted of four artists: Roger, Tyler, Emily, and Kevin. These four are all committed creationists, but their individual stories are not identical.

Roger is the creative director. He joined AiG in 2001 to lead the pro-duction of the Creation Museum after working for several years as a theme park designer in Tokyo. Before his work in Japan, his impressive résumé includes work on the 1984 Summer Olympics, the refurbishing of the Statue of Liberty in 1986, and Universal Studios' Jaws and King Kong attractions. As the creative director for the Creation Museum, his primary task was to manage the vision for the project as a whole, ensuring that every detail (e.g., exhibits, landscaping, music, lighting) proceeded according to plan and fit into the materialized storytelling. In the project's earliest phases, he was also the primary "scriptwriter," creating content for publicity materials, fund-raising texts, and exhibit plans. I found Roger to be reliably serious, mostly businesslike, and a consummate taskmaster.

Tyler was one of the first artists hired by Roger when the production of the Creation Museum got under way. He was the team's lead illustrator, producing "concept art" that bridged the team's initial brainstorming and final versions. He grew up in Brazil, the child of missionaries, returning to the United States at age eighteen to attend a Christian college. Before coming to AiG, he illustrated for a Christian educational book company and a non-Christian studio firm that contracted with major entertainment corporations like Milton Bradley and Fisher-Price. After finishing his work on the Creation Museum, he took a two-year hiatus from AiG to teach art at a Christian college in Florida. This last job created a very useful ethnographic effect; he was practiced at explaining his art while he worked and adept at articulating in more abstract terms his visions for individual art pieces. Throughout my fieldwork, Tyler was an ideal consultant: always answering questions thoughtfully, often preemptively showing me his latest work before I could ask, and always greeting me with a smile and an inquiry about my life and well-being.

Emily was hired in 2005 to help complete the production of the Creation Museum. She had returned to Ohio after completing a master's degree in theater design from the California Institute of the Arts, the private university founded by Walt Disney in 1961. Roger hired her specifically for her expertise in spatial, building, and set design. My ethnographic relationship with Emily remained uncertain throughout the fieldwork. Although she was always kind and often made time, like Tyler, to explain her work in detail even amid hectic schedules and looming deadlines, our interactions never lost a sense of caution. It was Emily who pressed me most about why I was interested in their work and what kind of book I planned to write. She made little effort to hide this caution, which echoed my primary impression of her: intense honesty. Of all the biographical interviews I did with the artists, hers was the most emotionally transparent. She shared intimate details about her life, including her only son's serious health problems as a newborn and infant.

Roger hired Kevin in 2005, two years before the Creation Museum opened. Kevin was eighteen at the time and had just completed his homeschool education in Michigan. In lieu of pursuing a college art degree, he decided to remain with AiG. When Ark Encounter opened in 2016, he was thirty years old, his résumé boasting the title of "lead production designer" on two major projects although he had no formal art training. His expertise is in sculpture and costume design. He is also the resident historian on the team, most interested in compiling bibliographic references for depicting "ancient cultures." Measured by minutes and hours, I spent the most time with Kevin. This was not intentional; it just happened that he traveled the least and spent less time in meetings than the others. He was the artist working at his cubicle most often during my days at the studio. I always found him to be good-natured and insightful, chattier than Emily or Roger, and less adept at explaining his art than Tyler.

### Collaboration

Since I first met the team in October 2011, I remained impressed that four individuals could be primarily responsible for designing a $150 million theme park and more than 100,000 square feet of exhibit space. What enables this kind of steady creative output? They did not know each other prior to starting work at AiG, and their lives outside the office mostly remained separate. For example, all are members of fundamentalist churches in the Cincinnati area, but none are members of the same church. Their productivity owed, in part, to their accumulated experience in collaborating as a team.

The team members jelled through working on the Creation Museum, learning to view their individual talents as a blessed mix. Usually with a smile and a short anecdote, Tyler, Emily, and Kevin would laud their complementary dynamic. Tyler and Emily are oriented more toward fantasy-inspired world-making and pushing the imaginative envelope—being "out there," as Emily described it. Also a fantasy fan, Kevin has more realist fidelities that owe to his interest in history. He is more conservative in his artistic imaginings than Tyler and Emily, more devoted to recapturing how things *were* than to how things *could* have been. This tension helped define their creative process and is one they enjoy negotiating together. Their assembly as a team was not accidental. As Emily phrased it during an interview: "I think that's why God put [Kevin] with us. [God] planned for that, to have that balance."

The team members developed their complementary dynamic through years of collaboration. Routinely, they worked in side-by-side cubicles five days a week, eight to ten hours a day. During deadline-looming stretches, the hours were more grueling. Tyler recalled that in the months preceding the Creation Museum's opening, they worked seventeen-hour days, often sleeping overnight at the design studio. Much the same was true for Ark Encounter.

Among their most impactful forms of team-building and creative inspiration was taking research trips together to destinations of interest and themed leisure attractions. A partial list Emily provided for me one day included China, Morocco, Germany, Trinidad, Bermuda, Alabama, Orlando, Los Angeles, Las Vegas, the Grand Canyon, Carlsbad Caverns, Atlanta, and South Carolina. Remembering and discussing these trips together was an active voice in their dialogic creativity. Consider an example from early May 2012.

To close the morning meeting, the team members told other AiG employees about their experience the previous day at the Lincoln Museum. It was the second time they had made the five-hour drive from northern Kentucky to Springfield, Illinois. The first had been during their design of the Creation Museum, and the experience was so helpful that they wanted an inspirational reboot for Ark Encounter. Roger described it as "the best museum out there, period." He added that this trip was especially good for reminding them to keep their focus on "the so what" of the Noah story. He reflected, "The Flood was an event in history, but so what, who cares?" Answering his own rhetorical question, Roger continued by stressing the creationist claim of a common ancestry that traces to Noah and his family: "None of us would be here if it weren't for Noah." He closed by returning to the question of park design and how to use "the so what" to create an immersive experience that would "make a linear row of boxes interesting."

The team members dispersed to their cubicles after the meeting. Before they started on the day's tasks, I asked Tyler, Emily, and Kevin about what they had gleaned from revisiting the Lincoln Museum. Roger had dominated the reporting during the meeting, and I wanted to hear how their impressions compared.

For Tyler, the most memorable part of the museum visit was seeing a time-lapse display depicting the Civil War's unfolding, complete with the rising death toll and names of battle locations. Emily focused on the experience as a whole rather than a single exhibit, and on how successfully the Lincoln Museum "told the story visually, mostly without words." This teaching style echoed a critique the team members consistently voiced of their previous work on the Creation Museum. They wanted Ark Encounter to rely less on text and signage, and more on embodied sensory experience. I asked if visitors needed to have much background knowledge about the Civil War to fully appreciate the exhibits and the storytelling. Kevin and Emily immediately said "no," the Lincoln Museum teaches to everyone equally well. Nearly in unison they reflected that this was a serious priority for Ark Encounter. They wanted all visitors, no matter their biblical literacy, to be fully immersed and to find the exhibits fully accessible.

The team's experience working on the Creation Museum and Ark Encounter and taking research trips together produced a shared sense of purpose and identity. As artists, as designers, and as creatives, the team members conceived of their task as a special one, namely, producing creationist content that is equal parts educational and enjoyable, edifying and entertaining, pious and playful, faithful and fun. Seamlessly combining these imperatives was a defining ambition in their production of religious publicity.

*Creationist Imagineers*

Early in my fieldwork at the design studio, I recognized a word that proved pivotal for understanding the team's special task: "immersion." No matter the specific content of design work, their goal was to create an immersive environment in which visitors can "experience" creationist teachings. The version of immersion the team abided by is dedicated to creating conditions in which visitors become active consumers in an environment where they can access the biblical past.[9]

For a sample of how the team talked about immersion, consider this excerpt from an interview I conducted with Tyler. He was discussing how, as artists, the team members approached the task of creating experiential conditions:

> *Immersion* is a huge part of the believability. Now, obviously, we are not so naive to think that somebody's gonna come into the park and think,

"Oh, I'm back in Noah's days today." No, they're gonna think, "Oh, this is like I'm going to Disney and Disney took me into the Pirates of the Caribbean and for ten minutes I'm looking at Jack Sparrow," or whatever. . . . It leaves us creatives in a world where we can kind of *dream up a world* that is believable because it did exist. . . . For us as creatives it leads into a world that we can explore, we can create, we never want to, we're never gonna go against what the plain written word is. But, there is that artistic liberty to *envision a world* that we can *immerse* somebody in. Of violence, of evil, a world that's kind of similar to maybe what we are dealing with today. But, *imagine a world* where nobody is doing right. Only one or two people, only eight people are doing right, and everybody else is out there, absolute hedonism, doing whatever they want to do. *Imagine a world* like that. I can't even *imagine* it. And, how do you pull that off in a theme park environment where you're not going to offend anybody? It's a tough task. (emphasis added)

This excerpt, which represents the team's reflexive discourse about its art and its immersive ambitions, incorporates three themes. First is the aim of "envisioning a world": the team members understood immersion to be about transporting the visitor away from the frame of everyday reality and to a frame defined by the creationist past. Second, the mention of artistic liberty that does not "go against what the plain written word is" points to the tensions between creative imagination and religious commitments that had to be navigated to successfully create the park. Third, the comment "for ten minutes I'm looking at Jack Sparrow" underscores a desired standard of industry professionalism. In an interview with Emily, she also used Disney terminology to describe their work: "My role on the team is, I, if you know what an imagineer is at Disney. That's what we do."

## Cocreators with God

The team members held their work to high standards of professional success, but they also discussed their work in a religious register, as entangled with their spiritual life and identity. This was another voice in their dialogic creativity: naming how their work of producing public culture was inseparable from their religious commitments. Emily provided this description of how her creative process works:

> We have the Word of God, which is a creative power in this earth. That's why we have the Bible, it's a creative, the words of God are creative power basically. God was a creator. I believe that all Christians are meant to be cocreators with God. When I go about creating an environment, even when I wasn't close to God and I didn't even remember my salvation, it's always just been something that, it's a gut just instinct, it's intuitive, where something or a vision comes to mind and you have an initial concept or idea and you just go about researching images or you draw something up or you sort of get all of the pieces or the information of what it's gotta be and then you go about, a journey. It's a process.

Similarly, Tyler described his artistry as a spiritual responsibility. In December 2013, I sent the whole team a *Christianity Today* story about "Christian art" via e-mail.[10] Tyler was the only one to reply in detail. In an 800-word e-mail he thoughtfully articulated a four-part response. The first part of his response unequivocally stated his understanding of the artistic calling:

> Art, first and foremost, should glorify God. . . . [For example, my mentor's] art is all about pointing to Christ, [and] the mastery in technique elevates him above virtually all other Christian artists in the marketplace. His art isn't dark or depressing. He believes art should elevate the spirit, similar to the way David played the harp for King Solomon when the evil spirits tormented him. His art generates high commissions, and he is a member of the National Society of Illustrators (membership by invitation only). My point is that the artist glorifies God the most when their aspiration is to be the best in their field because they are representing God (directly or indirectly) in their artistic exploits.

What does it mean to be a creationist imagineer? It means that your art, your creativity, and your labor are performed in at least two dialogic registers: one religious, one professional. Being an artist is a way for these Christians to enact their faith on a daily basis. With this dialogic relation in place, it then becomes imperative to produce high-quality work; anything less is not only risky for business but also a tragic misuse of God's blessings.

The central role of these two registers in the team's cultural production highlights an important social fact about modern fundamentalism. This is religion that is distinctly comfortable with the institutions of modern life, transforming and sacralizing them. Anthropologist Susan Harding decisively made this argument through her depiction of Jerry Falwell's institutional empire.[11] Much like Falwell's ministry, Answers in Genesis appropriates cultural resources and redeploys them for evangelistic ends. This work extends to the lives of labor inside Answers in Genesis, in which work and faith, talent and vocation are fused. This social fact runs against the grain of pietistic anxieties about the polluting effects of religion and this-worldly regimes, "the idea that religion is 'tainted' by coming into contact with money or commerce, as though there were an ideal religion, pure and unspoiled, isolated from the seamier sides of culture: money, sex, and entertainment."[12]

## The Studio

Describing the design studio as a physical space and an inhabited place sets an important context for the team's creative labor and process. The space itself was rather basic and functional, with few touches to make it overly comfortable but, as we will see later, plenty of touches to make it personalized.

Driving east on the I-275 loop that encircles the Cincinnati metro area—one exit past the Creation Museum and one exit before the Cincinnati/Northern Kentucky International Airport—one reaches the exit for Hebron, Kentucky. A right turn off the exit will take you into Hebron, a small town of approximately 5,000 people. A left turn will take you through a newly developed commercial strip that ends with Park West International, a collection of large warehouse spaces. The area is steadily busy, home to a mix of temporary renters and long-term tenants, such as an Amazon regional fulfillment center. Ark Encounter's rented warehouse-turned-design-studio resided in the middle of Park West International.

*Layout*

The studio's main entrance is a single door that that requires an electronic key for entry. Each team member has his or her own key attached to an AiG staff badge; without a key, you need to be allowed in by someone inside. The entry hallway remained sparsely decorated throughout my fieldwork, featuring only a series of promotional boards used for fund-raising and two topographic models: one of the Creation Museum, and one of the 800-acre site for Ark Encounter.

After turning left from the hallway, you enter the main boardroom. This was the site of morning meetings and any meeting involving the whole team. The room's dominant feature was a long table surrounded by ten black pleather rolling chairs. Concept blueprints for the ark's three decks hung on the boardroom wall throughout my fieldwork. A smaller boardroom space was located just beyond this, but it was rarely used by the team except to store old maps, blueprints, and early concept design materials.

A short hallway led to the main studio space. Along one side of this space were four offices with closing doors, including Roger's. His office's set-apart position mirrored his role as creative director. Along another wall were restrooms and the entrance to the kitchen space, another sparsely decorated room that screamed pure functionality. Along the back wall was a series of cloth boards, which the team used constantly to display concept art for whatever their current project was. In the center of the main studio area were the cubicles, twenty in all, which were organized into five blocks of four, with two cubicles facing each other on either side.

Through double doors in the back corner of the studio was a small workroom area where exhibit prototypes were assembled. Through another door there was a large construction area where larger exhibits were assembled and truck deliveries unloaded. This was the least occupied space for the creative team, and I spent most of my time in the main studio space.

*Sound*

Aurally, the studio was a mix of silence and ambient noises. We might expect a Christian workplace to feature some Christian music, perhaps the praise and worship variety of modern megachurches and religious radio, at least periodically, but that was not the case. No Internet radio, no iPod plug-in, not even a few bars from memory sung or hummed under one's breath. Only once did I hear a team member spontaneously break into song. Driving into work one morning, Tyler had heard Jefferson Starship's song "We Built This City" and could not banish the tune from his mind. Tyler and Emily shared facing cubicles, and throughout the morning they joked back and forth by periodically trading the song's main couplet: "We built this city, we built this city on rock and roll."

As an experiment, I spent part of one morning early in the project listing the collection of ambient and random noises that filled the space. The copier cover closes with a thud. The copier runs to make a few prints. A pencil sharpener revs. The overhead HVAC unit hums in stretches. Computer keys and mouse buttons click. Footsteps move across the floor. Pencil erasers are scratched on paper. Someone rustles in a chair. Hammering echoes from the back construction room. Cell phones ding with message alerts. The artists speak aloud but mostly to themselves: Emily chides the Internet connection, "Come on, you connect, server" followed by an "Ugh" of frustration; Tyler lets out a sigh of "OK" when transitioning to a new design task; and he wonders aloud thoughtfully about a new illustration, "OK, how'm I gonna do this? Do I want scared? Do I want excited? What do I want?"

It is not that the team members never interacted. Of course, they did. But they did so amid long stretches of silence and ambient noises. Their casual exchanges were usually brief, asking a question about a new piece of design work or giving editorial feedback on a design in progress. Often jovial, their interactions were mostly of the no-nonsense variety, focused on diligently completing the tasks at hand.

*Decoration*

The design studio's temporary and permanent decorations reflected the dialogic voices that informed the team's creative labor. The most prominent features within the cubicles were always the artists' own productions. They surrounded their work spaces with concept art. Some pieces were from previous projects, the Creation Museum or early Ark Encounter designs, but usually the art reflected the current project they were working on. I could always tell with a glance when an artist had shifted to a new major design task because there would be a nearly wholesale replacement of art on the cubicle walls. In this way, the team lived with one foot in the future: faced with exhibits in the making, concept art forecasting imagination not yet realized and labor still to come.

Next to every cubicle were one or two large, new wooden bookshelves. Each reflected the team member's shared identity as a creationist imagineer as well as his or her individual artistic acumen. For example, Kevin's shelves mixed his library of historical references with numerous Answers in Genesis publications. There were historical studies on subjects such as clothing of the ancient world alongside books by Ken Ham, issues of *Answers* magazine, and *The Genius of Ancient Man*. Another shelf was filled with technical design books and magazines. Some were focused on specific topics, such as how to illustrate characters in specific poses, while many others were about Hollywood blockbusters (e.g., art books on the production of *The Lord of the Rings*, *King Kong*, *Star Wars*, *The Last Airbender*, *Jurassic Park*, *The Chronicles of Narnia*, and *Avatar*).

Less pervasive, but strategically placed around cubicles and common spaces, were quotations. Some were attributed to famous persons; others were from unknown sources, anonymous, or written by one of the artists. These sayings served as dialogic reminders and as creative inspiration, such as the sign about good versus bad entertainment presented in the introduction. Atop Emily's file cabinet was a short, rectangular placard that read, "It's kind of fun to do the impossible," followed by the name "Walt Disney." Hanging above the coffeepot at a snack station, surrounded by posed and candid photos of the team, was a printed color sheet that read, "Making the simple complicated is commonplace; making the complicated simple, that's creativity. —Charles Mingus."

Perhaps not surprisingly, there were arks everywhere. Visually scanning the office, it was nearly impossible not to catch sight of at least one kind of ark model or drawing. Some were part of the team's work—miniature arks used for fund-raising and publicity materials. One particular genre of ark appeared throughout the studio. The team called these "bathtub arks," meaning the cartoonish representations that depict Noah's ark as nonhistorical and functionally implausible—useful to illustrate a children's tale but nothing more. This collection grew throughout my fieldwork and was a visible, material marker of a serious creationist critique. Bathtub arks are "cute, but dangerous," another node in the "secularist" conspiracy to attack biblical authority by trivializing the story and dismissing the historicity of Genesis.[13] Some of these same items reappeared on board the completed ark, material objects for an exhibit immersing visitors within the creationist present (see Figure 6.5).

## Creative Processes

To further explore the everyday creative labor at the design studio, we can identify six dynamics that characterize the team's work. Taken together, they flesh out the dialogic quality of the team members' creativity and demonstrate how it anchors their production of religious publicity.

### Tedium and Perfection

As my fieldwork progressed, I became acutely aware that a huge portion of the team's labor consisted of tedious action, such as filling in Photoshop drawing details and tinkering with concept art designs. The obsession with detail driving this tedium points toward a professionalized demand for perfectionism. In June 2012, Tyler was tasked with creating an advertising banner for a publicity event the following month where the team would promote and raise funds for Ark Encounter. A graphic designer who works on Creation Museum projects had created a rough draft, but Tyler did not like the design of the banner's text. He wanted the font to be the same as that used for other Ark Encounter promotional materials that were already circulating. For thirty uninterrupted minutes, Tyler adjusted and readjusted the font style, size, position, and color. Here, the production of religious publicity was informed by the logic of brand recognition, and artistic dissatisfaction compelled the dive into tedium.

This extended attention to design minutiae was not outside of the norm but instead was standard practice. For me, as an outsider to the world of artistic production, the tedium was compounded by the fact that investing long hours in a particular design is no guarantee of its success. Emily described this dynamic during an interview:

> You have to be willing to let things go. If you spend two days or fifty hours on a drawing that's not right, you gotta let it go. You cannot be rigid. You

have to be flexible with your work. Because if you're that way you might get a little upset. You have to learn to work as a team as well because that's the flexibility that's involved because you have to be able to come to a team meeting and have a unified vision of something.

One of Kevin's projects illustrates this flexibility and resistance to rigidity. Throughout my fieldwork, the team imagined a walking path—twenty feet wide, a third of a mile long—that would connect the park's Welcome Gate to the ark area. The importance the team placed on this path exceeded its physical dimensions. It would be a minor feature compared with the three main decks, but it initiated visitor immersion in "the pre-Flood world of Noah" and first introduced the "wicked society" that God punished with death. The team called it the Pagan Pathway.

From October 2013 through April 2014, Kevin worked on a design for the pathway. The idea was to use at least six steles (i.e., inscribed pillars), all of them eight to ten feet tall—to "tell the story" of pre-Flood life, from creation to the sinful world of Noah's day. Kevin produced several different stele styles for the team to consider in November, and from there he developed design concepts for the whole series. After six months of developing this idea, one the team members all agreed on, they decided to scrap the stele approach altogether and instead pursue the possibility of a painted mural. In June 2014, when I asked Roger why they made this decision, he said the reasons were purely pragmatic: a wall would be sturdier than steles amid the high winds that steadily gust on the Ark Encounter property, and it would be less expensive to paint an existing wall than to build and paint the steles.

When I first visited the completed Ark Encounter in August 2016, I found that the team members had later decided on yet another design direction. Instead of an outdoor pathway leading to the ark, they pursued the desired immersive effect on Deck Two. *Pre-Flood World* is a walking exhibit that winds among a mix of dioramas, signage, painted murals, and auditory annotations (see Figure 6.9). Perhaps this frustrated Kevin, or perhaps he took it in perfect stride as Emily suggests. In any case, scrapping design work after investing extensive labor was a regular part of the team's creative process. Again, the tedium of design highlights a commitment to professional perfectionism.

*Hierarchy*

The team members described their relationship as complementary and collaborative, but there was also an unmistakable chain of authority. Ultimately, Roger was the boss. Tyler, Emily, and Kevin were certainly free to argue the merits of their ideas, but when push came to shove, as it often did, Roger's vision was the one they followed. I observed a dramatic example of this dynamic in spring 2013, as the team finalized a new exhibit for the Creation Museum.

To welcome the summer tourist season of 2013, AiG wanted something new for museum visitors. The team members wanted something that would, in Kevin's words, "up the cool factor" but still teach creationist content. The idea they settled on was *Dragon Legends*, a walking exhibit that would fill the museum portico. The big idea of *Dragon Legends* is to demonstrate the plausibility of the creationist claim that humans and dinosaurs coexisted.

In early April, about six weeks before Dragon Legend's Memorial Day premiere, Tyler was stressed. He was behind on a deadline to finish the exhibit artwork. I sat with him at his cubicle desk as he explained all this. In addition to the actual artwork, the graphic files were massive (about "seven gigs"), which meant he was "living on edge all day hoping nothing crashes." On this morning, as he was finalizing the artwork for the Saint George legend (see Figure 5.9), Tyler uttered a series of adjectives to himself as he drew: "That's cool . . . That'll work. . . . That's pretty stinkin' awesome." He told me repeatedly that he was pleased with this display, even saying, "This one is my favorite." When I asked why, he responded, "I like the glow effect of the colors and the sense of movement." He suspected a few portions were too dark, but these were minor problems and did not diminish his enthusiasm.

At about eleven thirty we moved to the back workroom, where he used a carpenter's razor to cut a draft of the display from the printout and then pinned it up to view. A few minutes later Tyler called Roger in for his opinion. Immediately, Roger was unhappy. For the next thirty minutes they disagreed back and forth: Roger critiquing, Tyler defending, jammed at creative odds. In my field notes, I separated the exchange into four parts.

First, Roger explained his critique: "The values are too close." By "values" he meant the different colors used for elements that were touching. After several minutes Tyler asked with noticeable annoyance, "You can't tell she's chained up?," referencing the female character in the illustrated panel. Roger responded: "If I look real close, but at a glance, no. You're trying to do a graphic style that you think works, but I don't think it works. You're trying to be too subtle and too cool, and I lose it with what you're trying to do."

Second, Tyler compared this critique to a discussion years earlier when they were working on a different project. Roger affirmed the comparison, but only minimally, then shifted to a broader critique, saying that Tyler knew his deadline and needed to "think like a professional." As an observer in the room, I found that this comment noticeably elevated the tension. Roger reminded Tyler of his deadlines when working for the Christian book publisher. Sounding defeated, Tyler said: "I tried the simplest approach I could think of," to which Roger responded: "Your simple and my simple are like way . . ." Here, he stopped speaking and stretched his hands as far apart as they could go. Tyler noted that he understood what Roger was saying, "but it's not as simple as it looks. . . . I was going for a silhouette feel with the woman." More assertively, Roger returned to his basic critique: "That's not a silhouette. It's too complicated. It's a style, Tyler, you have a picture in your head, and I just don't think it's gonna work."

Third, their disagreement shifted from the color values to the printer. Tyler explained that the printer is not color calibrated. This sounded like it had a familiar ring, as if they had talked about this problem many times before. As a result, the printout looked different than what he saw on the screen. Tyler mentioned his time at the Christian book publisher, where the printer was more precise. Roger recognized this as a longer-term issue, something that needed resolving. It was a momentary respite from the creative clash.

Finally, they returned to Tyler's cubicle to view the version on the computer screen. Roger was not convinced, saying, "Even on this the values are too close." Tyler started experimenting with color changes, and Roger was immediately pleased: "Just like that!" Again, Tyler said that the change is not as simple as just swapping the color. Exasperated, Roger said in a raised tone: "You just showed me! For all intents and purposes, I can now read everything, just with that small change." Tyler continued clicking lines and color palettes and said, partly to himself, partly to Roger: "I don't know how I'm gonna pull this off." Roger, who had been standing behind Tyler and was turning to walk away, declared matter-of-factly without breaking stride: "You will."

The intensity of their exchange was as much about the stress of working under a tight deadline as anything else, but the dynamic it captured was always present among the team. Roger finalized all decisions, often in ways that resulted in additional work for Tyler, Emily, and Kevin. It is tempting here to reference how hierarchical authority is an established trait of fundamentalist religion.[14] Perhaps there is a parallel to make. Perhaps the team members are able to work so productively in the context of a rigid hierarchy because they have formed a disposition for such authority as part of a fundamentalist habitus. Perhaps. But the team's hierarchical dynamic owes as well to the nature of collaboration in late capitalist corporate culture, where every team has a director and most decisions are not made democratically.[15]

*Bureaucratic Clash*

Deadlines like the one Tyler experienced with *Dragon Legends* are typically not self-imposed by the team but instead come from the broader AiG ministry. The same is true with budgets. The team does not set its own budgets or perform its own fund-raising but must work within the financial constraints set by the ministry. All four team members regularly expressed frustration about the stress of deadlines and budgets, though the particulars varied: feeling rushed to produce too much art in too little time; being given too little notice about upcoming deadlines; having budgets reduced without warning; and receiving smaller budgets than requested or anticipated. A recurring clash centered on the ministry's profit motive and the team's creative commitments. Consider an example from May 2012.

To prepare for a private "land dedication" event on the Ark Encounter site in June, the team was asked to come up with a T-shirt design for ministry employees and invited guests. During the morning meeting, Steve, one of AiG's three cofounders and project director for Ark Encounter, informed the team members that at 4:00 p.m. staff from the

Creation Museum would arrive to discuss design possibilities. They had until then to produce some ideas. Cue the bureaucratic time crunch.

Immediately, the team members foregrounded the immersive imperative. The T-shirts should "make sense" vis-à-vis Noah's world. All color tones should be "earthy." To clarify, they noted that pastels like "orange and pink" were out of the question. The discussion flagged, and Roger asked everyone to spend at least an hour brainstorming on their own during the day. Before they all dispersed to close the meeting, the creative-bureaucratic clash reemerged between Steve and Roger. Steve stressed that the styles and colors that sell well in the Creation Museum bookstore are what the museum staff will advocate. Roger countered that having a "captive audience" who will "buy anything" is no excuse to not create a "really good" design. In a flat tone, Steve reminded Roger that it's all about "per cap for investors." Roger, in an equally flat tone, reminded Steve that it was "not all about per cap" for the team.

## "Cool"

As my fieldwork with the team progressed, I returned repeatedly to a curious absence. While the team members were all committed creationists and regular churchgoers, there was very little spiritualizing of the work they produced. Instead, when they were evaluating design ideas, works in progress, and finished concept art, the vocabulary they used was that of art, creativity, and entertainment. They assessed their work as "fun" or "boring," "inviting" or "distracting," "appealing" or "confusing," "interesting" or "simple," "engaging" or "blah," or, their most frequently used term of praise, "cool." This art talk, this discourse of cool, never ran out of steam. Moreover, work was never assessed as "inspiring" or "edifying," never promising to "bless" park visitors or bring them "closer to God." The artists were never overly pleased with their own productions; they were all perfectionists, but not once did I hear them say of any piece of work that it was "inspired by the Spirit."

Similarly, public prayer was largely absent around the studio. Morning meetings concluded with a brief prayer, but these were always divorced from the day's labor. They dealt mainly with prayer requests circulating throughout the AiG ministry and regular petitions for successful fund-raising. Only once did I observe a moment of spontaneous prayer. I was sitting with Tyler, Emily, and Kevin in Tyler's cubicle as they brainstormed an exhibit. Via e-mail, news came of a colleague's health problem. They prayed on the spot, asking for the man's healing and comfort and asking God to keep them alert to other spiritual attacks Satan might use to impede the success of Ark Encounter. The prayer was brief, and they returned to their brainstorming without further comment, picking up right where they had stopped.

I am not suggesting that the team engaged in any sort of bracketing behavior when it came to labor and religion. As discussed earlier, the team members understand their work as a religious vocation. Their faith is never not at work while they are at work. I make this observation about the presence of "cool" and the absence of spiritualizing art production to emphasize how matters of professionalism and entertainment are integral to their production of religious publicity.

## Culture Wars

While the discourse of "cool" dominated their talk about art, the team members' identity as fundamentalists appeared in other contexts of office talk. It was not especially frequent, but the team did incorporate familiar culture wars discourses into everyday life at the studio. Consider two examples, both occurring at the close of morning meetings.

A vital component of the modern creationist movement is what anthropologist Joel Robbins calls the "enchantment of science."[16] That is, creationists infuse modern science with religious meaning, reshaping science to fit their religious worldview. This practice concluded a brief exchange between Roger and Tyler in early December 2011.

It was only two months into my fieldwork, and I was still getting to know the team. Emily had asked me about the university courses I teach, and, responding to my answer, the team discussed how issues of cultural and historical "context" apply to their design work. The discussion prompted Roger to retrieve an evangelism lesson from his office that he recently heard on a television ministry. Jonathan Bernis's "Jewish Voice" focuses on "witnessing to the Jewish people" and helping Christians discover "the Hebraic roots of their faith." This particular lesson uses the Hebrew names of biblical figures from Adam through Noah to "spell out the gospel." The whole team was impressed. Roger closed his description of the lesson with a critique: "In English culture our names don't mean anything, don't have anything to do with who we are, [but in] Jewish culture all names mean something. . . . The problem with the Protestant church is that it has no history." Roger then tied this name lesson to their work on Ark Encounter; the whole point, he said, "is to get people thinking" and help them "realize the truth of the Bible."

Tyler had a chiropractic appointment scheduled directly after the meeting, but before leaving, he approached Roger and asked if he could see the name lesson again. Tyler thought that this lesson, if successfully presented, would be excellent for Ark Encounter: perhaps in the planned "preshow" film park visitors would view before boarding the ark, on a panel at the park entrance, or even on a small card that visitors could carry with them.[17] They agreed this lesson was "the perfect connector" between pre-Flood life, the post-Flood Old Testament, and the New Testament. Roger reflected, "There are no loose ends in the Bible." Tyler agreed, saying, "God has left his imprint on everything." He told Roger about a lesson he recently heard on YouTube by Louie Giglio, an evangelical celebrity and pastor of a megachurch in Atlanta's affluent Buckhead neighborhood. The video Tyler referenced was from one of Giglio's sermons, "Indescribable God," which went viral in 2008. In the sermon, Giglio described how the molecular element laminin (a protein structure that binds cells together) resembles the shape of a cross when viewed at the microscopic level and as scientific diagrams represent it. For Giglio and for Tyler, this was proof that the Word of God binds all of life together.[18]

Another core feature of American evangelicalism and fundamentalism is the sense of being culturally embattled. Sociologist Christian Smith argues that the movement's success derives from an ideological claim that "it is—or at least perceives itself to be—embattled with forces that seem to oppose or threaten it."[19] What AiG has done so successfully through its religious publicity is distill this sense of opposition and threat into one conspiratorial force: evolution. This cultivated disposition of being embattled was sporadically, but clearly, evident in everyday life at the studio. I was reminded of this one morning in March 2012.

I arrived that day to find the team seated around the boardroom table, talking casually after an abbreviated meeting. The conversation had turned to a new documentary film that would be released in select theaters at the end of the month: *Monumental*, starring the fundamentalist celebrity Kirk Cameron. One of the administrative assistants encouraged everyone to see the film and tell others to do the same. Cameron had self-financed the film, and if it grossed a certain dollar amount, a major media company would purchase the rights and distribute it nationally. *Monumental* repackages the standard fundamentalist narrative that America is in a state of national, moral, and spiritual decline.

Echoing the assistant's description of the film, Roger referred to America as "done," citing public schools as a prime example. Tyler and Emily seemed to want to change the tone of the conversation, adding that "God is sovereign" and that "everything will work out for the glory of God and for God's people." Undeterred, Roger continued that Christians never talk about "revival" and are failing to be any different than those causing the decline. With an eye toward the team's work of religious publicity, Roger reminded everyone that the lesson of *Monumental* is relevant for Ark Encounter: "That's why what we're doing is so important. It's going to be this weird little beacon of hope to remind people that we are different." With this, the team members dispersed to their cubicles.

## Constructed Dialogue

Planned and impromptu brainstorming sessions were a crucial part of the team's creative process. Some of my most insightful fieldwork moments occurred while listening to the quick back-and-forth of these interactions. As I listened, a marked feature of their brainstorming discourse emerged.

The team members regularly performed what linguistic anthropologists call "constructed dialogue."[20] That is, they imagined the various audiences who would visit Ark Encounter and then voiced the ideological stances they imagined these audiences would take when experiencing particular exhibits. In this way, team meetings were always distinctly polyvocal. Acts of constructed dialogue were not incidental to the team's creative process. They were pivotal, helping shape important artistic and design decisions. This was evident from my first full day of fieldwork at the studio in November 2011.

I arrived just after lunch and was informed that Roger had decided midmorning that the rest of the day would be "a regroup meeting" in which the team would review its progress on the entire park design. For me, this six-hour meeting was both very good ethnographic luck and a shove into the deep end of fieldwork. The team members were spaced evenly around the boardroom table, which was covered with scattered notepads, pens, yellow sticky notes, coffee cups, water bottles, Sharpies, lunch bags, architectural models of the ark, and Bibles (two translations: the New King James Version and the Defenders Study Bible, which is a King James Version).[21]

It was an absolutely dizzying day. I had met the team members once before, but I knew hardly anything about them. I had not yet learned how to pick up on their distinctive contributions, to Kevin's realist fidelities and Emily's keen eye for spatial design. I had not yet learned the discourse of "cool" or the ever-present hierarchy. Still, one pattern was obvious. Their discussion was filled with constructed dialogue, with team members voicing the stances of imagined interlocutors who were outside (and usually antagonistic to) their mission: "People think . . . ," "If I'm a skeptic . . . ," "For nonbelievers . . . ," "In people's minds . . . ," "The intelligent design people . . . ," "To the secular world . . . ," "Evolutionists always say . . ."

The team members' imagining of these audiences and their stances was oriented by what they hoped to achieve through their religious publicity: conversion. They used constructed dialogue to ask what objections various non-Christian audiences would likely raise and how their design work could preempt and challenge those objections. For them, Ark Encounter was about an opportunity to change common "misunderstandings of scripture." They hoped to show that Noah was not, as Roger phrased it that November afternoon, "a cave dweller rubbing rocks together." Noah was "sophisticated," wise, and learned from 600 years of living, fully capable of orchestrating the ark's construction. Experiencing Ark Encounter would help visitors discard "bathtub ark" images and seriously consider Genesis as literal history. Kevin said it this way during an interview:

> The purpose [of Ark Encounter] is to basically break down some of those barriers that people have so that they can get to the gospel. Because there's a lot of people that can't touch the Bible unless this is understood to them. They're like, "I can't touch the Bible unless I can know that this flood could've happened. Otherwise, this is just a silly fairy-tale book."

Kevin's constructed dialogue voices "people" at a crossroads, willing to be convinced but requiring certain explanations in order to transform their view of the Bible from "a silly fairy tale" to God's Word.

## Conclusion

This chapter brings together the key dynamics of the team's creative labor and process. To organize the analysis, I drew on the concept of dialogic creativity because it illustrates how the team members' work was embedded in numerous ideological and discursive networks. Their cultural production emerged from multiple sources, some reflecting their artistic identity and others reflecting their broader commitment to Protestant fundamentalism.

The team members worked against the backdrop of their experience as a collaborative unit. They learned about each other as artists, their relationship as a team, and lessons from previous success and failures. They mobilized experiences from producing the Creation Museum and various research trips to imagine Ark Encounter's creationist world.

They also fused two vocational registers, religious identity and professional identity. To borrow Emily's phrase, they understood themselves as "cocreators" alongside a fundamentally creative God. Their artistic talent is their blessing, and devoting their talents to the religious publicity of Answers in Genesis instead of to a "secular" studio allows them to enact their faith through their work. They demanded that their creative production meet or exceed industry standards. As creationist "imagineers," they compared their work to Disney and reached for Hollywood design books when seeking creative inspiration.

Finally, they integrated ideological conflicts between creationism and "evolutionism," and between Christian fundamentalism and "secularism." Collecting and displaying "bathtub arks" around the studio served as a constant reminder of how "skeptics mock the Bible" and "why what [they're] doing is so important." The culture wars appeared unexpectedly, but seamlessly, amid morning meetings. And performances of constructed dialogue invoked hostile, dismissive, and stubborn imagined audiences.

Understanding the team's dialogic creativity is about understanding the context of production for religious publicity. Before Ark Encounter could enter into the field of fundamentalist public culture, it had to emerge from the creative labor that filled the design studio. In the next chapter, we move to the team's organizing purpose: designing a creationist theme park that could convert non-Christians to Christianity and noncreationists to creationism. As we explore the team's model of conversion, we rely on the lessons learned in this chapter about the team members' identity as creationist imagineers and the nature of their creative process. So, what is their model of conversion?

4

Conversion as Play


The central visitor experience at Ark Encounter is the ark and its onboard exhibits. Likewise, these consumed the lion's share of the team's creative labor. If the park's primary purpose is to be a form of religious publicity, aiming for the conversion of non-Christians to Christianity and noncreationists to creationism, then experiencing the ark would be key to the conversion process.

Beginning with the public announcement in December 2010, Ark Encounter's publicity has made much ado about the project's scale. The largest timber frame structure in the world, nearly 4 million board feet of lumber, 510 feet long, more than 100,000 square feet of themed exhibit space, 800 acres of land: these are the numbers and claims that circulated widely through media releases, blog entries, and posts on Facebook and Twitter. The creative team was not exempt from being enamored with matters of sheer size. Office talk at the studio regularly included artist remarks that, for visitors, just seeing and being inside the massive ark would be affectively stirring. However, while size matters, it is not size alone that counts. For the team members, the embodied movement on board and engagement with exhibits were always most important. What kind of experience did they hope to create?

When boarding the ark, visitors snake through a themed queue that integrates signifiers of "pre-Flood society" and Noah's preparations for the Flood. The ark is raised twelve feet off the ground, and visitors enter from below. Part of the queue line experience is a short dramatic film in which Noah is interviewed by a snarky skeptic while final preparations before the storm are made. Visitors then pass through a "narrow door," allowing a "great reveal" of Deck One.[1]

From there, visitors are free to roam throughout the ark's three decks, filled with a mix of sculpted animals, the eight passengers in static and animatronic form, mural art, signage, interactive displays, multimedia exhibits, food vendors, restrooms, short films, and children's play areas. These three decks constitute the "more than 100,000 square feet of themed exhibit space."

Each deck teaches the creationist worldview and is organized by a particular affective experience. Deck One highlights the emotional drama of Noah and his family after the closing of the ark door. They are relieved to have escaped a terrifying storm, they have just witnessed mass death, and they are anxious about the weeks ahead. The team always talked about Deck One as the "darkest" of the decks, indexed sensorially by low levels of lighting. The storm is audible, as visitors hear sounds of wind, rain, thunder, and debris banging against the ark's sides. The first exhibit of Noah and family portrays them in the middle of praise and thanksgiving for their deliverance, with the auditory annotation of the raging storm and agitated animals in the background.

Deck Two extends the re-creation of everyday life on board the ark. Noah and his family are settled, going about their liminal living. Exhibits include the library, workshops demonstrating woodworking and blacksmithing, and feeding animals. The team envisioned Deck Two as the primary "how-to" deck, addressing numerous "practical" issues about the Noah story. How did they care for all the animals? What did they do with all the animal waste? How were air, water, and sunlight distributed? What did Noah's workshop and library look like? By addressing these questions, Deck Two materializes the pivotal creationist claim that "ancient man" was "brilliant and capable."

Deck Three continues themes from the first two decks and introduces several new experiences. More exhibits teach about animal kinds. More exhibits address everyday matters, such as what the passengers' living quarters might have been like. Deck Three also captures the salvific realization that God's wrath has been expended, the storm is over, the waters have receded, the eight passengers have been spared, and the whole world is now theirs. This affect encompasses further creationist teaching points about post-Flood life, such as the Tower of Babel dispersal of languages and people groups. Deck Three culminates in creationist typological theology, which presents Noah as a prefiguration of Jesus.

As visitors move through these three decks, a total of 132 bays (Figure 4.1) combine to tell an immersive story about the plausibility of a literal ark, the creationist rejection of evolutionary science, the steadfast faithfulness of Noah and his family, their deliverance, and ultimately the

Figure 4.1. Bay model built outside the Creation Museum to promote Ark Encounter. Photo by author.

evangelical gospel of salvation. The iconicity of moving from darkness to light, from judgment to salvation, was always a self-conscious strategy for the team members; they wanted visitors to experience this embodied progression. Through the story of Noah and his family, Ark Encounter teaches creationist history, theology, and politics. What model of conversion anchors this choreographed experience on board the ark? And how does this conversion model fit within the project's broader ambition to bolster creationism's cultural legitimacy?

## Literal Play

As the members of the creative team envisioned and designed the ark's three decks, plotting the experience for visitors, they counted on multiple audiences coming to Ark Encounter.[2] First, there are the devout: committed creationists who flooded the Creation Museum when it opened, who read Answers in Genesis books, subscribe to *Answers* magazine, attend AiG conferences, and generally consume everything the ministry produces. The team remained aware that the financial success of Ark Encounter relies on this audience visiting as families, congregational groups, and other organized collectives (e.g., to participate in pastor retreats, family vacations, homeschool outings, or church trips). While the team was excited for committed creationists to enjoy the biblical fun, and perhaps be further emboldened as outspoken creationists in the modern world, this audience occupied the team's attention least of all.

There are also well-meaning Christians who remain "blinded" by the "lies" of "secular evolutionists." They are saved, but their endangered faith is only salvageable by conversion to creationism. And there are spiritual seekers: the unaffiliated, the spiritual-but-not-religious, the "nones." These visitors are aware of creation-evolution controversies but are not invested in them. Certainly in need of salvation, they are not the primary antagonist of ministries like Answers in Genesis.

Finally, the audience that consumed most of the team's attention was the bête noir of creationists: skeptics, dogmatic evolutionists, and self-identified atheists. These are the scoffers, the mockers, those who ridicule projects like Ark Encounter and wish to rid society of creationism. The conversion of such hostile skeptics would testify most to the power of the Holy Spirit (and, perhaps, testify most to the team's creative success).

## Plausibility-Immersion

Whatever else the religious publicity of Ark Encounter amounts to, it is a $150 million act of witnessing. It is missionization, massively material-ized, performed in the key of biblical literalism. But the members of the creative team understood their labor as infinitely more complicated than merely explaining creationist doctrine to the public. After all, content-wise, there is very little at Ark Encounter that has not already been presented by the ministry in books, magazines, videos, online materials, and the Creation Museum.

The team's creative labor was organized by a two-part model of con-version. First, the team sought to demonstrate the plausibility of Genesis 6 through 9 (and, by extension, the historicity of scripture), beginning with the premise that it was physically and technologically possible for Noah to have built the ark described in Genesis. The project claims to use the exact dimensions detailed in scripture and only building materi-als that would have been available to Noah (namely, timber and iron). Through exhibits on board and throughout the park, the team portrays tools and techniques Noah might have used. Publicity materials repeat-edly explain that modern construction technology, such as cranes, was pragmatically necessary (e.g., to complete construction within the time frame required by building permits).

However, plausibility alone is not enough. Noah's story cannot merely be told; it must be felt. Success meant effectively engineering an affec-tive experience that would compel noncreationist visitors toward con-version. What was the pre-Flood world like, the one so wicked that God decided death was the only adequate judgment? What was it like to be surrounded by mass extinction? What was Noah's experience in build-ing the ark and preparing for the weeks on board? How did it feel to be inside the ark when the door closed, to hear the fierce storm outside and the cacophony of animals? What was the experience of living on the ark day after day? And what was it like when the dove did not return, to see the rainbow and be the center of God's saving grace?

An immersive experience promises to bridge the gap between plausi-bility and believability, and the logic of immersive entertainment is the engine that propelled the team's creative labor. This conversion model of plausibility-immersion exemplifies how Ark Encounter performs a deep cultural entanglement of religion with entertainment. This is not merely an instance of two cultural formations coming into contact, or the partial borrowing of symbols and resources. This is a thorough integration of dispositions from two social fields: modern entertainment and Protestant fundamentalism. Immersion is the primary example of such integration, as it is a primary strategy and imperative in our modern culture of entertainment.[3]

If the team could create an experience that demonstrates the reality of Noah's ark as a historical event and do so in a way that is fun for visitors, it will have established the conditions for conversions to happen. This approach both continues and departs from a long tradition of conversion via Noah's ark. Historian Larry Eskridge documents how American evangelicals throughout the twentieth century attempted to excavate physical evidence of the ark through archaeological expeditions. These searches were committed to the idea that discovering the ark's material remains would be a silver bullet for biblical literalism. Eskridge writes, "The revelation that Noah's old ship yet rested upon the heights of Ararat would cause the skeptic to reexamine his doubt and unbelief. . . . this great miracle would also serve to reveal to all the world who has been right all the while."[4]

The creative team capitalized on the symbolic power of the ark to convert but dramatically shifted the focus from archaeological remains to role play. The promise of conversion shifts from empirical evidence to experiencing Noah's world in an immersive scriptural environment. Demonstrating historical plausibility shifts from artifactual silver bullets to materialized re-creations of a literal biblical past.

To be immersed in the creationist past is to be immersed in a past where a universal flood killed everyone on earth except eight people. Six of these eight people, Noah's three sons (Shem, Ham, Japheth) and their wives, are the genetic ancestors for all modern humans. All the world's animals are the result of microevolution from the limited number of animal kinds brought on board the ark. In this past the age of the earth is roughly 6,000 years old, not the roughly 4.5 billion years determined by modern science. Human beings are a special creation of God, not the result of evolutionary processes. All animal kinds, including dinosaurs, coexisted with humans. Pre-Flood human life spans were dramatically longer, as illustrated by Noah's building the ark when he was 600 years old and living to 950.

The play of this experience is about being immersed in a history, biology, and anthropology that exists in direct opposition to that of modern science. At its core this immersive play is dialogic, working ideologically as a challenge to the scientific past of evolution. The creative team banks on park visitors becoming caught up in this past, igniting our capacity as *Homo ludens* to engage in playful reverence for biblical miracle, history, and truth.

## Religious Conversion and Play

Comparative ethnography tells us that Christian models of conversion rest on commitments to divine agency. Christians in widely different cultural contexts find ways of saying much the same thing: only God transforms people. But we also know that conversion is a sociocultural process that entails more than just what adherents have to say about it. In the anthropology of Christianity, conversion studies have focused on the trope of rupture. For example, there are excellent analyses of how continuities with a non-Christian past are managed alongside declaring a break from that past, and of the social costs when familial and social networks confront new religious difference due to conversion.[5]

The religious publicity of Ark Encounter requires a recalibrated focus on the nature of conversion as a human agentive process. While sincere commitments about the role of God in conversion are always present, conversion is always also a fundamentally social process. Through evangelistic projects, Christians creatively marshal strategies to foster spaces, moments, and opportunities that will create conditions for conversion.

Consider the example of Hell Houses, which are alternative Halloween experiences produced by evangelical, fundamentalist, and charismatic Christians.[6] Congregations and ministries design choreographed theatrical performances that diagnose moral pathologies and offer the evangelical solution of born-again salvation. For example, visitors witness scenes such as a young woman confronted with the choice of abortion, a gay male dying of HIV-AIDS, a teenager on a shooting rampage, drug abuse, marital infidelity, suicide, and date rape. The model of conversion at work in Hell Houses is about inciting an emotional and visceral condition of fear among visitors, to literally scare them into religious change. As with Ark Encounter, material and sensory channels are mobilized to conjure affective experience.

Consider, too, the example of Gospel magicians.[7] Like all illusionists, Gospel magicians deploy sleight-of-hand techniques and cunning. Unlike many illusionists, they do so in the service of a unifying narrative: the presentation of born-again theology. Gospel magicians turn tricks involving playing-card predictions into lessons about scriptural prophecy. The model of conversion at work for these magicians is that of enchantment, to wow audiences so much that they become open to sincerely listening to the evangelical message of salvation.

The example of plausibility-immersion joins fear and enchantment as a practiced, engineered model of conversion. In the analysis that follows, I examine some of the cultural production strategies the creative team marshaled to accomplish its goal of successfully immersing visitors in a creationist past. I also examine some of the creative tensions that arose as the team executed these strategies. Together, these strategies and tensions illustrate how the conversion model of plausibility-immersion is performed to produce Ark Encounter as a form of religious publicity.

## Strategies

How did the team members nurture the elements of plausibility and immersion in their creative labor? We can think of their work as a composite of strategies aimed at transporting visitors into a literal biblical past.

### Immediate Immersion

When should audiences first encounter elements of plausibility and immersion? The team answered this with no ambiguity: before arriving at Ark Encounter and, certainly, immediately upon their arrival at the park. This strategy is about engaging audiences as soon as possible, and it extends to the team's fund-raising and promotional work. Because Ark Encounter's donors and investors are already committed creationists, plausibility-immersion is used with them to bolster support for the project rather than to convert, but the team's creative labor is the same.

From December 2011 through May 2012, the team worked to produce a nearly sixty-page, glossy promotional book that was mailed to likely financial contributors and distributed at various fund-raising events. Roger was the primary writer for the book, but each of the team members edited and commented on numerous drafts. The "promo book" presents the basic rationale for Ark Encounter, explains the purpose of the three decks, and presents concept art for the exhibits. The language of immersive entertainment animates nearly every page. For example, donors were tempted to "imagine" boarding the ark through a sensorial appeal:

> As guests enter the impressive ark, all around them are cages filled with animals and props. Guests have entered the bottom of the ship. It is dark and dimly lit, and guests can hear the looming catastrophic events. As the wind begins to blow, objects bump against the Ark outside.

Further, they are assured of professional quality and consumer satisfaction:

> A background sound track of animal sounds will create the realistic sense of being surrounded by all the animals—it's not overwhelming, but a carefully choreographed cacophony of sounds to transform your visit into a truly one-of-a-kind experience.

Attention to a multisensory experience is clearly important. This emphasis recurs throughout the promo book, as well as in the team's broader creative labor. Ark Encounter is promised to be a feast for the eyes ("all around them are cages filled with animals and props"), ears ("a carefully choreographed cacophony"), and nose ("inhaling the delightful smells"). A sense of mood ("dark and dimly lit") saturates the play-infused invitation to "imagine."

This strategy of immediately engaging visitors in the core themes of plausibility and immersion was evident during an early team meeting in February 2012. The meeting lasted four hours, and its purpose was to brainstorm about the numerous park features that might be installed outside the ark itself. My field notes include three revealing summary remarks about the meeting.

First, budget constraints were a stable pillar of the discussion. Team members kept reminding each other that money was limited; Roger, for example, said they were aiming for "as cool as possible for as cheap as possible." Second, they continually recalled features from other theme parks, museums, and businesses as examples of what to do and what not to do. Many of these were places they had visited together as a team on research trips: Universal Studios, Walt Disney World, Silver Dollar City, Dollywood, the Columbus Zoo, Starbucks, the Creation Museum, Chick-fil-A, and the Indianapolis Children's Museum. Third, one comment in my field notes about the meeting captures a characteristic feature of the entire four hours: "The fluidity of their discussion killed me. One time they went from talking about how to create an attraction to talking about toilets at the entrance in a matter of seconds."

Much of the team members' talk concerned how to create an immersive effect throughout the entire park. In discussing the ark gift shop, they dwelled for several minutes on how to manage the kind of products that would be sold. Roger emphasized that it must be "a style that fits in pre-Flood culture." Briefly, Roger and one of the administrative assistants critiqued the Creation Museum on this account, noting that it resembles "any old Christian bookstore." All agreed that Ark Encounter needed to avoid this problem, extending the immersive experience to the gift shop.

On several occasions the team members returned to the question of food vendors and menu possibilities. They all liked the idea of bread being baked throughout the park. The aroma could foreshadow the eight passengers cooking on board and transport visitors via what the team members considered to be a universal sensation (i.e., the pleasurable, appetizing comfort of smelling freshly baked bread). In addition to the usual "hamburger, French fries, and a Coke," they wanted to offer "ancient" foods, like quinoa, tabouli, and hummus.

Toward the meeting's close, they discussed "script" possibilities for the bus ride connecting the parking lot to the ark site. Everyone wanted "the story" (i.e., immersion in Noah's pre-Flood world) to begin on the bus. They mapped the distance for this route and decided it would be half a mile, or a five-minute ride on a bus traveling at about fifteen miles per hour. Roger decided they would need to draft a script and practice it in the parking lot outside the studio, allowing them to gauge how much of the story they would be able to tell.

*The Authentic*

Plausibility and immersion are not separate imperatives in this model of conversion but instead are interlaced. Failures in the area of plausibility threatened to disrupt the immersive effect. With too many plausibility failures, immersion is not merely broken but lost. Just as immersion enhances the believability of the play experience, demonstrating the historical and practical plausibility of the ark would enhance the experiential immersion for visitors. Recall how Roger's critique of the teaser trailer included derision for using mass-produced "Lowe's" pegs instead of pegs that looked more "handmade."

The foregoing examples feature elements of plausibility, such as the use of "ancient" foods. There are also onboard demonstrations of plausibility, such as feeding and caring for the animals. An important example of plausibility for the team was Noah's use of technology, which is the focus for several exhibit bays as well as an interactive display proposed for outside the ark. The promo book described Noah's "construction site" as follows:

> [A] fascinating site [that] will contain other equipment, such as a pitch pot, a rope-making machine, and a peg-making machine . . . as well as many items needed for Noah's long journey ahead. The construction technology is on display to show that ancient man was not primitive at all, and that Noah had all the intelligence and technology he needed to build an Ark.

The plausibility of technology links directly to a key creationist teaching point: the "sophistication" of "ancient" peoples whose life spans far outlasted those of modern peoples.

The team's focus on plausibility was prominent in its critique of a different Noah: the one depicted in *Noah*, a blockbuster film starring Russell Crowe that was released in theaters in March 2014. Team members tracked the film throughout its production, knowing that they needed to see what "Hollywood" would come up with but remaining certain that the film was bound to disappoint theologically and in immersive terms of re-creating the biblical past. Here, the signifier "Hollywood" shifts from a creative exemplar to a "secular" recklessness with scriptural authority.

The night *Noah* was released in theaters, Answers in Genesis filmed a two-and-a-half-hour live webcast event that presented a theological critique of the film. The webcast was hosted by Ken Ham, one of AiG's cofounders and the ministry's most visible spokesman, several AiG "research scientists," and the lead "content manager" for Ark Encounter. What I found most revealing about the team members' reaction to *Noah* was that their critique diverged from the ministry's public discourse. While they affirmed the theological critique, their primary objection to the film was that it failed their measure of plausibility-immersion.

In early December 2012, images from the filming of *Noah* were released online. I e-mailed one of these images to Kevin—a close-up of Crowe on the set in full Noah costume—and asked for his evaluation. I was particularly interested in the clothing, since that was Kevin's area of expertise. He replied within a few hours:

> They're Hollywood, meaning they're going to do what looks pretty (to them), not what makes sense. The more I learn about this film the more I foresee a flop.

Eager to know more, I replied within the hour:

> Fascinating! Care to elaborate? What about their rendering of the clothing did not make sense?

His reply, just over an hour later, elaborated on his aesthetic and immersive critique:

> When an artist starts a project (I sometimes do this myself, and see many many artists do this as well), they figure what they want something to look like before finding out what it should look like. This is usually ok if you're doing a piece of art where the look is simply an interpretation, like a modern art painting or maybe a play. When it comes to a period film, play, painting or something similar, you have to just plain let go of what you want, and just be ready to learn about what it needs to be/look like. This could apply to a writer who wants to write a historical piece—let's say like Lincoln—they're either going to project themselves onto him, make him who they already have assumed he would be like, or they're

going to bite the bullet, forget themselves, and research and just be true to who he should be. So this is what happens with films that don't take the story seriously and they just want to project their own ideas onto it. I say to them, just go make a sci-fi! So specifically with the Noah movie, they don't take history seriously and so there doesn't need to be any connection between Noah's culture and the next culture—the Sumerians. So they just made him look like some Icelandic guy.

For Kevin, the film was doomed because it failed to "bite the bullet" and "take history seriously." The result, "project[ing] their own ideas onto it," falls short of the team's goal for its own projects of immersing the audience in a creationist biblical past. The stakes were high for Kevin: "some Icelandic guy" versus a believable Noah; a Noah who will impede conversion versus a Noah who would foster it.

### Before the Flood

As the team worked to create an immersive experience, its creative labor engaged in "world-building."[8] This is most striking in the team's imagining of life on earth before the Flood. In the creationist narrative, the Flood destroyed not just people and animals but also "culture." All was lost to the past, all but what Noah and his family brought on the ark, materially and through their collective memory. This makes the team's creative labor both more difficult and more open. On one hand, the team members lack physical evidence of "pre-Flood life." On the other, the lack of physical evidence means they are less accountable to referents of historical accuracy. Tyler described it this way during an interview:

> We can kind of *dream up* a world that is believable because it did exist. These people lived many, many, many times, many years more than we do. They lived seven, 800 years. So, *imagine* what somebody that had that much life span prior to this current age where you only live maybe 100 max, average is probably 70 or 80 years. *Imagine* what that amount of time of life would lend to just from a pure technological advancement. Through, just look, we've gone from just, in the few hundred years we've gone from farming to sending people to the moon. *Imagine* what

the technologies could have been like if you had hundreds of millions of people that were living really, really long life spans and the technology, *we have no clue.* (emphasis added)

World-building is prized by our modern culture of entertainment. Echoing Peter Stromberg's work in *Caught in Play*, the communication scholar Mark J. P. Wolf writes in his book *Building Imaginary Worlds*: "To invite an audience to vicariously enter another world, and then hold them there awhile is, after all, the essence of entertainment, which traces its etymology to the Latin roots *inter* meaning 'among,' and *tenere* meaning 'to hold.'"[9] In his analysis of world-building, Wolf observes that "the oldest and perhaps most common tool used to introduce a world and orient an audience is the map."[10] Michael Saler, a historian of the fantasy literature genre who agrees with Wolf, notes in his book *As If*: "Maps in particular were important for establishing the imaginary world as a virtual space consistent in all its details."[11] This strategy of mapping worlds is evident from Thomas More's *Utopia* in 1516 to A. A. Milne's *Winnie the Pooh* in 1926, J. R. R. Tolkien's Middle Earth in 1937, George R. R. Martin's *A Song of Ice and Fire* in 1996, and a great many other works.

By imagining Noah's pre-Flood world, the creative team joined this world-building tradition. In January 2012, I sat with Tyler while he worked on a map for the promotional book (Figure 4.2). His eyes darted back and forth between dual monitors. One screen featured an early version of the map in Photoshop, and he busily clicked keyboard keys, redrawing rivers, erasing mountains. The second screen displayed an online version of the New King James Bible open to Genesis 4.

Tyler's map reappeared in numerous publicity and fund-raising materials in subsequent years leading up to the park's opening. During the February 2012 meeting described earlier, the team spent a few minutes discussing where to place the map in the park. Everyone agreed it should be featured prominently, helping to instigate the immersive experience.

The map represents the Garden of Eden area from the pre-Flood earth. Tyler's task, he clarified as he worked, was to engage the biblical past on creationist terms while using his artistic imagination to fill in details not provided by scripture. After all, the text says very little about

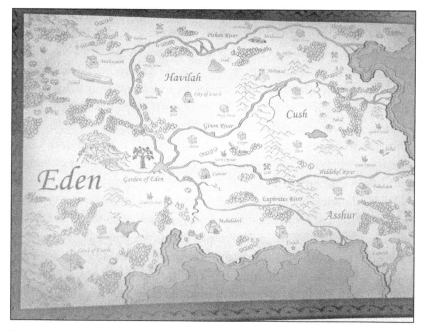

Figure 4.2. Map of pre-Flood Eden. Photo by author.

this land. It says the garden was east of Eden and names a few places, rivers, and minerals. Tyler did the rest. He considered his work as parallel to creations like Tolkien's Middle Earth and the world portrayed in the film *Avatar*, except he was representing an actual world. More accurately, he continued, his work was closer to Mel Gibson's depiction of the Mayan world in the film *Apocalypto*.

As an earnest biblical literalist, how do you construct a map when the coordinates are so few? The literalism of this map is not in its physical coordinates but in the history it presumes to capture: a past place that did exist because scripture says so, but that no longer exists because God said to Noah, "I am going to put an end to all people, for the earth is filled with violence because of them. I am surely going to destroy both them and the earth."[12]

If literalism animates the signified, fantasy is the chosen signifier. Many who see Tyler's map are immediately reminded of the maps of Middle Earth in *The Lord of the Rings*.[13] This is not accidental; Tyler kept a matted version of Tolkien's map in his cubicle for creative inspiration and reference throughout the process of designing this Eden. What I never saw at the studio, or heard reference to, were previous creationist attempts to render spatial representations of Eden. In her book *Paradise Lust*, Brook Wilensky-Lanford surveys the historical effort to locate and replicate the Garden of Eden.[14] The creationist maps Wilensky-Lanford presents operate primarily in the register of political geography (e.g., referencing longitude and latitude, naming current nation-states). Compare this with Tyler's map, which speaks solely in the register of fantasy world-building (Figure 4.3).

Tyler's double-voiced map suggests an elective affinity between biblical literalism and world-building. Both are geared toward immersing adherents/consumers in an experience that is not empirically available. We can never know what the pre-Flood world looked like, but with the help of Tyler's map, we can imagine. Imagine the beauty of an Eden with dew still on it. Imagine 800-year human life spans, the accumulated intelligence and skill born from 600 years of learning from your own mistakes. Imagine a world so wicked that it incited God's wrath. Imagine the end of the rain and the power of God's grace. Imagine . . .

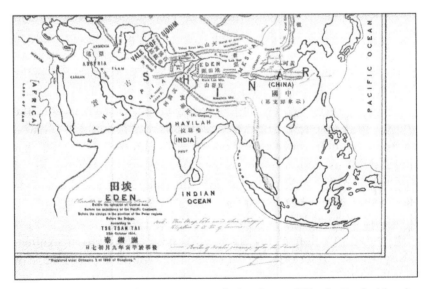

Figure 4.3. Realist-oriented creationist map of Eden. Source: Wilensky-Lanford (2011).

## Tensions

The team maintained well-defined strategies for crafting conditions of plausibility and immersion. While individual artistic and design preferences sometimes diverged and clashed, it was clear that the team members shared a common creative vision and a commitment to realizing that vision. Still, performing strategies of plausibility-immersion was not always straightforward or uncomplicated. Several tensions persisted around how to re-create the creationist past in ways that would successfully integrate the imperatives of fundamentalism and modern entertainment.

### Family Friendly

One tension emerged from competing imperatives. The first imperative derived from the demands of creationist theology and plausibility-immersion. The team members were intent that their representation of "pre-Flood" society be true to their reading of the biblical narrative. God sentenced everyone but the righteous Noah and his family to death, and the team wanted to seriously address the theme of judgment-worthy sin. This theme opened up a wide range of creative possibilities. As Ann Pellegrini notes in her analysis of American evangelical Hell Houses: "Sin makes for much more interesting spectacle and narrative than goodness."[15] However, the team was equally aware of a second imperative derived from the demands of the leisure industry and tourist economy. As a form of public culture, Ark Encounter must be acceptable for all ages. In market terms, families are a key profit-making demographic for a successful theme park, no matter its inspiration or content. So: *how do you depict the most sinful period in human history in a way that will be fun for the whole family?*

Consider an example from my first full day of fieldwork at the design studio. In the middle of the six-hour "regroup meeting," the team devoted one hour to brainstorming the Pagan Pathway (a walking path that would lead visitors into the ark). Like Tyler's map and the bus ride from the parking lot to the ark site, the pathway fed the immersive experience because it would be one of the first park features that visitors encounter.

The team members explored a series of design possibilities. They could include pre-Flood people teasing Noah, sin evidenced by disbelief. Sitting there, I couldn't help but think how this neatly affirmed their own work, first with the Creation Museum and now with Ark Encounter, both of which receive regular and unapologetic public ridicule.[16] Emily cited Disney's Pirates of the Caribbean as a useful model for how to depict sin and still be entertaining. Tyler worried about making the scene look too much like any particular historical place or era; they wanted to capture the uniqueness of the world before destruction. But how do you use known materials to create the unknown?

Much of their time was spent imagining symbolic possibilities. What about Venus-type statues to show hypersexuality? What about perversions of nature, such as half-human/half-animal forms? Maybe tribal masks could work? Tyler liked the idea of using a currency to symbolize rampant greed. Would blood and teeth be good? What about cannibalism? Roger, remembering something in his office, left abruptly and soon returned and placed a series of pictures on the table. All of the images depicted ritual scenes and objects from tribal societies, primarily African. He asked the team to consider these images for cues and clues. Breezily, ancient sinfulness and the "pagan" were invoked via the cultural Otherness of non-Western indigeneity.

Emily worried about losing "the reveal moment." They wanted to obscure the ark so visitors would not rush through the pathway. The ark is too large to hide completely, but they needed to distract the eager gaze of visitors desiring the main attraction. Roger suggested vertical flags of different colors and designs. Everyone liked this idea. Henry, the director of park construction, suggested a painted fence. Everyone was skeptical. Tyler summarized their hesitation: "A painted fence looks like a painted fence. You don't want to defeat the experience. No camouflage either; it will look like a military depot. Nothing can be modern." Lighting presented just such a modern dilemma, but Roger had anticipated this. He pointed to a large salt crystal on the table, one he had brought in specifically for this meeting, which could be used to hide electronic lights.

And so on, back and forth, until the team members were satisfied they had created a workable set of possibilities to resume with later. The design direction for the pathway continued to change (first to the series of stele monuments designed by Kevin; then, perhaps much to Henry's delight, a painted mural lining the pathway; then to the *Pre-Flood World* exhibit on Deck Two), but the creative vision never detached from concerns about what was appropriate for a broad visiting public of parents and children.

The question of how to ensure a family-friendly environment appeared again during production of the promo book. Tyler was illustrating concept art for a four-minute live-action preshow film, which visitors would view before entering Deck One. In the film's earliest iteration, the approach was to depict scenes from Noah's final pre-Flood days: Noah meeting with Methuselah before his death, Methuselah passing scrolls to Noah, Noah being tempted by "harlots," Noah preaching his final sermon, and the start of the rain.

Tyler's progress slowed as he worked on the "temptation scene," in which Noah is approached by "two harlots" on his way to the ark after visiting a dying Methuselah (Figure 4.4). Tyler explained that this scene's main goal was to demonstrate Noah's righteousness through his resistance to "seduction." The trick Tyler faced was to make the seduction seem real, but in a way that would be acceptable "for kids." Sitting with

Figure 4.4. Concept art for preshow film temptation scene. Photo by author.

Tyler as he worked, I noted that he spent extra time on one specific feature of the concept art. First he raised the hemline of the woman on the
left, exposing more of her leg. Then, he lowered it, covering more. He repeated this several times, raising and lowering the hemline. Eventually,
he settled on what is visible in Figure 4.4. He was pleased with how his
depiction of the partly exposed thigh turned out; it was suggestive, but
no more so than in many G-rated films and advertisements that are part
of the public's everyday media consumption. He had successfully negotiated, if only momentarily, the family-friendly tension that animated the
team's work of religious publicity.

*Surprise*

A second tension that arose in team meetings and individual creative
moments related to teaching creationist content while also continually
"surprising" audiences. For noncreationists audiences, the story of Noah
is well known and easily accessible. For creationists as well, Ark Encounter presents very little new content. It teaches what Answers in Genesis
has been teaching since its founding in 1994, which varies little from the
modern creationist movement that began in 1961 with the publication
of *The Genesis Flood*, which was not altogether different from George
McReady Price's books dating back to 1902.[17]

This tension of surprising audiences was also tied to the team members' suspicion that non-Christian audiences were prepared to dismiss
the park as religious kitsch.[18] Their desire was to generate impressive
professional work, "Hollywood quality," defeating judgments of poor
taste and making audiences pause when they experienced the unexpected sophistication. Emily gave voice to this hope and danger during an interview. We were discussing her sources of creative inspiration,
and she turned to metaphor: "Stuff that inspires me is stuff that has all
the right pieces in the right level that are just blended together like an
orchestra or a great football or basketball team. Do you know what I
mean?" When I asked her to elaborate on what Ark Encounter's orchestra pieces were, she responded:

> Well, on this project one of my main goals is to, and I've expressed this
> to our team, is that I don't want it to be a stereotype that's been created of

like biblical themed environments. . . . It's in *breaking those stereotypes*, not just in the architecture, but also in how we portray the figures, the characters, Noah and his family, how we tell the stories, how we do the pre-show, for example, or, I mean even to the aging of the wood and the textures, because that *can go really bad*. We want to make sure and keep a firm eye on that, and that goes back to art direction. So, at the end of the day that'll be our fault. If we hire a scenic company to do any texturing or aging, if it *comes off like plastic or cheap looking*, that's our fault that we didn't do a *better job* at directing that. In this, an important piece to the puzzle would be in portraying Noah the right away. That his character comes across the way that God would want it to come across . . . I mean, that's the important piece, the story. Making sure the ark isn't *hokey or just weird* and too *stereotypical* of what a lot of the church tries to do. Out of just, because they, not saying what they do is wrong, they do it with good hearts, they do it to try and portray something visually, but maybe it's *not their talent* or something. It's kind of *hokey*. That's sort of our goal. We're always trying to *do something better*. (emphasis added)

Emily hopes to surprise audiences by exceeding "hokey" stereotypes of "biblical themed environments." Gently, she critiques "the church" for well-intentioned but ill-suited attempts to present the Bible "visually."

Kevin voiced the same critique, though less gently. Toward the end of a fieldwork day at the studio in January 2014, I told him that I had plans to visit the Holy Land Experience in Orlando, Florida, an attraction that is frequently derided by religious and secular critics for being the epitome of kitschy religious entertainment. Working at the desktop computer in his cubicle, Kevin glanced at me and said wryly, "I'm sorry." I asked what he meant, and he added, in an unambiguous tone, "It's so cheesy." As we talked more, it was clear that religious attractions like the Holy Land Experience were an explicit creative Other for the team, an example of what it must avoid if Ark Encounter is to be successful as a form of public culture. So, how do you surprise an audience amid these conditions of a deeply familiar biblical story and perceived public expectations about kitsch?

In early May 2012, I ate lunch with Tyler in the design studio kitchen. We talked candidly about the planned script for the preshow film. He thought the current approach was "good," but he was feeling dissatisfied and was certain that a "better, more creative" idea could still be discovered. When I asked what he meant, he explained that depicting Noah's final pre-Flood days would "work just fine," but he thought it was "too event-driven." The "so what" was being lost. Without further prompting, Tyler recalled a film he had recently seen—*Remember Me*, a romantic drama set in New York City—that he thought could work as a model. He described the film without giving too much attention to plot details. When I read a summary of the film later that day, it was clear his retelling was partial. But, the film's particulars were less relevant for Tyler; it was the film's ending he cared about.

Although viewers know the film is set in contemporary times, no exact date is provided. The final scene shows the main character staring out the window of one of the World Trade Center towers. The camera zooms out to set the towers against a clear blue sky. The scenes that follow depict the first reactions at street level on the morning of September 11, 2001. Ash floats down through the air. Another central character, a policeman, barely manages chaotic traffic. Each of the central characters is shown looking upward, but the object of their fixed stare is never revealed. It would be unnecessary, even gratuitous, to do so. Tyler "loved" how this dramatic ending "totally changed" his viewing of the entire film. He wanted to show it to the team and to adopt this logic of audience surprise to revise the preshow script away from "giving everything away up front."

I don't know if Tyler ever showed *Remember Me* to the team, but the preshow script was not revised in this direction. In fact, the team scrapped the original script in favor of an interview between Noah and a skeptical reporter and outsourced the labor to a Christian film company.[19] Still, Tyler's hesitation and critique help make clear how the tension of surprising audiences informed the creative process and the team's hopes for successfully realizing the model of plausibility-immersion.

## Conclusion

This chapter has explored how the team's model of conversion fits within Ark Encounter's ambitions as religious publicity and fundamentalist public culture. The team members' design choices were organized by two interlaced imperatives: to demonstrate the historical plausibility of the Noah story and to immerse visitors in a creationist biblical past.

I noted earlier that the team members always envisioned a variety of audiences coming to Ark Encounter. While they sometimes differentiated among these potential visitors, they also erased the lines of difference when it came to how audiences would be successfully engaged. The model of plausibility-immersion would satisfy each audience they anticipated because modern consumers are all equally primed with an "aesthetics of persuasion" instilled by our shared culture of entertainment.[20]

All of Ark Encounter's potential audiences demand to be entertained. They are a predisposed public, accustomed to being "caught up" in different experiential worlds by popular media productions (*Star Trek*, *Star Wars*, *The Lord of the Rings*, *The Chronicles of Narnia*, and *Game of Thrones*, to name just a few) and the affective turn in re-creating the past (e.g., the examples of museum education described earlier).[21] Moreover, they are a discerning public, expecting Hollywood and Disney quality. If the team failed to achieve the high bar set by secular productions, the conversion model of plausibility-immersion would not be achieved. Skeptics would remain skeptical, seekers still seeking, the lost still lost.

Plausibility-immersion is fundamentally about play. Following Stromberg, "play" refers not generically to leisure activities but specifically to the experience of being caught up in a reality different from that of the everyday.[22] Throughout the process of cultural production, the team debated how best to create conditions that would enable visitors to play at Ark Encounter. They wanted visitors to play in the creationist past: a world in which the earth is 6,000 years old, humans and dinosaurs coexisted, and humans lived as long as 900 years, and in which a universal Flood killed all but eight people from whom all modern humans descended.

The team's desire for visitor play resonates with a long-standing relationship between religion and play. Ritual contexts work as a space for play, in which adherents are transported to a sacred space-time.[23] Anthropologists of Christianity have observed this function to be especially resonant in the ritual travel of pilgrimage. For example, ethnographies of American Christian pilgrims to Israel-Palestine feature vivid examples of how natural landscapes allow visitors to play in biblical history and "walk where Jesus walked."[24] Moreover, play affords multiple relations with ritualized space and activity. In their ethnography of the English Marian shrine at Walsingham, for example, Simon Coleman and John

Elsner highlight how pilgrims perform irreverence and irony. These travelers deem the site's High Anglican past "vulgar" not to reject it but to engage in "gay explorations of campness."[25] Pilgrims cultivate a critical and humorous distance from this past, while still maintaining a religiously meaningful experience.

In their comparative study of religious toys and games, religious studies scholars Nikki Bado-Fralick and Rebecca Sachs Norris extend the concept of religious play.[26] They argue that popular religious commodities help to cultivate lived religion in everyday life through embodied channels. As people use religious toys to engage in play, the line separating devotion and fun blurs and, at times, disappears. While the fun of religious toys can be used to teach and evangelize, fun also introduces more ambiguous elements into religious life. "Fun is dangerous" for its potential to cultivate critical and creative thinking.[27]

In her ethnography of American charismatic Christians, anthropologist Tanya Luhrmann documents how the use of play and the "as if" imagination has become a dominant, mainstream method for training middle-class Christians to experience God.[28] In the "pluralistic, science-oriented West," in what some have called "a secular age," Christians can no longer take for granted the authority and unquestioned legitimacy of a biblical worldview.[29] As a response to their awareness of competing epistemologies, these charismatics "encourage a deliberatively playful, imaginative, fantasy-filled experience of God."[30] This fantasy-filled experience works as an invitation: *just* try it. The creative team's invitation to play at Ark Encounter suggests that the fondness for religious play extends beyond the personal and the congregational to the consumer-centered religious publicity of a creationist theme park. *Just* imagine . . .

The team's ambition for religious play speaks to the comparative study of religious conversion. The model of plausibility-immersion, and the experience of play it entails, organize Ark Encounter's promise to convert. Alongside other ethnographic cases, such as Hell House theater performances and Gospel magicians, the example of Ark Encounter illustrates something of the human agentive and creative side of producing conditions for conversion.

Connecting the concept of play with the study of conversion also returns us to an instructive debate. Luhrmann pitched part of her project as a critique of Susan Harding's research among fundamentalist Baptists.[31] Harding argued that conversion begins with learning religious language. As potential converts learn to think in fundamentalist categories and use the tradition's scripturally inflected vocabulary, they are initiated into the process of conversion. While recognizing the importance of religious language, Luhrmann argued that the learning involved with conversion is more expansive. Learning to be a culturally competent Christian, in particular a Vineyard-style charismatic, means learning to train the body, emotions, and cognition as well as your language.

Ark Encounter's model of plausibility-immersion, grounded in the experience of play, echoes both Harding and Luhrmann. Playing in the world of Noah entails adopting the rhetoric and literal historicity of creationism, and it also entails a multisensory, affective experience. It is an embodied experience of the creationist past. I continue with this theme in the next chapter, which examines how the team members' work as imagineers reveals a particularly creationist way of re-creating the past.

5

## The Past Is Not History

### The Debate

Fundamentalist Protestants live in a present that anticipates an apoca-
lyptic future. As an everyday experience, this functions as "a specific
narrative mode of reading history; [they] do not inhabit the same historical landscape as nonbelievers."[1] Creationism, bundled in the same
fundamentalist temporality, also positions believers in a sacred space-
time. In the creationist world the earth is roughly 6,000 years old,
humans and dinosaurs coexisted, pre-Flood human life spans could
extend for nearly 1,000 years, and a universal flood 4,000 years ago
killed all but eight people from whom we all descended. But creationist
temporality is not reducible to a timeline of events; it is about conjuring
a particular historical landscape in the present. It is this creationist past
that the team sought to produce at Ark Encounter, inviting visitors to
play in an inhabited historical landscape.

There is a jarring difference between how creationism and evolutionary science imagine and narrate the past. I begin this analysis by stepping slightly back in time to February 4, 2014, and a widely publicized
"debate" between Answers in Genesis cofounder Ken Ham and science
celebrity educator Bill Nye. This event, part of AiG's arsenal of religious
publicity, was viewed by millions of people that evening and has been
viewed by millions more through YouTube and other media. The debate
was held at the Creation Museum—in Legacy Hall, the same space where
the team and I watched the ark trailer. Answers in Genesis released 900
tickets, the hall's capacity, for public sale a month before the debate. Tickets sold out in minutes. Thanks to good fortune and the quick telephone
dialing of a colleague, we secured two tickets.[2]

Driving to the museum, I balanced a curious excitement for the
event and an anxiety about the weather: a threatening winter storm

was primed to blanket the Cincinnati region with heavy snow and ice. I arrived an hour before the scheduled start time to find a mostly full parking lot and a bustling scene. Heavy, wet flakes had begun to accumulate, and I hustled inside alongside others who had secured one of the prized tickets. My colleague had already picked up our passes from the museum admission booth, along with two glossy orange and black cards. The larger card had a debate itinerary on one side and a list of "procedures" on the other (e.g., "Please refrain from cheering, applause, or other disruptive behavior"). The smaller card could be filled out, directed to "Mr. Nye" or "Mr. Ham," and submitted during the final forty-minute debate portion in which the two men would answer audience questions.

I had been to the Creation Museum at least a dozen times before that night and this time was immediately struck by the number of handlers on-site: employees and volunteers spread throughout to direct traffic, keep the crowd moving, and check wristbands. Purple wristbands were for the more than seventy media personnel in attendance, who were directed to reserved seats close to the stage. Orange wristbands were for the rest of us. Museum handlers were easy to spot because all of them wore the same orange and black T-shirts that had been designed especially for the debate.

We found two seats in a back corner of Legacy Hall, affording a complete view of the room. The crowd seemed to skew younger and was composed primarily of married couples and their school-age children. Most faces were phenotypically white, with only a few noticeable exceptions. A few other couples stood out because they wore traditional Mennonite clothing, a common sight whenever I have visited the museum. Some Bill Nye supporters displayed their allegiance on screen-printed T-shirts that read, "Bill Nye is my homeboy," with the outline of a bowtie printed just below the crew neck. Settling in, we noted that the stage and podium were covered in orange and black signs. The utterly consistent color wash reflected the marketing and branding prowess of Answers in Genesis. In the museum bookstore a few months later I would find DVDs, T-shirts, books, and coffee mugs for purchase that kept this visual theming alive (Figure 5.1).

The 150-minute debate began with 5-minute opening statements from Ham and Nye. After a coin toss to determine the order, Ham spoke first.

Figure 5.1. Nye-Ham debate T-shirt for sale in the Creation Museum bookstore. Photo by author. A sign above the rack recontextualizes a debate quote from Ken Ham that circulated widely in ministry publicity materials: "THERE IS A BOOK."

In his statement, Nye began with a humorous family anecdote about how his grandfather learned to tie a bowtie, now Nye's signature fashion accessory, and then proceeded to articulate a fundamental difference between creationism and evolutionary science.

Answers in Genesis distinguishes between two kinds of scientific activity: "observational" and "historical."[3] The former refers to actions such as microscopic analysis of DNA, in which scientists "directly" observe the empirical world. The latter refers to practices such as fossil analysis, in which scientists "indirectly" observe the past by making inferences about the empirical world. This is where Mr. Nye began his case for evolution and against creationism:

> The question tonight is "Does Ken Ham's creation model hold up? Is it viable?" So let me ask you all, what would you be doing if you weren't here tonight? That's right. You'd be home watching *CSI. CSI: Petersburg?* Is it coming? I think it's coming. [audience laughs] And, on *CSI* there is no distinction made between historical science and observational science. These are constructs unique to Mr. Ham. We don't normally have these anywhere in the world except [at the Creation Museum].[4]

Bill Nye spoke in concert with the mainstream scientific community. Only creationism works with this distinction; it is not a recognized or operative set of categories used in science. Mainstream scientists see creationists' use of this distinction as a strategy to undermine the authority of evolutionary theory. It is a rhetorical maneuver designed to instigate doubt: "Historical science is more uncertain, more open to debate than evolutionists let on, and don't let 'em tell you any different."

It is no accident that Bill Nye began by rejecting any legitimacy for a division between "historical" and "observational" science. The fact that creationists and noncreationists view the past in remarkably different ways is marked by the respective promotion and rejection of this divide. These two groups do not inhabit the same temporal landscape. To understand the team's cultural production of the creationist past and how it is performed through its religious publicity, we will use the concept of history-making to analyze a Creation Museum exhibit designed by the team and launched on Memorial Day 2013: *Dragon Legends.*

## History-Making

If history is, as it may be, a tyranny over the souls of the
dead—and so the imaginations of the living—where lies our
greatest well of inspiration, our greatest hope of freedom
(since the future it totally blank, if not black) we should
guard it doubly from the interlopers.[5]
—William Carlos Williams

This passage from the American poet William Carlos Williams captures
a pivotal social fact. The past is contestable, and defining history is an act
of power. Creationists and evolutionary scientists both work to "guard"
the production and public circulation of history. To understand this
work of guarding history, history-making serves as a revealing concept:
a field of practice through which claims about the past are produced and
invested with ontological, political, and moral significance. This concept
resonates with other conceptual efforts to understand the social processes through which "versions of the past . . . assume present form" and
become socially ratified.[6]

History-making pivots on the difference between "the past" and "history." Scholars across disciplines insist on this distinction. For example,
museum studies expert Mike Wallace writes: "There is no such thing as
'the past.' All history is a production—a deliberate selection, ordering, and
evaluation of past events, experiences, and processes."[7] In their ethnography of colonial Williamsburg, anthropologists Richard Handler and Eric
Gable stress the discursive production of history: " 'The past' exists only as
we narrate it today. The past is above all the stories, not objects."[8]

Distinguishing history from the past presents a fundamental tension.
The past is gone, yet it is always with us through constant remembering, forgetting, and rediscovering—forever and densely mediated by the
production of histories. In forms of public culture, history-making is a
social and ideological accomplishment achieved through material projects, such as museums and theme parks. The study of history-making
confronts important questions: How are different relationships to the
past cultivated? What strategies and resources are marshaled to perform
history-making? And what is at stake ideologically and materially in
competing acts of history-making?

When it comes to science's history-making antagonists, fundamental-ists play a leading role, largely due to creationism's persistent presence in the public sphere: introducing pro-creationism or antievolution bills to state legislatures, revising textbook standards to undermine evolu-tionary theory, and supporting multimillion-dollar projects like the Creation Museum and Ark Encounter. The creationism-science clash is heightened by the fact that both groups are committed to the uni-versal legitimacy of their respective projects. Both desire to "create a totalizing understanding of the world . . . one that is valid for all cul-tures and nations at all times."[9] This totalizing drive reflects a shared commitment between creationism and science: knowledge about the past matters dearly for life in the present. Like natural history muse-ums, creation museums affirm that "understanding our origins will tell us important information about who we are today."[10] These shared com-mitments underscore the contested nature and authoritative stakes of history-making.

The religious publicity of Answers in Genesis forcefully returns us to William Carlos Williams and the process of naming interlopers and guarding history from them. The past is ideologically contested, and even the most authorized histories can be actively and creatively chal-lenged. As the historian Raphael Samuel writes, "History is not the prerogative of the historian, nor even, as postmodernism contends, a historian's 'invention.' It is, rather, a social form of knowledge; the work, in any given instance, of a thousand different hands."[11] Moreover, those thousand hands do not work in concert, which means the present hosts multiple historical narratives vying for cultural authority. Anthropologi-cally, our calling is to understand whose hands are doing what, and how the struggle for authority unfolds.

## Dragons as Dinosaurs

By May 2013, fifty or so highway billboards had been erected throughout the Kentucky-Ohio-Indiana tristate region. These billboards advertised the Memorial Day opening of the Creation Museum's newest exhibit: *Dragon Legends*. Ark Encounter fund-raising was proceeding more slowly than the ministry had anticipated. As of October 2015, the park's opening date had been pushed from its initial "spring 2014" to summer

2016. While waiting for funding to be secured, the team devoted its creative labor to other projects in the ministry's religious publicity machine. Enter the dragons.

When you enter the Creation Museum's main building, the first space you encounter is the "portico": a curving walkway, about ninety paces long, that guides visitors to the ticket booth, bookstore, café, and Main Hall. The spatial position of the portico is significant. It provides the first experience the visiting public consumes, and it is free to consume because it is walkable without purchasing an entry ticket. The contents of the portico establish a frame for the remainder of the museum for every visitor who come through its doors.

When the museum opened in 2007, a trademarked Answers in Genesis teaching mnemonic—"The 7 C's of History: Creation, Corruption, Catastrophe, Confusion, Christ, Cross, Consummation"—filled the portico. This alliterative theological shorthand condenses the past into seven pivotal events in creationist cosmology. "Confusion" to "Christ" moves from the Tower of Babel (Genesis 11:1–9) to the New Testament Gospels. "Cross" to "Consummation" elides the Acts of the Apostles and all of the Epistles. And, of course, closing with "Consummation" leaps straight to Revelation's new heaven and new earth, eliding 2,000 years (and counting) of human endeavor. These temporal jumps work for creationists because this adheres to a Bible-centered presentation of history.

The 7 C's remain an Answers in Genesis trademark, but the team explained to me that the ministry wanted to instill a new portico exhibit to open the 2013 summer tourist season. They were determined to "up the cool factor" while still teaching creationist content. Like the 7 C's, the new exhibit would establish an interpretive frame and be grounded in history-making.

*Dragon Legends* presents the creationist argument that the coexistence of humans and dinosaurs is validated by the fact that stories involving human encounters with, or sightings of, dragons are told in different areas of the world by different cultures from different time periods. The website promo for *Dragon Legends* uses this teaser written by Roger:

> Regale yourself with delightful artwork and other beautiful adornments as you stroll beneath the colorful Chinese dragons in the museum's portico. Learn about encounters with these incredible beasts from China to

Africa, Europe to the Americas, and Australia to the Middle East. Discover what ancient historians have written about these creatures, and examine armaments that may have been used by valiant dragon slayers. Why are there so many dragon legends from cultures around the globe? Why do descriptions of these magnificent animals often sound similar to what we call dinosaurs? How could our ancestors carve, paint, or write about these creatures if they have truly been extinct for millions of years? Evolutionists struggle to explain the intriguing evidence that people lived at the same time as dinosaurs. God's Word indicates that dinosaurs and man were created on the same day, so biblical creationists are not surprised to uncover clues that ancient man had indeed seen these beasts.[12]

The critique of evolution is both subtle ("our ancestors") and overt ("Evolutionists struggle"), and the creationist blending of stylistic ("delightful artwork," "beautiful adornments"), scientific ("explain the intriguing evidence," "uncover clues"), and religious ("God's Word," "biblical creationists") registers is diligent and savvy.

The creationist argument unfolds as follows. Individual dragon legends are rooted in past events that have varying degrees of factuality, but all were inspired by something real. At some point in the past, humans interacted with animals that resembled the dragons of lore. Human conceptions of the actual creatures became more fantastical over time through storytelling. The most likely real-life inspiration for dragon legends were the animals we now call dinosaurs.

Several biblical texts provide the scriptural basis for this dragons-as-dinosaurs argument. Creationists begin in Genesis 1 and 2, which describe God's creation of all animals, land and sea, alongside humans. The literalist interpretation is that every animal for which there is fossil evidence must have coexisted with humans, including dinosaurs. From here, they go to Job 40 and 41. As God reprimands Job, chastising him for forgetting the vast gulf between human fallibility and divine glory, God describes two beasts. First:

Look at Behemoth, which I made along with you and which feeds on grass like an ox. What strength it has in its loins, what power in the muscles of its belly! Its tail sways like a cedar; the sinews of its thighs are close-knit. Its bones are tubes of bronze, its limbs like rods of iron.[13]

Then, there is "Leviathan":

> Its snorting throws out flashes of light; its eyes are like the rays of dawn. Flames stream from its mouth; sparks of fire shoot out. Smoke pours from its nostrils as from a boiling pot over burning reeds. Its breath sets coals ablaze, and flames dart from its mouth.[14]

Creationists interpret these texts to mean that Behemoth and Leviathan were both dinosaurs. These two scriptural animals represent the creatures that humans interacted with and told stories about; eventually, they became the stuff of elaborate legends.

Dinosaurs hold a strategic place in AiG's religious publicity. The image of the dinosaur is immediately recognizable to the mass public and an undeniable source of fascination (think: *Jurassic Park*). The claim that humans and dinosaurs coexisted is also a feature of the creationist past that is utterly foreign to the evolutionary past. Read anything critical of creationism—scholarly, popular, measured, or jeering—and you will likely find reference to the "bizarre" claim that dinosaurs lived alongside humans.[15]

The dragons-as-dinosaurs argument is a narrative and epistemological shift in the development of modern creationism. When dinosaurs became part of the popular consciousness in the nineteenth century, many creationists initially denied their factuality, claiming that dinosaur fossil discoveries were forgeries staged to advance evolutionary theory. As dinosaurs gained their enigmatic popularity, the dominant creationist argument shifted to recognize the authenticity of dinosaur remains, now classifying them as creatures from the pre-Flood world that were extinguished by Noah's Flood.[16] Contemporary creationists now include dinosaurs as being among the animals that Noah brought on board the ark. It was in this post-Flood world that dinosaurs were outcompeted and hunted to extinction by humans, which explains their presence in the fossil record.

The dragons-as-dinosaurs argument is now a staple of creationist history-making. A version of the argument appears throughout creationist literature and in most of the world's creation museums. For example, the Akron Fossils and Science Center uses a four-shelf bookcase to present the argument. *Dragon Legends* is the creative team's imagineered version of this history-making argument, conjuring a mosaic past through three display boards and eight display cases filled with a mix of material culture replicas crafted by Kevin and images illustrated by Tyler. The exhibit runs the length of the museum portico, with about thirty feet of space separating adjacent displays. The team designed *Dragon Legends* so that visitors could consume the exhibit at their own pace, studiously examining everything or leisurely inspecting a sampling.

When you enter the museum from the door closest to the parking lot, you experience the exhibit in order of the argument narrative (Figures 5.2–5.11).

*Dragon Legends* is animated by imagination and ambiguity. Were dinosaurs dragons? To immerse visitors in this question, the exhibit moves among archaeological replicas, mythology, folklore, fiction, tall tales, scripture, scriptural Apocrypha, and historical documentation. Read from a certain angle, *Dragon Legends* could be problematic for fundamentalists. After all, if the Bible tells us that humans lived with dinosaurs in the books of Genesis and Job, what else do we need to know? What happened to the plenary sufficiency of scripture? But this reading misunderstands the religious publicity at work. One reason the team chose dragons for the new portico theme is because of dinosaurs' popular appeal: immediate familiarity and fascination for a mass public. As we will see in the next section, dragons afford the creative team more artistic agency precisely because this theme extends beyond the pages of scripture.

## Producing *Dragon Legends*

*Dragon Legends* occupied the team's creative labor for seven months, from October 2012 through the Memorial Day 2013 opening. In the weeks preceding the opening, the team regularly worked twelve- to fourteen-hour days. When Tyler led me on a tour of the exhibit, ten days after its public premiere, he reflected that the significant and stressful investment of time was well spent. He considered *Dragon Legends* a huge improvement over the 7 C's installation: the prior portico exhibit was "too empty" and less "colorful." Tyler's nod to color drew me back to the hours I had sat with him as he tediously adjusted palettes and, of course, to his creative dispute with Roger concerning the aesthetic approach to the Saint George panel.

Figure 5.2. Display 1 profiles "dragon depictions around the world." The use of questions and qualifying language (e.g., "dinosaur-like creatures") mimics the exhibit's rhetorical strategy of inviting visitors to question the past and consider "the intriguing evidence." The display invokes the authority of archaeological science. While the interpretation of the remains as evidence of dinosaurs is contestable, the fact of the remains is not.

Figure 5.3. Display 2 profiles four "dragon legends," crossing freely between mythology, biblical apocrypha, and folklore. The dragons-as-dinosaurs argument is less grounded in the historical truth of every legend, and more in the global presence of legends as reflective of actual encounters with dragon-like creatures from the past. Their sum is more important than any single legend.

Figure 5.4. Displays 3 and 4 are designed as a pair, serving the same narrative function. The two examples depicted here—John of Damascus and Marco Polo—are "eyewitness accounts" from the historical record. Tyler chose to depict all four eyewitnesses with quill in hand. Writing and its materiality function indexically, collapsing the divide between "legend" and the recording of an actual past. This sense of realism is reinforced by Kevin's historical replicas, which include strategies like the artistic weathering of an explorer's map.

An interview with Tyler early in the design process helped me understand how the team negotiated historical accuracy and creative license. We talked in his cubicle while he worked on panel design prototypes. He was quick to specify the truth-value of *Dragon Legends*: "We're not showing any reality, and we're not saying [legends] are proof [of dinosaurs]. It's more, we're asking, 'Could it be?' " The strategy of "just asking" reproduces a long-standing creationist rhetorical device, which urges public audiences to question the presumed authority of evolutionary science and accuses "secularists" of censorship if doubt is prohibited.[17] Tyler continued, explaining that *Dragon Legends* "is a more playful, fun thing; just a fun, expressive way to tell stories." He contrasted this approach with the team's work on Ark Encounter, which he described as "hyperrealism," offering fewer opportunities to "go stylized."

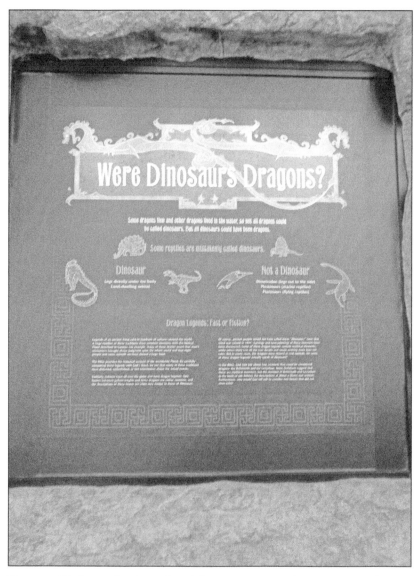

Figure 5.5. Display 5 is the closest the exhibit comes to a complete narrative rendering of the dragons-as-dinosaurs argument, but even this does not explain the logic step by step to visitors. This reflects the team's desire to rely less on explanatory signage and more on embodied experience to make the exhibit "intriguing."

Figure 5.6. Display 6 uses a map that mixes realism (the relative size and location of continents) with cryptozoology. For example, the legend of Mokele Mbembe, a dinosaur alleged to have existed in the African Congo as late as the mid-twentieth century, has been told and retold by creationist explorers (Loxton and Prothero 2013). *Dragon Legends* never uses "cryptozoology," a term that marks the legendary creatures as not historically factual, but leaves the actuality of cryptids as uncertain: questionable but distinctly possible.

Figure 5.7. Display 7 presents the most text of any display, namely, the two chapters from the book of Job that are read as scriptural proof of human-dinosaur coexistence. The quill-in-hand strategy repeats from the "eyewitness accounts," creating a visual bridge between the more authoritative scriptural display and the historical ambiguity of nonscriptural eyewitnesses. The "Behemoth" image extends the creationist argument, providing a visual depiction of the reasoning that humans hunted dinosaurs into extinction after the Flood.

The decision to prioritize a more imaginative approach over strict historical accuracy happened early in the creative process. Tyler described the initial design approach as "a more classic" style and illustrated this by showing me an artistic rendering of the Saint George legend on his computer, one more in line with the tradition of depicting a smaller animal and Saint George stabbing downward. The team decided against a "classic" approach because its representational style was too realist. For Tyler, creating *Dragon Legends* in such a style would require visitors to work overly hard in the exhibit experience to discern "what's real and what's not." The team wanted the exhibit to immerse visitors in a "playful, . . . fun, . . . expressive, . . . stylized" version of the dragons-as-dinosaurs argument, not require them to visually distinguish truth from

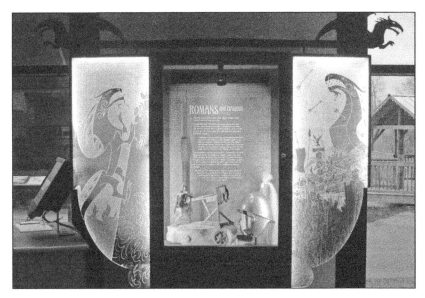

Figure 5.8. Display 8 illustrates a Roman folkloric tradition of encounters with dragons. The replica of a ballista-firing machine integrates an element of historical realism.

fiction. This helps explain why an imagineered Saint George differs so radically from the more commonly rendered version.

As an alternative artistic approach the team chose a style "akin to *Secret of the Kells*," an animated feature film released in 2009. The film is an adventure story set in eighth-century Ireland that fictionalizes the making of the Book of Kells, a lavishly illustrated copy of the four Gospels and a significant artifact in Irish national, religious, and artistic history.[18]

The team's decision regarding which intertextual aesthetic inspiration was right for *Dragon Legends* helps us understand the creative process in this act of creationist history-making. The team members regularly used contemporary film animation as a model for their original designs. During interviews, Tyler, Emily, and Kevin all named animation companies and individual artists as important influences on their creative development. As we have seen, art books from Hollywood and Disney films (e.g., *Jurassic Park, Star Wars, The Lord of the Rings, The Prince of Egypt, The Chronicles of Narnia, Avatar, The Last Airbender, King Kong*) were continually on the move between bookshelves and cubicle desks around the design studio. In this case, it was not just any animated film

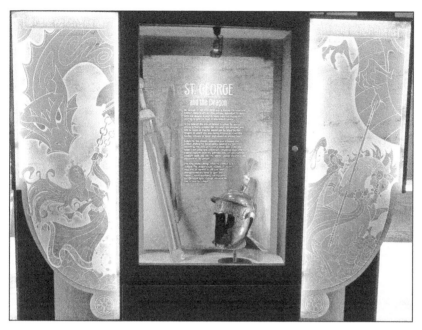

Figure 5.9. Display 9 narrates a version of the widely told legend of Saint George and the Dragon. The narrative portion highlights Saint George as not only a dragon slayer but also a "devout Christian" who successfully converts an entire "city." The team's imagineered version of this legend is striking for its contrast to more typical depictions. In most artistic representations, such as those that are ubiquitous throughout the city of Bethlehem in Israel-Palestine and in Ethiopian Orthodox churches, Saint George is looking and stabbing downward into a much smaller creature.

but a film that portrays a time period resonant with *Dragon Legends* and the making of biblical artistry. By naming *Secret of the Kells* as the center of creative gravity, the team members effectively cast themselves within a venerable Christian tradition that integrates art, faith, storytelling, and representations of the past.

As Tyler worked on the display panel art, Kevin worked on the material culture replicas for each display case. In late January 2013, I spent the morning sitting in his cubicle as he searched potential materials for the Saint George display. His searching process was patterned. He began by typing a search term into Google Images, then read the Wikipedia page for the search item. Sometimes he proceeded to several other Internet sources or his shelf of history books (most published by Answers

Figure 5.10. Display 10, which references the epic poem *Beowulf*, makes two distinctive rhetorical moves within the exhibit. First, it constructs a similarity between *Dragon Legends* and the famous poem, both of which blend "accurate information" and "fiction." Second, it makes explicit reference to the museum's history-making antagonists: "those who believe dinosaurs lived millions of years before man."

Figure 5.11. Display 11 concludes *Dragon Legends* with a modern legend set in the American West. Consistent with the rhetorical strategy of the exhibit, it ends not with a declarative explanation but with a question that asks visitors to explore whether or not the legend is "just another tall tale" or evidence of something else.

in Genesis, but with a few secular university and popular press titles sprinkled in). In one instance, he puzzled for several minutes over which cross symbol would most likely have adorned Saint George's shield. He searched on "Chi Rho," assessed the Wikipedia entry, and determined this was probably not the right cross. He also devoted time to comparing different helmets. The display cases did not have enough room for full armor, but Kevin was certain that "a helmet will give a good character to the period." Eventually, he concluded that he would need to sculpt the helmet by hand because all the affordable replicas were off by at least two centuries. Twin imperatives governed Kevin's decision making about how to create the exhibit experience: avoiding historical anachronisms and crafting single replica items that could effectively represent a specific historical period.

Kevin would eventually fashion most of the replica items in the exhibit, such as the cowboy hat and gloves for the American West display. He explained that a good replica hat cost between $300 and $500, but a basic hat that he could craft to look worn and weathered was only $30. Given Kevin's reliance on Internet sources, I asked how he "vets the credibility of different websites." His response contained six points: the best source for researching *Dragon Legends* is a rare book that costs $600, but that exceeds the project budget; he never uses dates from sites that sell replicas because there is too much danger of misinformation; he is cautious when there is a lack of specificity in period marking (e.g., when "Roman" is not qualified); he does not prioritize sites that end with the suffix ".edu"; he does prioritize reenactor sites; and, finally, as he explained it, "I can usually smell out the fishy stuff. . . . You know it when you see it."

I sat with Kevin again in early March 2013, less than three months before *Dragon Legends* would open. He was working on the "Romans and Dragons" display, crafting small details of the miniature soldier figure. He wanted the soldier to be captured mid-action, viscerally engaged in battle. To achieve this effect, he chose to depict the soldier firing a ballista dart, with his mouth open in midscream.

Kevin worked in a digital sculpting program to design the soldier before printing it as a 3-D model. For reference, he kept eight images of human faces open on his desktop. Two were of men screaming—one straight on and one a side view—and the other six were of "Italian men" in different manners of repose. He dedicated more time, though, to working with the soldier's hands, which operated a lever and a trigger cord of the ballista dart. Kevin wanted the hand to look "right," which meant grasping the cord tightly with a fist, with no separation between the fingers. I asked what material the original cord would have been made of, and he said perhaps hemp or twine. He was unsure and seemed unconcerned with the accuracy of this particular detail.

Tyler and Kevin led the art direction for *Dragon Legends*, but the content writing for the displays was the labor of another team member, Andy, a former pastor who joined Answers in Genesis in 2010. Initially, Andy wrote primarily for the ministry's website, but in early 2013 he was officially transitioned to work with the creative team to develop content for Ark Encounter. The timing of this shift meant that he would also work on *Dragon Legends*. As the content writer, Andy conducted historical research on the different legends and coordinated his display text with the artists' work. In an interview, Andy said that his biggest challenge was "trying to figure out, are [the legends] really talking about something that we would call a dragon? And is the source in any way reliable?" He joked that his mandate was to be "legendarily accurate."

For example, *Beowulf* specifies that the dragon was wounded under its left wing, so Andy made sure that Tyler's panel illustration depicted this detail. The most challenging research process was for "Romans and Dragons." The Answers in Genesis book that served as the basis for the entire exhibit uses the word "dragon" for this legend, but the earliest historical accounts use the Latin word for "serpent." The animal's length in these accounts is 126 feet, so for Andy it was (and remains) ambiguous whether the account was a tall tale about a snake, a dinosaur-dragon reference, or something else. The most vexing display for him was "Cowboys and Dragons." Although he loved the artwork Kevin and Tyler produced, this "tall tale" was "too much of a stretch" to seriously consider as even remotely an actual human-dinosaur encounter.

What are these legends describing? Were dragons dinosaurs? Were dinosaurs dragons? Did humans coexist with dinosaurs? Are creationists right about the Bible, history, science, and evolution? *Dragon Legends* was rhetorically and aesthetically choreographed to provoke visitors to question the past in this way. The exhibit's oscillation among the actual, the potential, the implausible, and the unknown past was anticipated by the team's creative process. Tyler decided against a "classic" approach to representing dragons in favor of a style inspired by animation. Kevin used minute details of historical authenticity to craft materials that could mark a particular past, while the authenticity of other items was left unmarked. Andy wrestled with how to be "legendarily accurate."

*Dragon Legends* performs the reality that creationists do not inhabit the same temporal landscape as noncreationists. Visitors experience, walk through, and interact with the creationist past, which is designed and presented in opposition to the mainstream past of evolutionary science. This creationist history-making ultimately works to construct legitimacy over and against the authority of the evolutionary past.

## Creationist History-Making

History-making reveals the inescapable fact that our relationship to the past is forever and densely mediated by the production of histories. In turn, the anthropology of history-making confronts searching questions: What social, ideological, and material work goes into constructing different relationships to the past? What strategies and resources are marshaled to perform history-making? What are the social, ideological, and material stakes when multiple forms of history-making compete for public loyalties?

With these questions in mind, we might pause and scrutinize the relationship between creationist history-making and our analytical imagination. Anthropologists Eric Hirsch and Charles Stewart theorized a companion concept to history-making, "historicity," which refers to the social processes through which "versions of the past . . . assume present form" and become socially ratified.[19] They write that "all history is ethnohistory since it is composed according to cultural principles."[20] Yet, not all pasts carry equal weight in pluralistic societies. Some pasts are celebrated, others decried. Some pasts are accepted as fact, others contested, and still others dismissed. Why? Why is creationist history-making not simply just one more ethnohistorical variation, akin to numerous indigenous histories that diverge from scientific accounts, another thread in the beautiful tapestry of cultural diversity?

The answer is power and authority. While other pasts may differ from scientific history-making, they do not challenge science in the public sphere. They do not openly vie for the loyalty of public audiences. They do not create a zero-sum game, in which legitimacy and authority are construed as hanging in the balance. Creationist history-making is locked in a contentious dialogue with the history-making of mainstream

THE PAST IS NOT HISTORY | 133

science, and the religious publicity of the Creation Museum and Ark Encounter intensifies this contention.

The incommensurability of creationist and scientific pasts, and the public authority at stake in their history-making contest, were put front and center by both Ken Ham and Bill Nye in their February 2014 debate. Nye's five-minute opening statement began by describing how the Creation Museum's distinction between historical and observational science is unique to creationism, not part of mainstream science. Ham's five-minute opener asserted just the opposite. He began in the register of conspiracy, saying that "the word 'science' has been hijacked by secularists." He continued by directly rejecting evolutionary science (presented in creationist caricature):

> There's different types of knowledge, and I believe there is where the confusion lies. Molecules-to-man evolution belief has nothing to do with developing technology. You see, when we're talking about origins we're talking about the past. We're talking about our origins. We weren't there. You can't observe that, whether it's molecules-to-man evolution or whether it's the creation account. When you're talking about the past, we like to call that origins or historical science.[21]

Ham went on to highlight "science textbooks being used in public schools" as a key site where "secular evolutionists . . . force the religion of naturalism on generations of kids."

History-making plays a pivotal role in Ham's rhetorical and ideological framing of the debate and its public consequences. The same is true for Nye, whose most durable framing before, during, and after the debate has been that creationism is dangerous for America's youth and, by extension, for America's national future. In a two-minute clip he recorded for the *Big Think* series in 2012, the video that prompted Ham's invitation to debate, Nye culminates with this thought:

> When you have a portion of the population that doesn't believe in [evolution] it holds us back. . . . I say to the grown-ups: "If you want to deny evolution and live in your, in your world that's completely inconsistent with everything we observe in the universe, that's fine. But don't make your kids do it, because we need them." We need scientifically literate

voters and taxpayers for the future. We need people that can, we need engineers that can build stuff, solve problems.[22]

In the 2014 debate, Nye concluded his opening statement with this same framing of the public stakes of history-making:

Here's my concern. What keeps the United States ahead, what makes the United States a world leader is our technology, our new ideas, our innovations. If we continue to eschew science, eschew the process and try to divide science into observational science and historic science we are not gonna move forward. We will not embrace natural laws. We will not make discoveries. We will not invent and innovate and stay ahead.[23]

Nye's fear-for-the-future framing reprises previous defenders of science in staged creation-evolution debates. In 1982, Russell Doolittle (PhD in biochemistry from Harvard University) opposed Duane Gish (PhD in biochemistry from the University of California, Berkeley) in a nationally televised debate filmed at Jerry Falwell's Liberty University (then known as Liberty Baptist College). The previous year, twenty state legislatures had introduced education bills requiring public schools to give "equal time" to creationism in science classrooms.

Doolittle began his opening statement reflexively, explaining, "I'm here this evening against the advice of many of my colleagues." He then listed the numerous reasons such debates are a "no-win situation" that grants free "publicity" to creationists. But this was only a prelude to his primary framing:

The reason I'm here tonight is that I really am a concerned citizen and I'm worried about the future of education in America. I'm very much worried about what has happened during this past year in Arkansas and Louisiana, where in fact the state legislatures have seen fit to award the equal time teaching of creation and creation science in the science curriculum. To me, this is a travesty.[24]

The durability of this fear-for-the-future frame and the religious publicity of Answers in Genesis punctuate the fact that the past is ideologically contested. The Creation Museum, the Ham-Nye debate, *Dragon Legends*, Ark Encounter: all are creationist efforts, recalling William Carlos Williams's warning to "guard [history] doubly from the interlopers." To understand this struggle for authority, I turn to a framework outlined by the French anthropologist Pierre Bourdieu.

A hallmark of modern society is the struggle for symbolic power, described by Bourdieu as "the competition [among different social actors] to impose their particular visions of the social world."[25] One example Bourdieu used to illustrate how this competition works is the struggle to define legitimized language, such as projects of language standardization and the naming of different varieties as nonstandard (i.e., deviant, bad, incorrect, handicapping). Another example is what I have explored here, namely, the competition to define legitimized history.

In struggles over symbolic power, Bourdieu outlines two different social conditions: doxa and orthodox-heterodox.[26] Doxic conditions are those in which a single dominant position persists in an unchallenged and taken-for-granted way, in which alternative positions are so marginalized that they are silenced in the public sphere and even unthinkable for many social actors. This condition has not been true for the creationism-evolutionary science debate for a long time. Before the impact of Charles Darwin's *On the Origin of Species* in 1859, Charles Lyell's *Principles of Geology* (1833) and the popularization of Scottish theologian Thomas Chalmer's 1815 theory of gap creationism challenged the authority of young-earth literalism.

The evolution-creationism debate is a case of orthodox-heterodox struggle. Evolutionary science occupies the orthodox stance in American public life; it is more authoritative because it is invested with more legitimacy in more publicly influential sites. As we have seen, while nearly 26 million Americans may identify as committed creationists, arguing for creationism will prohibit you from winning National Science Foundation funding or earning a science degree from any non-fundamentalist-affiliated university. Creationism occupies the heterodox stance: a socially real intrusion on the "universe of possible discourse."[27] Ministries like Answers in Genesis simultaneously work to advance the legitimacy of creationism while trying to corrode the legitimized status of evolutionary science. Through its religious publicity, Answers in Genesis seeks to disrupt the existing orthodox-heterodox order.

Because they exist within this condition of struggling for power, institutions like the Creation Museum and Ark Encounter operate as safe havens. Creationists can visit these spaces and consume their heterodox history without being confronted with the orthodoxy of scientific evolution. Kevin provided a sense of this dynamic during our first recorded interview in December 2011. When I asked him about his artistic influences for creating representations of the past, he answered:

> The secular world owns probably 99 percent of all the material out there. So, you have to like reinterpret most of it. And, you've got all these years you have to, in a sense, compact into 6,000 years because that's, you know, my biblical worldview.

Answers in Genesis seeks to nurture a refuge from this imbalance. The Creation Museum and Ark Encounter are sites where heterodox practices like reinterpretation, secular-to-creationist translation, and reading between the lines become unnecessary. This sense of living in a world that is 99 percent contra to your identity fosters the disposition of feeling embattled and prompts the Answers in Genesis slogan that is reprinted on merchandise throughout the museum gift shop: "We're Taking Dinosaurs Back!"

### Playing in a Heterodox Past

The religious publicity of Answers in Genesis is grounded in the struggle for symbolic power. This struggle is fundamentally about claiming authority and legitimacy and wresting it away from evolutionary science. *Dragon Legends*, the Creation Museum, and Ark Encounter complement the long-standing creationist strategy of influencing public school curricula to either support their heterodox past or grant it legitimacy. This strategy began after the repeal of the Tennessee Scopes law in 1967 and the enactment of a new Tennessee state law in 1973 that required "equal time" for evolutionary science and creationism in public school science curricula. These efforts continue in the present. For example, the documentary film *The Revisionaries* (2012) explores this struggle as it plays out in the form of textbook adoption policies by the Texas State Board of Education.

Public education is certainly a key site in the orthodox-heterodox struggle for authority. Cultural critic Andrew Ross, writing about local school board struggles in Disney's Florida town of Celebration, argued: "In the absence of a national religion or shared cultural traditions, the public school has long been held up as the unique source of American national unity. It has ended up serving too many agendas as a result."[28] The powerful valence of public education helps explain why creationist attempts to introduce antievolution and/or pro-creationist material into K-12 curricula are so vehemently contested. However, power in modern society is diffuse and variable. Civic institutions, such as education, are not the only sites where hearts and minds are won and lost. The history-making religious publicity of *Dragon Legends* reflects the power that is up for grabs in the field of museum education.

Museum studies expert Mike Wallace wrote in the mid-1990s that "Americans crowd into historic sites, collect antiques, consume historical novels, take in costume epics and movies about time travel, and devour innumerable docudramas and documentaries on television."[29] Now, twenty years later, nothing has changed on this score. Americans seem to never tire of the past, and they love to consume cultural products that depict, retell, reenact, and explore histories.

This inexhaustible public appetite for the past has been seized by a particular hunger in recent years. Historian Vanessa Agnew describes an "affective turn" in the consumption of the past, in which consumers desire histories that can be experienced more than analyzed.[30] A public turn toward the affective is illustrated by entertainment strategies of immersion, simulation, play, and fun. Educational is good; edutaining is better.

This affective turn brings us back us to an earlier observation. Modern entertainment is not just dominant compared with other cultural forms; the logic and values of entertainment have actually infused other cultural forms. Peter Stromberg describes this dynamic as "survival of the most entertaining," a new Darwinian contest visible in politics, education, advertising, religion, and other contexts.[31] We have observed several museum examples where immersive entertainment strategies are used to tell specific histories: Atlanta's Center for Civil and Human Rights, the U.S. Holocaust Memorial Museum in Washington, DC, and an Indiana living history museum. Other examples abound, from colonial Williamsburg to natural history museums.[32]

*Dragon Legends* shifts the affective register from the deep emotional resonance with collective trauma, as with the Atlanta and Washington, DC, examples, to the fun of imaginative discovery. The team mobilized numerous entertainment strategies to engage museum visitors in an experience of the creationist past. A map displays the global fact of dragon legends; replica swords, helmets, and maps reference actual, possible, and fictional pasts; artistic representations depict scenes of human-dragon encounters. Taken together, the displays of *Dragon Legends* use entertainment to invite visitors to play in the heterodox past of creationism, a past that clashes with and rejects the orthodox past of evolutionary science. This is the power that is up for grabs in the museum experience of history-making and the work of religious publicity, the power to successfully edutain visitors.

In the ongoing orthodox-heterodox struggle between evolutionary science and creationism, pressing questions linger. Can productions like *Dragon Legends* immerse visitors in ways that trump secular evolution museums? In contrast to the hotly contested field of public school curricula, where symbolic capital derives from scientific legitimacy, can creationism score a victory in the court of public entertainment, where creative capital speaks in an artistic and affective register? *When it comes to history-making, is creationism more fun than evolution?*

## Conclusion

History-making is at the heart of the team's creative labor and the ministry's public ambitions. I was reminded of this fact in September 2013. I had traveled to Washington, DC, for a professional conference and was returning to Washington National Airport in an Uber vehicle. On the way the driver asked me questions about my life as a university teacher and anthropologist. I spent a few minutes describing Ark Encounter and my fieldwork with the creative team. He seemed to listen attentively and finally responded with a short statement: "I think [Ark Encounter] is a good idea, especially for the kids. Good story about Noah."

A few weeks later at the design studio, I relayed this anecdote to Roger. I suspected he would enjoy it and hoped that he might value my remembering and choosing to share it with him. Roger laughed gently, honing in on a familiarity in the driver's response. He reflected silently for a moment, then said: "It's always about the kids, kids or animals. It's actually a terrible story. Billions of people dying. It was a genocide. That's the hard part, to tell the full truth." We have seen up to this point the team's creative labor and its approach to telling the full creationist truth. In the next chapter, I turn to the experiential possibilities on board the ark. How is "the full truth" choreographed for visitors?

# 6

## A Walking Poetics of Faith

*August 2016.* Nearly five years since my initial visit to the design studio, I made my first trip to Ark Encounter on a sunny Thursday in late August. The park was an eighty-mile drive from my home, south through Cincinnati, across the Ohio River, and down I-75. During the drive my mind flitted among various questions. Will it be crowded with other people? How will visitors interact with the park as a whole and with individual exhibits? Will the food be any good? Will the park resemble the Creation Museum? How will it compare with other attractions that materialize the Bible? More than any of these, I was fixed on a single line of questioning. After focusing closely on the team's creative labor, what will the actual experience be like? Will the park and its exhibits seem successful, given my fieldwork behind the scenes? Will I get caught up in the immersive play of creationist history-making?

After nearly seven hours, I drove away, my field notebook filled with an excited jumble of observations. Chief among them was this: the creative team members had impressively executed their entertainment imperatives. Not always, and not equally on every square inch, but they had created an affectively rich environment that affords multiple immersive possibilities.

The "massive" size of the ark did not disappoint, as the years of publicity had promised and Figure 6.1 attests. There is indeed a wonder in approaching the structure, each step providing a further sense of scale, and walking alongside it, seeing the timber bones bulge from the inside out at the bow and stern angles. But many small creative touches here and there were also striking, although they did not register immediately. For example, I had been exploring the three decks on board for several hours before I noticed a scratch on the floor. I bent down to look closer. In fact, it was not a scratch at all but three small claw marks printed as an indentation in the floor paneling. Throughout all three decks, the marks are present to evoke

Figure 6.1. Ark Encounter as seen from the staged viewing area, a choreographed photo opportunity. Photo by author.

the path of small animals boarding two by two. Or, perhaps, they signify critters that scurried loose before being recaptured by Noah?

\*\*\*

This chapter draws together several data sources to explore the immersive possibilities afforded by Ark Encounter, particularly focusing on exhibit choreography and the mobilization of material and sensory channels. Ark publicity materials, Creation Museum exhibits, historical moments from the American creationist movement, observations from other attractions that materialize the Bible, and interviews with the creative team and creationist visitors—all have been valuable. Reading across these materials, I integrate two frameworks for understanding consumption at the attraction.

First, I adopt religion scholar David Morgan's approach to the "gaze" in religious visual culture, which he describes as "a form of sociality, prompting a disposition toward groups and institutions as well as presenting others as objective realities meeting one's look."[1] The choreographed space of Ark Encounter elicits and encourages a fundamentalist gaze, a way of seeing that reifies creationist truth claims and re-creates the movement's moral critique of evolutionary science. Like other religious gazes, it "opens up the possibility of seeing what non-participants will miss or fail to recognize. Belief is a disposition to see, hear, feel, or intuit a felt-order to the world."[2] Walking the decks of Ark Encounter affords an embodied fundamentalist gaze, a material register of belief performed through sensational forms and the frame of immersive entertainment.

Second, as this gaze fosters a "felt-order to the world," it mirrors what anthropologist Susan Harding calls a "poetics of faith." She argues that the religious authority accrued and displayed by fundamentalist leaders of the Religious Right is not merely a product of individual charisma, the power of the role being occupied, or something passively granted by devoted adherents. Authority, trust, and commitment are actively produced in an ongoing dialogic exchange between movement leaders and their religious public. Harding writes:

> Fundamental Baptist interpretation rests on a poetics of faith—absolute faith—not a hermeneutics of suspicion. The Bible is entirely true in the ordinary sense of accurately depicting historical events. The rule of inerrancy extends, not explicitly and by no means irrevocably (as it does to the Bible), to the preachers and other "men of God." Specifically, everything Jerry Falwell authors is true. But truth is not automatic, transparent, unmediated. It is the outcome of continuous exegetical exchanges between the Bible and its readers, a preacher and his people. A preacher's God-given authority, like the absolute truth of the Bible, is produced by a community of believers through its interpretive practices. It is as if Falwell, in his varied storied manifestations, were telling his followers, "Read me as you read the Bible. I appear in many versions. There are differences between the versions, and there are awkward silences and anomalies within them. My tales are troubled and they are troubling. Harmonize my discrepancies. Close my gaps. Overcome my troubles. Make me whole. Make me true."[3]

Just as Falwell relied on a listening public to "close [his] gaps," Ark Encounter relies on a visiting public to get caught up in the fundamentalist gaze. At the park, we see a walking poetics of faith in action. As creationist audiences move through the park, they are asked to participate in the experiential choreography, fill the intertextual gaps between literal scriptural history and the creative team's artistic imagination, and reconcile what secular skeptics dismiss as irrevocable scientific problems.[4] The fundamentalist gaze at Ark Encounter is coproduced between the expressive culture of materializing the Bible and adherents keen to interact with a materialized version of their faith commitments. As we will see, this walking poetics of faith is organized by two frames of immersive experience: a creationist past and a creationist present.

## Immersion

Devoted supporters of Ark Encounter, vehement critics, and curious onlookers tracked the project's progress on its website, and the park's immersive possibilities began through this virtual portal. In particular, the Ark Encounter blog accumulated more than five years' worth of publicity for the attraction, nearly 400 posts between December 2010 and the opening in July 2016. The blog continually asked readers to "imagine" the world of Noah and to play in the creationist version of biblical history. Consider this example from September 2015:

> Taking a trip through the Ark design studio warehouse reveals just how much things are beginning to pile up. Many of the exhibits, cages, and cargo boxes await the day when we can start shipping things down to the Ark site to be assembled inside the Ark. *Imagine* Noah's faith. Not only did he build the Ark according to God's specific dimensions, but can you *fathom* the logistics involved in gathering enough food and supplies for his family and all of the animals? *Imagine* all of the space all of these items would take up as the Ark was being prepared. *Did* he need to build storehouses just for these items? *Did* animals arrive early to give Noah's family time to study their habits so that they *would* know what kinds of food and how much of it to bring? How much space *would* they require? Noah's responsibilities involved so much more than building the Ark itself. (emphasis added)

Immersive entreaties ("imagine," "fathom," "would") are stitched together with literalist language ("did") and the typological hermeneutic that circulates widely among fundamentalists ("we" is aligned with "Noah's responsibilities").[5]

A little more than a year earlier, in June 2014, the ministry used an image of Tyler's fantasy-oriented map of Eden to accentuate a post, "Imagining the Pre-Flood World." The text is composed primarily of questions, such as "What were the earth's climate and geography like? Were there subtle environmental indicators of the coming catastrophe? Where were the rivers, hills, and seas? Did the early earth have jungles, deserts, or savannahs?" The exhibits on board Ark Encounter do not try to address each of these questions individually, but the goal of the blog was not to prepare visitors to hunt and peck for every answer to every question. The aim was to enliven the imagination of visitors, to instill the fundamentalist gaze before arrival, to find the path for the walking poetics of faith.

## The Creationist Past

Ark Encounter's central promise is that it provides a "life-like" window into a creationist-themed biblical past. Come and see the "full-size" ark, the "ingenious" systems on board for housing and caring for the animals, and the rooms for the passengers' liminal life during the storm: library, blacksmith work space, woodworking space. Come and see how Noah and his family lived. The exhibit that pursues this promise most elaborately is *Living Quarters* on Deck Three.

Several placards hanging next to the exhibit entrance explain what awaits inside, including an introduction to the eight people who lived on the ark. Consistent with the teaching style throughout the ark, these signs pose questions to aid visitors' imagining and present answers in the register of plausibility:

> Why are the living quarters so nice? Illustrations of Noah's Ark rarely give any consideration to the living arrangements for Noah and his family. What might their rooms have been like? Would they be simple, housing only the bare necessities, or would they have taken great care in building their rooms, just like they did with the rest of the Ark? There are many

reasons to think their living quarters were quite nice. As far as we know, the Lord did not inform Noah how long they would be on the Ark, so the family would probably have prepared for an extended time inside the Ark. Also, they worked hard caring for the animals every day. Having a comfortable place to relax and refresh would be extremely beneficial for keeping up morale and energy for all the hard labor they faced.

Another sign on board is titled "Artistic License" (two other signs on board also bear this title). Here, visitors are asked to close the intertextual gap between a literalist ideology of scripture and the creative team's artistic labor in re-creating a literalist ark:

> Other than the identities of their descendants in Genesis 10, the Bible tells us very little about Noah's family. We don't even know the names of the women on the Ark. Since we don't have a time machine, we can only make educated guesses about the looks, skills, and personality of each individual. Any attempt to represent historical events necessarily involves using artistic license, and we took great care not to contradict biblical details. As you explore these living quarters, you'll get to meet your ancestors as we have imagined them. How did they spend their free time? What hobbies and interests did these individuals have? How did the couples meet? What were their lives like prior to the Ark project? To distinguish biblical truths from the story we have created, Bible references are included whenever the information is directly from Scripture.

This metacommentary on the creative process aims to bolster immersion, not impede it, by assuring visitors that while certain details are fictionalized, the spirit of the exhibit maintains the literalist commitment to scriptural authority. The immersive frame is momentarily broken in hopes of enhancing it. We are brought backstage into the design process before we are returned to the immersive world of plausibility questions.

Entering the *Living Quarters* exhibit, you walk by four rooms, one for each of the four couples: Japheth and Rayneh, Shem and Ar'yel, Ham and Kezia, and Noah and Emzara. The rooms are flush with minute details, from beds and cushions to replications of tools and mementos to busy, lived-in work spaces. They look cozy and enjoyable, a sufficient mix of necessities and creature comforts. For example, the first room features Japheth and Rayneh (Figure 6.2).

The details of each room are paired with imagined biographies. Rayneh, the sign explains, is "artistic" and "enjoys making crafts and adding some flair to their surroundings, such as painting intricate designs on pottery." A still, life-size figure sits on the floor, enacting the scene described on the sign, surrounded by her artistic materials. Rayneh's character portrayal opens further intertextual gaps, which visitors can close with their own imaginings:

> Rescued by Noah from a life-threatening situation when she was a little girl, Rayneh grew up around his family. She helped Japheth with his farming responsibilities, and the two eventually became husband and wife. She put her seamstress skills to good use during the Ark's construction, creating many of the clothes and tapestries seen on board.

The room also features numerous drawings of plants and small potted plants, which mark Japheth's acumen. He stands in the corner playing a flute, perhaps delighting, perhaps annoying Rayneh with a tune. Overhead, flute music plays. The description imagines his talents and a character that is not one-dimensional:

> Japheth inherited Noah's adventurous spirit, although it is not very compatible with his agricultural work. Growing up around the Ark site has not afforded him the opportunity to explore, but he longs to set out once the Flood ends and has composed songs about these dreams. The oldest and tallest of the sons, Japheth excels in farming, just like his grandfather, Lamech. Because of this, Noah charged him with growing, preparing, and storing the food for the Ark. The plants in the room, the indoor garden, and the vast stores of grain, seeds, and nuts throughout the Ark provide evidence of his success in this area.

Just beyond the first two passengers' rooms are a series of common areas linked by the theme of food: garden, kitchen, storage, and dining (Figure 6.3). They looked well stocked and appealing, brimming with brightly colored produce and ample supplements like strands of hang-

Figure 6.2. Passenger room inside the *Living Quarters* exhibit. Photo by author.

Figure 6.3. Food area inside the *Living Quarters* exhibit. Photo by author.

ing garlic. Display signs explain that Noah and his family were sustained by a vegetarian diet while on board the ark. One placard shifts registers twice, from a literalist proof text to immersive detail and then to plausibility:

> The Lord said all foods that are eaten were to be gathered (Genesis 6:21). Noah and his family probably received most of their sustenance from foods that could have been stored for the many months aboard the Ark: grains, root vegetables, legumes, and nuts. Fresh fruit was likely not on the menu, but dried and preserved fruits may have been. Conditions during the flood blocked large amounts of sunlight, but the Ark's third deck would have still received some natural light. The large window would allow the family to grow a variety of vegetables and herbs throughout the top floor to supplement their diet.

Across from the garden display are the kitchen and dining room. In each, passengers are present to create an embodied feel for the space. Standing in the kitchen, Ar'yel "uses a mortar and pestle to grind tea leaves." Ham and Kezia work in the dining room to prepare beans for a meal:

> The table and benches in the dining room provide the perfect place for Noah's family to eat their meals. The family also gathers here for prayer, meetings, and games. Here we see Ham delivering a basket of vegetables as his wife, Kezia, shucks them in preparation for a meal.

Two subtle details aid the immersive play in the creationist past. First, all the signage is written in the present tense. One sign says that Ham is "delivering" a basket—not that he would have delivered, used to deliver, perhaps delivered, or any other such past or conditional formulation. Second, because we see Ar'yel, Ham, and Kezia here, we do not see them in their own rooms. The eight characters appear only once on each of the three decks; after all, they could not have been in two places at the same time.

The *Living Quarters* exhibit fosters the fundamentalist gaze by recreating scenes from everyday life on board the ark. Other displays contribute to the creationist past in less explicitly guided ways. For example, consider the animals. Throughout the three decks, though primarily on the first two, a variety of sculpted animals are perched in cages. Some are familiar—bear, deer, bats—but most are not unless you are learned in paleozoology. The team wanted to prioritize now-extinct animals rather than modern species. The preparation for this experience of the fundamentalist gaze began before the park's opening through the online publicity of the Ark Encounter blog.

From April 2014 through February 2015, the blog posted a nine-part series, "Forgotten Fauna," that introduced readers to the creationist theological-biological category of "animal kinds." The series discussed examples of animals that are now extinct, but ones for which there is fossil evidence and that therefore would have been on the ark. The presentation of each animal profile is formulaic, including similar information about its size, where fossil remains have been found, distinctive physical characteristics, and comparisons with nonextinct animals for scale and reference. Each post is framed with the same note that these animals are "varieties of creatures Noah interacted with that we do not." The team presented the extinct species as animals unfamiliar to visitors, which require the imaginative creativity of the team to "bring to life,"

Figure 6.4. Extinct species displayed on board Ark Encounter. Photo by author.

from skeletal fossils to three-dimensional figures. These posts contribute to the immersive experience of the creationist past by previewing a series of unknown animals that visitors would be surrounded by on board the ark.

Visitors encounter animals such as this on Deck One (Figure 6.4). Each species is accompanied by a sign that presents anatomical and behavioral details for the unfamiliar specimen. The sign next to Figure 6.4 also integrates the crucial event for Flood geology:

THE CASEID KIND
Status: presumed extinct
Adult lengths: 3.9–14 ft (1.2–4.3 m)
Representative shown: *Cotylorhynchus*
- Caseids were rather bizarre looking, with proportionately small heads, sprawling stances, and massive, plant-processing guts.
- As with all other non-mammalian synapsids, they are known only from rock layers deposited by the Flood.

- Caseids laid eggs, but may not have been covered in overlapping scales like most reptiles.

Walking through the Ark Encounter decks and inspecting these "presumed extinct" animals is less like being at a zoo and more like being immersed in an alternative past. In this creationist past, the animals were alive and well and collected by Noah. Part of the walking poetics of faith is about filling these gaps: getting caught up in the creationist zoological world of the ark, along with the family's everyday life on board.

### The Creationist Present

Exhibits are also choreographed to invite visitors to play in the creationist present. More precisely, visitors are immersed in the creationist worldview, complete with its "enchantment of science" and critique of the "secular evolutionist" conspiracy that poses a moral and spiritual danger to the world.[6] On Deck Two, the *Fairy Tale Ark* exhibit powerfully invokes this immersive frame.

Approaching the exhibit, your visual field is immediately drawn upward to a series of animals lining the top of the entrance (Figure 6.5). They are certainly cartoonish, but they somehow exceed that description. In my initial field notes I described them as looking "zany, even slightly imbalanced or crazed," signified by their eyes, facial expressions, and jumbled arrangement. The longer I stared at them, the more an unsettled, suspicious affect sank in.

Unlike some other exhibits, where a wooden rail prevents visitors from entering the space, you must step into the *Fairy Tale Ark*. Once inside the small room, there are two dominating features. The smaller of the two, positioned on the wall to your left, is a sign encircled by a snake. The figure is bright red with a dragon-like head, designed as an exact copy of the snake from the Garden of Eden display at the Creation Museum. The sign reads ominously, dialogically voiced as Satan himself: "If I can convince you that the Flood was not real then I can convince you that Heaven and Hell are not real."

The primary display is positioned directly in front of you, covering the entire wall. It is a collection of nearly 100 children's books on Noah's

Figure 6.5. Entrance to *Fairy Tale Ark* exhibit. Photo by author.

ark, most of them written in English but some in Spanish or French. They are arranged neatly on six shelves, interspersed with other ark-themed kids' toys and games, housed directly behind glass panes. Two textual annotations frame visitors' reading of the collection. First, three rows up from the bottom, a series of small books are lined up side by side. They resemble an antique collection of fables, and they present the "7 D's of Deception." For example, "Destructive for All Ages" explains: "The cute fairy tale arks are not only marketed to children, thousands of items featuring whimsical arks have been made for adults too. The abundance of these fanciful objects attacks the truthfulness of Scripture."

This strategy innovates and riffs on AiG's trademarked "7 C's of History," which is the organizing pedagogical theme of the Creation Museum and numerous AiG publications. At the center of the display is a larger book, also looking like a fable, that is voiced in a rhyming, fairy-tale register. It begins: "Once Upon a Time, there was an old man of God. His name was Noah and his task was quite odd. One day, the Lord said to build a little boat, 'Make it nice and cute, but who cares if it will float . . .'" The cartoonish, simultaneously playful and ominous aesthetic teaches a singular lesson. A literalist reading of Genesis—complete with an actual Flood, actual ark, and actual Noah and family—is lampooned every day by the ubiquitous circulation of "fairy-tale" arks.

This lampooning is no accident, but who is to blame? The snake-encircled sign suggests devilish agency. The bounds of responsibility widen in the text of "Discrediting the Truth," which identifies "many atheists and other skeptics" as directly culpable. The "abundance" of un-realistic ark representations targets children, affects everyone, and is an orchestrated "attack" on the authority and historical plausibility of liter-alist scripture. It is, in short, conspiracy.

Answers in Genesis persistently claims that "evolutionists," "secular-ists," "atheists," "non-believers," and others campaign to silence "Bible-believing Christians" as legitimate readers of scripture and practitioners of "creation science." This familiar fundamentalist refrain appears here as a materialized effort to expose and make obvious a taken-for-granted creationist social fact: the Bible is "under attack." The assembly of child-hood artifacts performs a creationist critical discourse analysis of the modern secular antagonism to fundamentalism.

The *Fairy Tale Ark* exhibit adopts the same discourse of conspiracy that helps to organize the Creation Museum. As Ella Butler describes in her ethnographic analysis of the museum, "The creationist is here positioned as a kind of knowing subject who is enabled to see the truth behind the façade presented by authority figures."[7] Answers in Genesis as a ministry, and the creative team as cultural producers, create these enabling conditions through their choreographed exhibits. The creation-ist critical discourse analysis of *Fairy Tale Ark* directly reprises *Lucy*, an exhibit added to the museum in June 2012.

The partial skeleton of *Australopithecus afarensis* excavated in 1974 in Ethiopia's Awash Valley, given the name Lucy, is a celebrated discovery among evolutionary scientists. As a testament to Lucy's fame, natural science and natural history museums throughout the world use re-creations to show visitors how her body frame and bipedal locomotion place her between earlier hominins and modern humans (Figure 6.6). It is precisely displays such as this from the Field Museum in Chicago that prompted the Creation Museum to install its own reimagined Lucy (Figure 6.7). The portrayal of Lucy as a knuckle-walking ape will either

Figure 6.6. *Lucy* at the Field Museum. Photo by author.

Figure 6.7. *Lucy* at the Creation Museum. Photo by author.

baffle or enrage anyone committed to evolutionary science, but what is most striking about the Answers in Genesis Lucy display is the visual framing that accompanies this portrayal.

The display stands as an island in the middle of a room. In addition to the standard creationist rejections of evolution (e.g., "Man's word says humans and apes evolved from a common ancestor, but God's Word says there's no ape in your ancestry!"), two features visually perform the creationist critical discourse analysis. Scattered in a mixed-up, but fully discernible, mess under Lucy's feet and knuckles are images of different ways in which Lucy has been represented by artists in evolutionary contexts. This presentation is complemented by the rear side of the display, which compares a replica of the cranial portion of the skeleton with five different representations of Lucy's flesh-and-hair face. Signage beneath the faces explains that no facial representation can ever be fully accurate, and that the ideological "starting points" of the artist will determine how the face is brought to life.[8]

The combination of visual and textual strategies in this exhibit works to fertilize not just doubt about the evolutionary argument of who Lucy was but suspicion about the motives behind erasing other representational possibilities. As with *Fairy Tale Ark*, the creationist visitor is positioned as a knowing subject discovering the secular evolutionary conspiracy to censor creationists. Here, we see an immersive continuity generated by the Creation Museum and Ark Encounter, where the fun-

Figure 6.8. Fundamentalist cartoon "Another Pied Piper" from the 1920s.

damentalist gaze bridges visitor participation in the creationist present across the two attractions.

As forms of religious publicity, Ark Encounter and the Creation Museum join a long history of creationist visual culture. The conspiracy-saturated critiques in *Fairy Tale Ark* and the *Lucy* exhibit are contemporary renditions of images such as E. J. Pace's "Another Pied Piper" cartoon from the 1920s (Figure 6.8). Pace was an early pioneer of the Christian cartoon genre whose work appeared widely from 1910 through the early 1940s in publications like the *Sunday School Times* and *Moody Monthly*. "Another Pied Piper" depicts young boys and girls who have been seduced by the "Darwinian Hypothesis of Evolution" and led to "Disbelief in the God of the Bible." William Jennings Bryan reprinted the cartoon in *Seven Questions in Dispute* (1924). It appears on the first page of the final chapter, "The Origin of Man," in which Bryan argues in terms that could be plucked directly from Answers in Genesis books, blogs, or exhibit signage at the Creation Museum and Ark Encounter: "The evolutionary hypothesis is the source of the poison which is bringing disorder into the Church. Scratch a critic of the Bible and you are sure to find an evolutionist."[9]

## Sensory Annotation

The fundamentalist gaze at Ark Encounter is organized by two immersive experiential frames: the creationist biblical past and the creationist present. As visitors alternate between these frames, a walking poetics of faith is performed. It is useful to consider how that gaze is embodied, that is, how the visual experience is annotated by other sensory registers. Recall David Morgan on the dynamics of religious visual culture: "Seeing is not disembodied or immaterial and vision should not be isolated from other forms of sensation and the social life of feeling."[10] Through sensory annotations, the affective force of the immersive play is heightened.

There is an incredible amount of aesthetic, theological, and ideological continuity between Ark Encounter and the Creation Museum, but the sensory choreography at the ark marks an important experiential difference from the museum. Scholarly critics have argued that the Creation Museum "privileges sight over the other senses," so much so that it produces "a certain sensory exhaustion."[11] I have experienced a similar feeling of fatigue whenever walking through the main series of exhibits at the museum, mainly because most exhibits include extensive signage to read, often in a way that spatially engulfs the visitor. Scholars, however, are not the only critics of the museum.

As we saw earlier, a refrain among members of the creative team was that they wanted Ark Encounter's exhibit teaching to rely less on signage and more on embodied experience. In an early interview with Emily she remarked that the museum "is successful and it looks awesome and people love it, but we see all the stuff we want to do better." A few minutes later, I asked what they hoped to improve:

> EMILY: One of the big deals for us was that a lot of the text and writing was a lot and overwhelming for people. Or, it wasn't enough of a big picture.
>
> JAMES: So, visual teaching?
>
> EMILY: Yeah, visual teaching and big picture. To where, if people want to explore they can, but if not they still get it.
>
> JAMES: And they don't get lost in the details?
>
> EMILY: Yeah. Because the Bible in itself is intense if you're not gonna sit down and study it and be diligent about understanding it from Genesis to Revelation. . . . In the museum, it was very technically based on things from Genesis. For just the layman, it's hard for them to understand and those are the people we want to reach in the Ark project. So, in a way it was good for us because we're like, "Hey, the Creation Museum is for the technical people that want to go deep and get more information. When we open the Ark Encounter we want every man to be there, Christian and non-Christian alike, to come and hear this gospel presentation." And anybody can understand it.

For Emily, recalibrating the exhibit pedagogy from textual reading to aesthetic learning was a strategy for reaching the broadest possible public. However efficacious its work might prove to be for converting visitors, the team did successfully create an embodied fundamentalist gaze.

## Auditory Visuality

The *Fairy Tale Ark* is directly preceded by exhibits that portray scenes from everyday life on the ark: Noah at work in his study, the library full of scrolls, Japheth doing woodworking, and Ham showcasing black-smithing technology. So it goes throughout the three decks: as a visitor, you are asked to shift between the two frames of immersive experience, a creationist present and a re-created literal biblical past.

Along the way, there are plenty of distractions that might disturb the immersive play. A cleaning crew might be wheeling around a large trash can. A snack stand sits at the back edge of Deck One, which struck me as reminiscent of an airport kiosk. Trash cans, restrooms, and security cameras are located throughout, requisite but blatant breaks in the immersive frame. Despite these breaks, Ark Encounter's immersive coherence is renewed by its auditory choreography.

The onboard soundscape is among the more indelible imprints of all my observations at the park. The baseline instrumental sound track—composed uniquely for the ark and written to connote a "Middle Eastern" style—first becomes audible as you approach the outside queue to board the ark. Running on a constant loop, it plays throughout the three decks. However, as you walk through selected exhibits, this baseline sound track is complemented or replaced by auditory annotations to the visual experience.

This auditory shift happens immediately upon entering Deck One. You are surrounded by animal cages stacked one on top of another, and the narrow walkway turns sharply to wind among the cages. One sound track, playing at a lower volume but directed nearer to you as a visitor, features an indiscernible mix of animal sounds. The animals are lively, even a bit unhinged by the storm. On the second sound track, playing louder but projecting from a greater distance, is a loud, unnerving mix of booming thunder, cracking lightning, and pouring rain.

Both of the examples just discussed—*Living Quarters* and *Fairy Tale Ark*—feature auditory annotations. As you move between the garden and kitchen portions of the *Living Quarters* exhibit, you hear Ar'yel at work. The orchestration streams down from overhead: she hums peacefully, even happily, while a knife chops vegetables methodically and scrapes them to the side. It is the sound of contended work. When you enter the *Fairy Tale Ark*, the upbeat baseline sound track shifts to a very different tune. It reminded me of a dream sequence in a film, perhaps an animated film, where something terrible is about to happen. Interspersed throughout the dreamy instrumental is the sporadic sound of children laughing. Their voices steadily increase in volume and transform from the voices of young children playfully giggling to teenagers laughing in mockery. The exhibit's ominous message of a secular conspiracy is enhanced by this eerily disturbing auditory annotation.

During my fieldwork with members of the creative team, they spent significant time discussing how to immerse visitors in the "pre-Flood" world of Noah. While the "wicked" nature of the world that God judged is referenced throughout the decks, it is most concentrated in Deck Two's first exhibit, *Pre-Flood World*. A winding walkway moves through five spaces: creation, the Garden of Eden, the Fall, "Descent into Darkness" (i.e., a portrayal of the extravagant sinfulness of the generations preceding Noah), and the Flood. These spaces and themes are displayed through elaborate dioramas and a series of colorful murals, some with minimal textual framing and scriptural verses. The striking visuality of the murals is annotated aurally. The baseline sound track shifts to peaceful sounds of nature as you approach the creation murals (e.g., birds chirping) and shifts again with each new space. One of the three largest murals depicts a dramatic scene of "pagan" ritual (Figure 6.9). Overhead, a cacophonous loop plays: raging fires, raucously cheering crowds, a duel of sharp colliding and sliding swords, and human screams. There is little interpretive space to imagine anything but death by combat in view of a bloodthirsty public. It is unmistakably violent, but nothing more than PG-13.

## Haptic Visuality

While the integration of sight and sound is the primary sensory annotation at Ark Encounter, it is not the only one. There is also haptic visuality, the relation of sight to touch. This sensational form pervades both everyday religious practice and choreographed attractions like museums. Devotional objects such as rosary beads, altar items, and prayer cloths create tactile opportunities to enact religious commitment,

Figure 6.9. Mural art in the *Pre-Flood World* exhibit. Photo by author.

display identity, and cultivate belief through bodily engagement.[12] In the context of science museums, "interactivity" has been an imperative since the opening of the Exploratorium in San Francisco in 1969. Designed by Frank Oppenheimer, that attraction broke from the dominant museum model of "look, but do not touch" by creating fully interactive exhibits. In an early essay explaining the Exploratorium's rationale, Oppenheimer wrote that "the gap between the [science] experts and the [public] laymen" could only be bridged by "apparatus which people can see and handle." He continued: "Explaining science and technology without props can resemble an attempt to tell what it is like to swim without ever letting a person near the water."[13] As Ark Encounter mobilizes haptic visuality to foster the fundamentalist gaze, it reproduces a strategy learned from both everyday religiosity and professional museum design.

Throughout the three decks, there is only one explicit tactile prohibition: "Do Not Touch the Animals." Otherwise, visitors are free to physically engage different onboard features, from running your hand along cages to touching storage pots, ropes, and engraved wooden signs. Deck

Two consists of a series of interactive digital displays that advance creationist teaching points about the historical plausibility of the ark. As a visitor, you approach large, high-definition screens that provide a cross section view inside the ark. When you place your hand on a sensor, a digital demonstration shows how Noah and family could have used different technologies, for example, how the wave-powered purifier generated potable water or how solid waste removal functioned.

One of the more affectively stirring experiences of haptic visuality is the structure of the ark itself (Figure 6.10). From various vantage points, your visual field is drawn to the sunlight streaming down from rooftop windows and the layered depth of the large space. This is particularly striking on Deck Two, on which you can look over, down, up, and back. Your touch is drawn to the massive timbers forming the building's bones: each one is utterly unique up close, with splits, knots, and dried sap streaming out. If you are so inclined, the physicality of the space affords the visceral possibility to "imagine" the vessel during the Flood, perhaps just as Noah and his family experienced it.

Figure 6.10. A visual field inside Ark Encounter. Photo by author.

There is no signage orchestrating this particular affect, but it was encouraged by publicity materials. A video interview with the owner of the timber frame company that provided the ark's construction materials was released on the Ark Encounter website and YouTube channel in December 2015. Speaking in an ethical register of environmental sustainability, the owner describes with awe his experience of interacting with the large timbers: "Everybody who comes through [the ark] can enjoy the character and the size and the magnitude of these logs."

The significance of the wood's materiality resonated especially well with one of the individuals I interviewed in early 2016 before the park's opening. Matt, a lifelong creationist in his early twenties, is an amateur woodworker who crafts presents for friends and family for birthdays, Christmas, and other occasions. For his sister's wedding, he built an arch under which the couple recited their vows. When I showed Matt the timber framing video, he said that it answered questions he had about Ark Encounter's "environmental impact" and heightened his enthusiasm for visiting the park. Instead of the other promotional videos that explained the park's design and teaching exhibits, Matt was more excited about seeing the publicity video celebrating the ark as an architectural feat. This preference was not merely about marveling at modern construction; it was about accessing the creationist past through this sense of awe.

Matt could have revoiced this publicity material in a devotional register. He might have imagined the tactile engagement with the wood as a unique material conduit for praising God. But this is not what he did. Instead, he used the video to bolster his expectation that Ark Encounter would demonstrate creationist claims about the Bible's literal historicity and offer a glimpse into the experience of being on board during the Flood. This marks an important pattern: Ark Encounter mobilizes haptic visuality for pedagogical, not devotional, ends. To clarify, consider how another attraction that materializes the Bible engages this sensational form.

As noted earlier, the Holy Land Experience is a fifteen-acre "living, biblical museum" in Orlando, Florida. Amid its various re-creations of sites in modern-day Israel-Palestine, people can pin their prayers to a cross (Figure 6.11).[14] At the attraction's Testimony Cross Garden, visitors write out prayers on small slips of paper and attach them to a

Figure 6.11. Testimony Cross Garden at the Holy Land Experience. Photo by author.

wooden cross. This ritual form involves several constitutive material acts. There is the writing itself. As when one keeps a daily prayer journal or submits a prayer card to a popular ministry, spiritual power is harnessed by putting pen to paper and externalizing human interiors. This extends the associations between writing technology and faith emphasized by other Christian performances, such as when one sings the opening lines of a southern gospel music standard: "When God dips his pen of love in my heart and writes my soul a message he wants me to know." Then, there is the folding. Each prayer is bent: some loose and uneven, some tight and perfectly aligned. Folding eases a tension between the public quality of the cross and the secrecy of each paper's contents ("This is just between me and God"). Once the paper is folded, there are the bodily acts of kneeling and stretching to attach it. The power works via iconicity: the park map that each visitor receives when entering the Holy Land Experience prompts you to "nail your burdens (prayer requests) to the cross."

The materiality of this ritual transforms a prayer into a thing: a small piece of writing. A sign not far from the Testimony Cross Garden reads: "Have your personal prayer requests placed between the ancient stones at Jerusalem's Western Wall. Monthly transportation to Israel provided free of charge." When these prayers become small pieces of writing, they become something that can be gathered, packed together, and transported easily. The destination of these traveling prayers is not incidental. Jerusalem's Western Wall is a pivotal site for Protestant pilgrims to the Holy Land.[15] Ritual practices at the wall, such as inserting written prayers into its fissures, participate symbolically in the ongoing contest over biblical land, as the wall also receives the devotional labor of Jewish and Muslim supplicants. Transforming prayer into a thing is a matter of efficacy. The power of your request or report is intensified when you write it out on a small square of colored paper; it is further intensified when the paper is pinned to the cross and intensified again when the paper travels to a crevice in Jerusalem. As prayers become things, they forge a link between two places: a "living, biblical museum" in Florida, and the Holy Land sites that inspire Orlando's materialized re-creations.

While individual visitors may devise something similar, the kind of devotional act and process fostered by the Testimony Cross Garden is not part of the spatial and sensory choreography at Ark Encounter. At the ark, the focus is pedagogical, mobilizing the fundamentalist gaze by alternating between immersive experiences of the creationist past and the creationist present.

*Multiple Itineraries*

On my second tour of the *Pre-Flood World* exhibit, I got caught up inspecting the minute details of a diorama display that depicts a bacchanalian scene. Small 3-D printed figures of burly men hoist chalices while draped with seductive women. One man has collapsed facedown from a few too many chalices and scattered a plate of food. Two women dance together, enticing a pleased onlooker. As I absorbed the display, a woman and her two teenage daughters paused beside me to view it. One daughter pointed to the passed-out man, chuckling at the spectacle. The mother, in a slightly graver tone, recontextualized a bit of scripture to assess the scene: "There's nothing new under the sun." And then they moved on.

I have examined the fundamentalist gaze constructed at Ark Encounter through a composite of materials: my experience on board mixed with the team's aesthetic choreography and observations from other attractions that materialize the Bible. Moments like the mother-daughter exchange in front of the diorama suggest that the walking poetics of faith can work rather cohesively. Other observations of visitor engagements suggest the same. For example, in the food storage area of the *Living Quarters* exhibit, an older husband-and-wife pair traded an approving couplet in the register of literalist plausibility: "Noah had grape vines because he made wine," to which she replied, "And he would have had seeds."

Committed creationists dutifully filling in the gaps may be the dominant visitor experience at Ark Encounter, but it is certainly not the only possible one. As the park continues to develop, it will be important to compare the multiple itineraries that visitors bring with them as they move through the ark. In their ethnography of English pilgrims to the Catholic and Anglican shrines at Walsingham, Coleman and Elsner observe how visitors act as "bricoleurs." Visitors find ways to engage the place that are not bound by "a generic, impersonal and potentially alienating form of liturgy," including agentive practices of subversive irony, humor, and unscripted devotion.[16] How might creationists perform similar tactics while playing in the creationist past and present? Likewise, it will be important to track the social contexts of consumption and how these shape the experience. Do visitors come alone? As a family? On a friendly outing or a romantic date? For a homeschool assignment? With church groups? As part of a pastor's retreat? Or, as a friend of mine who teaches at a Christian college told me in early October, as a surprise "team-building event" with colleagues?

Of course, committed creationists are not the only park visitors. Skeptics will visit, as they have visited the Creation Museum, to confront an ideological Other and take pleasure in mocking the materialized worldview. What consumptive tactics will they employ to make their way through the exhibits? How might they negotiate the walking poetics of faith that the site tries to choreograph? How will they integrate the experience into their skeptical lifeworld?

A clue to how skeptics might respond was apparent in a report published in October 2016 by the National Center for Science Education (NCSE), a leading public institution devoted to advancing science literacy and challenging antiscience movements.[17] The president of the Kentucky Paleontological Society, Dan Phelps, composed an extensive review of Ark Encounter for the NCSE, including forty-eight high-quality images from the park. He has a long history of public activism against Answers in Genesis that began in the late 1990s when he contributed to blocking AiG's attempt to secure land adjacent to a fossil-rich state park as the initial Creation Museum location. Since then, he has written numerous repudiations of AiG, the Creation Museum, and Ark Encounter for regional news outlets (e.g., the *Lexington Herald-Leader*).

The review includes plenty of humorous jabs, such as this description of the ark's appearance: "The AiG version does look more attractive, if not as seaworthy, than a rectangular barge, and since the entire thing is an invention based on an ancient myth, it probably doesn't matter." Alongside scientific refutations of creationist history-making claims about flood geology, the review is full of interpretive moments that decode the aesthetic choreography. In response to the queue video of "The Noah Interview," Phelps writes: "I suspect the video is Ken Ham's swipe at reporters who have asked him uncomfortable questions about the Ark and tax rebate incentives." There are very few moments where he does not see dangerous silliness, plain and simple, except when noting with approval the quality of the production value. He observes that the *Living Quarters* exhibit "showed a great attention to detail and were obviously carefully constructed."

What other itineraries might develop in addition to the ideological antagonists of committed creationists and critical skeptics? In particular, what are the possibilities for other committed religious actors who share a literalist biblical past but are not embraced by creationists? Will Mormons and Jehovah's Witnesses visit Ark Encounter? How might their walking poetics of faith both coincide and clash with a space designed by fundamentalists who reject these other claims to authentic Christianity? The next wave of research on Ark Encounter and the Creation Museum will need to examine the fact of multiple and competing itineraries to further our understanding of religious publicity.

## Conclusion

We have now completed a journey: from behind the scenes with the creative team to inside the Answers in Genesis re-created ark. In analyzing the completed Ark Encounter, I have developed a twofold argument. First, the park is choreographed as a walking poetics of faith, through which a fundamentalist gaze is constructed by two frames of immersive experience. As visitors move between these frames, they are asked to fill the intertextual gaps between literal scriptural history and the creative team's artistic imagination. Second, the affective force of this immersion is heightened by a series of sensory annotations that work to embody the fundamentalist gaze.

To close, we can observe how this gaze must also absorb a commercial gaze. Though it originates from the field of market capitalism, outside the cultural orbit of fundamentalism, it nonetheless impacts Ark Encounter's potential to succeed among committed creationists. This finding emerged from a shared concern voiced by both prospective visitors and the creative team. One of my visitor interviews was with Jaime and Sara, a young creationist pastor and his wife, who were excited to visit the park with their three children. We had finished reviewing their spiritual life histories, and I was arranging the publicity materials for them to view. As I queued the videos up to play, Jaime expressed a worry he harbored about the park: that it would be "cheesy," and that die-hard fundamentalists would support it despite mediocre production values. Sara promptly agreed, explaining that if the park was not "high-quality," she would be hesitant to invite "nonbelievers" as guests. After a moment's pause, Jaime reflected: "I think a lot of Christians eat bad cake because it has Jesus sprinkles. Do you know what I mean?"

The members of the creative team obsessed over this same concern, though in their own register of professionalism. Recall their agonizing about whether or not the ministry's audiovisual staff would achieve "Hollywood quality" in the sixty-second promotional trailer for which they had designed the film set. In audio-recorded interviews and informal conversations around the design studio, the artists described their aim to surprise audiences by creating a sophisticated park experience. Recall Emily's reflection about her hopes for the park, in which she describes her ambition that Ark Encounter not be a "hokey stereotype."

For Ark Encounter's cultural producers and creationist visitors, quality was a paramount concern. For Jaime and Sara, their personal enjoyment of the park and their willingness to use it as a witnessing tool likewise hinged on whether it satisfies a certain standard of consumer quality. For the creative team, professional quality is an imperative for the park's success, both financially and in terms of public legitimacy. On one hand, this demand for quality makes sense in the context of capitalist consumption. Customers expect to get their money's worth, and as a for-profit entity, the park wants visitors to want to return (and to want to invite others). But are other cultural layers also relevant?

Two historically constituted and interlaced contexts further ingrain this concern for quality. First, as Jaime's metaphor of "bad cake" and Emily's critique of other attractions attest, there are entrenched attitudes about the hierarchy of goods in the Christian cultural marketplace. In her book *Material Christianity*, religion scholar Colleen McDannell examines this hierarchy.[18] As early as the 1860s, Catholics were arguing about what constituted acceptable devotional art. The category of "kitsch" entered the American cultural lexicon of taste judgment in the 1930s, offering a readily accessible label for goods that did not meet a perceived standard of artistic quality.[19] Popular, mass-produced religious commodities and styles were often relegated by Catholics and Protestants alike as substandard, unworthy of serious religious application. Judgments of taste such as "kitsch" served as ways for religious authorities and leaders to police what the religious public ought to consume. Contemporary creationists are attuned to the social fact of this hierarchy and recognize as well that there are high stakes in failing to meet commercially determined standards of quality.

A second context has to do with a broader social condition that frames judgments of taste among American creationists. The condition is made legible with this question: Who are fundamentalists? Or, more precisely: What is the dominant cultural reputation of fundamentalists? Susan Harding argues that the invention of "fundamentalism" as a category rested on:

> an escalating string of oppositions between Fundamentalist and Modern—between supernaturalist and reasoning, backward and progressive, ignorant and educated, rural and cosmopolitan, anti-intellectual and intellectual, superstitious and scientific, duped and skeptical, bigoted and tolerant, dogmatic and thinking, absolutist and questioning, authoritarian and democratic.[20]

From H. L. Mencken's unrelenting editorials during the Scopes Trial in 1925 to representations of Dayton, Tennessee, locals in the film *Inherit the Wind* (1960) to polemical diatribes like comedian Bill Maher's *Religulous* (2008), the archetypal fundamentalist in the American imagination is a rural, white, uneducated southerner.[21]

This cultural symbol resonates with other discourses that marginalize nonmainstream whites who either do not fit or refuse to accommodate middle-class dispositions, namely, the figure of "poor white trash."[22] For the creative team, exceeding public expectations about Ark Encounter's quality is about defying this historically constituted symbol and evading its stigmatizing baggage. To avoid judgments of religious kitsch by performing professional sophistication, Ark Encounter as a form of public culture hopes to rescue fundamentalism from class-inflected objectifications like those portrayed in a cartoon from the *Columbia Daily Tribune*, a Missouri newspaper. This image circulated widely in the wake of intelligent design legislation controversies in 2005, two years before the opening of the Creation Museum in Kentucky (Figure 6.12).

Figure 6.12. Newspaper cartoon that reproduces antimodern fundamentalist cultural symbolism. Note the stigmatizing semiotic elements of racialized poor whiteness: bare feet, tattered overalls, misshapen physical features, pot belly, and grossly nonstandard spelling.

These two conditions—judgments of taste and the cultural symbol of the antimodern fundamentalist—create the fertile social-ideological backdrop for concerns about quality to flourish among creationist cultural producers and consumers. For the fundamentalist gaze to work at Ark Encounter, it must absorb the commercial gaze of an entertainment-savvy public that is poised for accusations of religious idiocy.

# Conclusion

*Dallas, Texas.*[1] In 2007, the Institute for Creation Research relocated from San Diego to Dallas, America's fourth-largest metropolitan area. Since 2011, it has been raising funds and coordinating designs for a $30 million facility: the Discovery Center for Science and Earth History. Publicity materials pulse with the language of market competition and channel the spirit of Frank Oppenheimer's Exploratorium: "This is going to be like unlike any other hands-on educational center in the world," and "Our exhibits are going to be fully interactive, state-of-the-art experiences, tools that will excite students, families, and educators; a place of exploration and inspiration." One of ICR's lead researchers, a former Answers in Genesis employee, describes the proposed planetarium in the double-voiced register of religion and entertainment: "This is a fully immersive, 3-D presentation; it's going to be like a movie, but where people will see how God is glorified in what He has made in the universe."

*Treasure Valley, Idaho.*[2] In June 2011, the Northwest Science Museum was announced to the public. The facility was proposed for a yet-to-be-named site near Boise, and its 350,000 square feet promise a "full-scale" replica of Noah's ark. Again, publicity brims with claims of distinctiveness for the ears of investors and potential visitors: "Every once in a while an opportunity comes around that seems to be larger than life"; "[It] is different from anything that's ever been done before"; and "[It is] unique amongst creation based museums because it will be designed as a true science museum." Promotional materials invoke scholarly legitimacy and embattled fundamentalist conspiracy in equal parts: "The museum will be full of scientific evidence from over 32 fields of science," and "The purpose of the museum is to show censored science that's not shown in state-sponsored museums."

*Moose Jaw, Saskatchewan, Canada.*[3] Rumors about a biblical theme park in the prairie land and plains of western Canada began circulating in 2015 and were confirmed in September 2016. The as-yet-unnamed attraction was proposed by a Chinese entrepreneur, a former Buddhist who became a born-again Christian in 2008. At an estimated cost of $1.2 million, the park will cover five acres of land, adjacent to a local cemetery. The proposal includes four phases. The first will feature a "full-scale" replica of Moses's Tabernacle, complete with Ark of the Covenant and ritual implements. Next, further scenes from the Hebrew Bible will be added, as well as biblical landscapes (e.g., a re-created Jordan River and Sea of Galilee). The third phase will add a "full-scale" replica of Noah's ark. Finally, displays will be installed inside the ark, focusing on animal life and a digital experience that re-creates scenes from the life of Jesus.

*Berlin, Germany?*[4] In 2008, an interdenominational group announced Genesis Land, a roughly seventy-five-acre park estimated to cost $120 million. The project is a trans-European collaboration: led by a Dutch financier with offices in Switzerland, architects from Lichtenstein, an animation company from Austria, and seeking a location in urban Germany. Publicity materials highlight the formative role of Genesis 6 through 9 in the venture: "At the beginning, we knew we wanted to create something unique, something that doesn't yet exist anywhere in the entire world. And, because we wanted to bring to reality something from the Bible, we quickly hit upon the idea of Noah's ark." Along with the re-created ark, the park will be organized around four themed "pavilions," aligning natural elements with materialized scripture in a fundamentalist temporality: Earth ("multimedia" presentations of the days of creation), Water (a "large and impressive" simulation of Noah's Flood), Air (re-created scenes from the life of Jesus), and Fire (literalist imaginings of the book of Revelation). In terms that directly echo Answers in Genesis materials and the words of the AiG creative team, one of the project directors envisions the visitor experience this way: "It also fascinates people to find themselves actually standing in the front of the ark and to say, 'Wow, what a huge thing it is!' When you look at different pictures of the ark, you can see a little ship with some animals peering through the windows. This will certainly not be the case here."

\* \* \*

The race is on in the global creationist movement to build sites of religious publicity, all hyped with ambitions of ever-increasing sophistication. These projects integrate the literalist imperative of fundamentalism with an enthusiastic embrace of modern entertainment. The four attractions just noted are in various stages of development. Others, there is every reason to suspect, will follow in the years and decades to come. I have focused here on Ark Encounter to explore how such attractions mobilize the power of religious entertainment. Ultimately, I hope this book will make three lasting contributions.

First, Ark Encounter demonstrates how fundamentalist public culture can emerge from a thorough entanglement between religion and entertainment. The strategies and imperatives of immersion are leveraged to solidify and enliven the creationist counterpublic, convert the noncreationist public, and make claims to popular legitimacy. We have seen how the choreographed experience at such attractions is about playing in the creationist past and present. And we have seen how discourses and resources from "Hollywood," fantasy world-building, affective history, and edutainment are directed toward those re-creations. From Ark Encounter to the proposed Genesis Land, these attractions do not simply teach creationism. They teach creationists to be proud of creationism, and they demand that noncreationist audiences take notice. As forms of religious publicity and public culture, they seek to claim and proclaim cultural authority.

Second, Ark Encounter exemplifies the global phenomenon of materializing the Bible. Throughout the world and across centuries, Christian communities have transformed the written words of scripture into physical, experiential, and choreographed environments.[5] These attractions work aesthetically, mobilizing the senses through bodies, technologies, objects, and places. They combine play and piety, fun and faith, leisure and devotion, imagination and morality, affect and religious pedagogy. Perhaps most of all, they make promises to visitors: of access to the sacred past and of intimacy with traditions of belonging. There is a desire to experience scripture, not just read it, and in the process cultural commitments of scriptural authority and relevance are reproduced. This phenomenon highlights valuable questions for future research about the potential feedback loops among scripture's transmedial expressions, such as how might visitor engagements with choreographed places impact their subsequent acts of studying the written Bible?

Finally, Ark Encounter provides an opportunity to expand our understanding of creationism and fundamentalist public culture. The figure of the "creation scientist" has dominated comparative scholarship about this conservative Christian movement, as have creationist strategies for appropriating the language, symbols, and materials of science. There is good reason for this dominance, and these issues deserve continued attention. However, religion-science need not persist as our only analytical frame for understanding creationist identity and ambition. This book has performed a recalibration, making the frame of religion-entertainment the center of analytical gravity. In doing so, I have aimed to make creationism newly legible. The figure of the "creative creationist" offers distinctive insight into how durable fundamentalist dispositions (e.g., embattlement, conspiracy, literalism) shape cultural production and are performed to advance religious publicity. Moreover, the figure of the creative creationist places the power of religious entertainment squarely within our vision.

In closing this book, I reflect here on how Ark Encounter's self-identification as a "theme park" fits into the broader scheme of fundamentalist religious publicity. In these final pages, I will work toward a reprised question about the future of competing claims to the public trust.

## "Fundamentalism"

The modern theme park emerged as a "medium of mass communication" from cultural predecessors like carnivals, world's fair expositions, and landscape gardens.[6] This new genre of place was inaugurated by the opening of Disneyland in California in 1955, which was described as "a new kind of cultural experiential product" in which "the carefully controlled sale of goods (souvenirs) and experiences (architecture, rides, and performances) [is] 'themed' to the corporate owner's proprietary image."[7]

Ark Encounter exemplifies the modern, Disney-esque theme park in selected ways. A coherent theming exists throughout the park to organize the visitor experience ("throughout" is no hyperbole: even the paper bag my lunch was served in contributed to the immersion, printed with details about Noah's wife and a quiz based on onboard exhibits). What is fantasy at the Magic Kingdom or nostalgic nationalism on Main Street USA is biblical literalism and fundamentalist politics at Ark Encounter.

There is a choreographed effort to immerse visitors in an experiential frame distinct from everyday life, especially what Answers in Genesis would call the everyday attack on biblical authority by "evolutionism." There is also a dedicated ambition to attract the broadest possible public. Families with children and tour groups are the target audience, not any specialized niche or elite demographic. Of course, it is also worth observing that the creative team constantly engaged with Disney as a creative and professional exemplar. Recall the parascriptural reminder displayed in Emily's cubicle: "It's kind of fun to do the impossible. Walt Disney."

Considering the expansion of sites like Moose Jaw and Genesis Land, a further parallel between the modern theme park and fundamentalist parks remains an open question. By the mid-1990s, the popularity of themed attractions had begun to influence the creation of other cultural products. For example, "Cartoons and films [were] being styled at early stages with potential theme park attractions in mind, the relevant question perhaps being 'will this story be good to ride?'"[8] At present, it seems that biblical stories are materialized in service of existing cultural systems (e.g., Noah and creationist Flood geology). But could the promise of theming and the power of entertainment have a lasting structural influence on how the Bible is engaged? Will the materializing potential of biblical stories figure into the calculus of which stories become fixed in the collective memory of religious communities? Perhaps: "Will this scripture be good to experience?"

But in other ways, Ark Encounter is a decidedly fundamentalist theme park that diverges from its industry counterparts. The earliest theme parks were "places where modern people [could] alleviate the anxieties in their lives and the crises in their societies."[9] Disneyland and Walt Disney World have always promised a kind of escapist leisure. Not so with Ark Encounter. Here, creationist-diagnosed crises not only are present but are integral for the immersive experience, such as with the *Fairy Tale Ark* exhibit. The fundamentalist theme park thrives on naming and critically dissecting its cultural antagonists.

Ark Encounter also fosters a different attachment to the past than do other modern theme parks. As historian David Lowenthal writes, "Vagueness is a prime virtue that theme parks share with the past. A modicum of knowledge is plenty, the less precise the better."[10] The creationist past imagined and performed at Ark Encounter marshals every possible detail, fills in the rest with "artistic license," and then invites visitors to fill the intertextual gaps so that scriptural authority is solidified.

Finally, Ark Encounter is choreographed by religious pedagogy, whereas the spatial design of the modern theme park is devoted to capitalist consumption.[11] Visitors still exit through the gift shop, but the sale of goods does not orchestrate the flow or content of exhibits on board the ark. Rather, the park aims to immerse visitors in the creationist past and present through its aesthetic arrangement.

In short, Ark Encounter is fully recognizable within the modern genre of "theme park," yet it is not beholden to all of that genre's expectations. Much like the use of the term "museum" for the companion facility in northern Kentucky, embracing the identifier "theme park" makes Ark Encounter recognizable as a cultural and touristic place. But what else might this association do?

Anthropologist Susan Harding has argued that the meaning and rhetorical force of the term "fundamentalism" was invented by the Scopes Trial in 1925 and redefined by the Religious Right in the late 1970s and 1980s.[12] By "invented" she does not mean that the term was created ex nihilo. It was in use as a self-descriptor as early as 1920, inspired by the publication of *The Fundamentals* beginning in 1910. She means that the Scopes Trial saturated the category of "fundamentalism" with a particular meaning and launched it onto a particular trajectory in its public circulation. Harding writes:

> In Scopes-trial histories, the word and all persons and things called "fundamentalist" are riddled with pejorative connotations, while those who interrogated the literal Bible, those who "won" the battle even though they lost their [legal] case, carry off the prestigious associations—educated, scientific, rational, progressive, urbane, tolerant, in a word, modern.[13]

We saw as well how this ideological baggage helps shape the demand for "quality" in religious entertainment experiences among creationist cultural producers and consumers.

Harding hoped that her analysis would "open up a space in which other accounts, not only of the trial but of 'fundamentalism,' might emerge."[14] Other accounts have emerged, including her own exploration of how fundamentalist poetics fostered religious authority and galvanized political action among the Religious Right. She subverted the limiting interpretive frame of modern/antimodern to explain how fundamentalism achieved success as a public religion.[15]

This book enters this space of different accountings of fundamentalism, namely, by recentering the analysis within the frame of religion-entertainment. A fundamentalist theme park is a prism, much like the Scopes Trial and the poetic discourse of leaders like Jerry Falwell. It reflects the repertoire of fundamentalist dispositions (literalism, hierarchy, embattlement, conspiracy, devotional consumption, etc.), but it also reflects and refracts immersive entertainment, creativity, scientific authority, history-making, aesthetic preferences, consumer capitalism, and the ambitions of religious publicity. We must grapple with all these if we hope to clear an ark-shaped space in our representations of fundamentalism.

Harding's argument also has a reflexive dimension. It is not only about who fundamentalists are and what they hope to achieve but also about how a nonfundamentalist self is forged through the representation of fundamentalism. As she explains, "Through polarities such as ['belief and unbelief, literal and critical, backward and progressive, bigoted and tolerant'] between 'us' and 'them,' the modern subject is secured."[16] Perhaps, then, there is also a reflexive dimension to understanding Ark Encounter as a form of fundamentalist public culture that mobilizes the power of religious entertainment.

At the outset, I highlighted Peter Stromberg's observation that entertainment is not just dominant *compared with* other cultural forms but has actually *infused* them. According to Stromberg, "As Darwin argued for the survival of the fittest, we now have survival of the most entertaining."[17] I noted that creationist and secular history makers engage the same strategies and imperatives of immersion and building affective attachments with the past. What I did not note is that secular museum professionals are equally aware of this new Darwinian contest. Their production staffs confront the same questions as the Ark Encounter creative team about integrating art, entertainment, and claims about the past in order to attract and compel audiences.

In his book *Stuffed Animals and Pickled Heads*, Stephen Asma goes behind the scenes at Chicago's Field Museum. Asma was interested in

how exhibit designers managed the dual imperatives of fun and learning, and how they balanced the competing pressures of satisfying and
educating consumers. He found a hesitant anxiety: "Many [curators,
designers, and developers] were very concerned that the cost of some
of this increase in entertainment might be a decrease in scientific content."[18] This sentiment echoes a prescient worry voiced in the early 1990s
by Stephen Jay Gould, one of the most vocal and popular opponents of
antievolution movements:

> Museums exist to display authentic objects of nature and culture—yes,
> they must teach; and yes, they may certainly include all manner of com-
> puter graphics and other virtual displays to aid in this worthy effort; but
> they must remain wed to authenticity. Theme parks are gala places of
> entertainment, committed to using the best displays and devices from the
> increasingly sophisticated arsenals of virtual reality to titillate, to scare, to
> thrill, even to teach. . . . If each institution respects the other's essence and
> place, this opposition poses no problem. But, theme parks represent the
> realm of commerce, museums the educational world—and the first is so
> much bigger than the second. Commerce will swallow museums if educa-
> tors try to copy the norms of business for immediate financial reward.[19]

If a secular logic closely polices the categories of "museum" and
"theme park," then Answers in Genesis and other fundamentalists follow
a different path. They meld these genres together in their history-making
productions. The Creation "Museum" is full of theming, Ark Encounter
is full of teaching exhibits, and visitors can purchase a discounted two-
day pass to consume both attractions as a tandem experience. While
others may implement the strategies and imperatives of entertainment
with trepidation, fundamentalists do so with gusto, bending the genres
to their public ambitions. Perhaps there has been a cultural shift since
the 1990s when Asma and Gould were writing. Perhaps science and history museum professionals have allayed anxieties and caught the gusto.
In 2015, the DoSeum opened in Texas as a science and discovery center
for children, advertising to the public: "Visit San Antonio's theme park
for the brain!"

As fundamentalist theme parks and museums continue to proliferate—
as ICR's Discovery Center, Genesis Land, and other proposals indicate—we

must wonder how secular cultural producers and history makers will be shaped in turn. How will the interplay between fundamentalists and their antagonists impact their respective expressions of public culture? To reprise a question from an earlier chapter: *Whose past will be more fun?*

Throughout this book, I have interrogated both the strategies and the stakes of fun. Entertainment, conceived as immersive play, is the engine that fuels the fun of Ark Encounter's fundamentalism. This biblical attraction draws from a global Christian tradition and the modern genre of theme park to conjure a distinctively creationist world. Grounded in physical experience—the testimony of the senses—Ark Encounter is oriented by the ongoing process of claiming and proclaiming cultural legitimacy. Ultimately, the promise that this will be successful is the power of entertainment.

## ACKNOWLEDGMENTS

This book was six years in the making, and throughout this time I received tremendous support. First and foremost, I recognize the grace of the Ark Encounter creative team; the hospitality of church members at Cornerstone Assembly of God; and the assistance provided by guides and caretakers at attractions that materialize the Bible. This book could never have happened without them.

The Department of Anthropology at Miami University continues to be an ideal home for my life as a teacher-scholar, and I am grateful for the collegiality there. Jeb Card, especially, has been a lively and encyclopedic conversation partner. Also at Miami University, the Humanities Center provided instrumental support, and Rory Johnson, Nathan French, Jon Otto, and Walt Vanderbush have given friendship and intellectual inspiration. Many students added value to this project; in particular, I want to recognize the contributions of Amanda White, Kimberly Blake, Claire Vaughn, and the students in my course ATH185: "Cultural Diversity in the United States" in the fall of 2014 for helping me explore the power of entertainment.

NYU Press, once again, has been an ideal publisher for my scholarship. Jennifer Hammer's editorial wizardry immensely improved the manuscript, as did critical feedback from two anonymous reviewers. I also want to recognize other manuscript reviewers, whose insight benefited this book. Select portions of several publications were revised for inclusion here: chapters in *Lost City, Found Pyramid: Understanding Alternative Archaeologies and Pseudoscientific Practices* (2016); *Christianity and the Limits of Materiality* (2017); *The Bible in American Life* (2017); *Ethnographies of Waiting: Doubt, Hope, and Uncertainty* (2017); and the articles "Replication as Religious Practice, Temporality as Religious Problem," *History and Anthropology* (2016), and "Biblical Gardens and the Sensuality of Religious Pedagogy," *Material Religion* (2017).

My life as a teacher-scholar is enriched beyond measure by treasured colleagues around the world. For support on this particular project, I thank Andreas Bandak, Tim Beal, Jon Bialecki, Anderson Blanton, Tom Boylston, Saliha Chattoo, Simon Coleman, Omri Elisha, Matthew Engelke, Jackie Feldman, Jeff Guhin, Grey Gundaker, Paul Gutjahr, Naomi Haynes, Eric Hoenes del Pinal, Tina Howe, Brian Howell, Hillary Kaell, Rebekka King, David Morgan, Crispin Paine, Katja Rakow, Joel Robbins, Don Seeman, Charles Stewart, Matt Tomlinson, Michael Walker, Steve Watkins, Travis Webb, Joe Webster, and Vincent Wimbush.

Local coffee shops provided reliable sanctuary for writing the bulk of this book. In particular, the staffs at Kofenya and Oxford Coffee Company in Oxford, Ohio, and Joe's in East Atlanta Village inspired with their hard work and hospitality. Always inspiring are two dear friends who, every Friday night, throw their unlocked doors open and welcome any who come: Brandon and Heidi, you are irreplaceable. My family—Judith, Mary, Roger, JD, Roger, Charlotte, Sam, Ed, Clay, Dave, and Mary Ann—I work, in part, to offer you pride. And, to Sara: my love, you changed my life. Every day I strive for better, for you and for Simon, who changed our lives. Si, we can't wait to rediscover the world with you.

Songs, prose, and prayers kept this project (and its author) from unraveling. Among many others, I am grateful for Caitlin Canty, Guy Clark, Sam Cooke, Miles Davis, David Grisman, Gregory Alan Isakov, James McMurtry, Van Morrison, John Prine, Sturgill Simpson, Todd Snider, John Steinbeck, Wallace Stegner, and the prophet Habakkuk: though the fig tree may not bud and no grapes grow on the vine, I will rejoice and be joyful.

*The Ark and the Anthropologist*

The research for this book spanned more than five years, beginning in April 2011 and concluding in Septemebr 2017. It took unexpected turns, from the creative team's design studio to a small congregation north of Dayton, Ohio, to sites around the world that materialize the Bible, and back to Ark Encounter. This methodological appendix details the project's fieldwork journey and, in doing so, highlights research decisions that I hope other scholars studying religious publicity and processes of cultural production will find valuable.

ACCESS

Throughout this project, I participated in numerous professional conferences in anthropology and religious studies. The most common question I received during question-and-answer sessions and in collegial conversations following a presentation was this: How did I secure the backstage access?

Like anyone interested in American religion, I was intrigued by Ark Encounter's announcement in December 2010. I was further intrigued because the ministry was based only an hour's hour drive from my home. I had just concluded a different ethnographic project and was wondering what direction my research might take next. I was intrigued, but not immediately sold.

The idea of studying creationism was not inherently appealing. Works like Christopher Toumey's *God's Own Scientists* had masterfully analyzed the modern creationist movement.[1] Out of anthropological curiosity, I visited the AiG Creation Museum twice in 2009, which was certainly a stunning experience. Because I had not yet visited other creation museums, I did not fully appreciate the production quality, but the AiG museum was clearly sophisticated and well financed. Still, the cultural identity being performed there was utterly consistent with what Toumey and others had already captured.

If creationism per se was not the motivating interest, what was? It was the promise of getting behind the scenes, of seeing how a project like Ark Encounter was made, start to finish. My thinking in early 2011 was this: gaining access to the production of a creationist theme park would be an anthropological story worth telling.

I initially contacted Answers in Genesis in April 2011 and received my first reply a month later. The e-mail came from Ark Encounter's main administrative assistant, who connected me with Steve, project director for the ark. I conducted an interview with him in late August 2011, after three months of e-mails and rescheduled meetings. I learned a number of useful details about Ark Encounter, but the interview was really more about Steve acting as a gatekeeper for my research proposal.

Six weeks later, in mid-October 2011, Steve gave me a tour of the design studio. I discovered toward the day's end that this kind of backstage peek was usually reserved for deep-pocketed donors. The team members were there working, and I met them briefly. Looking back at my field notes from the day, I was most struck by the labor intensity of the production process. There were models and design sketches everywhere: intricate and impressive, yet clearly only preliminary and conceptual.

I returned two weeks later for the first full day of fieldwork. It was then that I presented my research project to the creative team. Roger welcomed me, introduced everyone, and gave a shorthand explanation of what Ark Encounter aimed to teach: showing people that Noah and the Flood were "real events in history," that "the Bible is true," and that the story "could have happened." There was no probing session of questions from the team about my intentions. After the introduction, the team members resumed their meeting, and I sat down to begin taking field notes. Roger did outline two nonnegotiable conditions for the research. First, my presence could continue only if I did not "disturb" their creative process. And, after I asked about photographing concept art, he agreed, so long as the pictures did not "appear on some website denouncing us."

In short, gaining access to the team's process was relatively straightforward. There were three gatekeepers: the administrative assistant who first fielded my e-mail; Steve, who approved my initial access to the team; and Roger, who approved my continued access. Why was it not more complicated or rigorous? Consider three possibilities.

First, on my second full day of fieldwork, the team asked an inevitable question: Are you a Christian? I am, though the team members did not press me to specify any further. I am not an evangelical, a fundamentalist, or a creationist. If anything, I am best described as an ecumenical, liberal Protestant interested in interfaith dialogue. I affirm the scientific validity of evolutionary theory and see no conflict between this fact of natural history and ontological commitments tied to religious tradition. However, the team members never pursued a more precise answer. For them, knowing I identified as Christian seemed to suffice.

Second, the team was accustomed to attention from outsiders, with its creative labor on both the Creation Museum and Ark Encounter widely covered by journalists. Unlike previous ethnographic projects, where the Christian groups I studied were some mix of surprised, flattered, and delighted that a scholar wanted to write about them, the creative team was familiar with the spotlight. Demonstrating to the team members that my work differed from the journalism they were used to was an important context for the development of our relationship.

Third, as the old saying goes, there is no such thing as bad publicity. In allowing my continued presence, perhaps the team members were obeying this maxim. Perhaps they assumed that a professional anthropologist, Christian or not, working at a public university was an "evolutionist." Perhaps they believed me when I assured them that had I no interest, "evolutionist" or not, in writing any kind of exposé. Whatever the case, perhaps they were unconcerned with what I would produce; it only mattered that their work would be written about in yet another venue for yet another audience.

BEHIND THE SCENES

When I was granted fieldwork access, the research design focused on the process of cultural production. The plan was to follow the team's work all the way through until the park opened. For forty-three months, until June 2014, my research progressed according to this plan.

The backbone of the fieldwork was the team's daily creative labor. I spent mornings and afternoons at the design studio while the team members drew freehand, illustrated concept art, worked with raw materials, sketched exhibit schematics, edited and critiqued each other's work in progress. I talked with the artists at their cubicles, took notes during planned and impromptu team meetings, documented lunch-time work talk, and photographed the ubiquitous art sitting on tables, hanging on walls, and discarded in trash cans. I arranged semistructured interviews with team members, but the majority of audio recordings and field notes addressed the work of a small team working from small desks: usually tedious, frequently under deadline, ever-conscious of budgetary constraints, and constantly seeking the next imaginative breakthrough.

While this book is only possible because of the unprecedented access I was given to the production of a creationist theme park, the fieldwork was far from ideal. I was not granted completely open access and had several requests denied, such as attending Answers in Genesis board meetings, audio-recording selected interviews and meetings, and at-tending selected fund-raising events. Akin to Matthew Engelke's de-scription of a portion of his work with the British Bible Society, my fieldwork with the team was "anthropology by appointment."[2] Each visit to the design studio had to be arranged weeks ahead of time. The proj-ect's greatest frustrations ensued from this requirement. On numerous occasions, arranged visits were canceled or rescheduled, often with little advance notice. On a few occasions, I arrived at the studio only to find most or all of the team away for the day.

Although less than ideal circumstances defined this fieldwork, I did clear two qualitatively significant obstacles. The ethnographic record is filled with anthropologists recounting their mistaken or assumed iden-tities in the field: as spies, missionaries, and colonial officials, among others. With the team members, I was not mistaken as a journalist, but I believe my initial presence was slotted into their most readily available category: a journalist who is here briefly to collect a story, take a few pic-tures, and leave to publish something dismissive or critical. Despite my attempts to explain the nature of anthropological fieldwork, it was only my continued presence that convinced them that this project was some-how different. I recall arriving at the studio one morning in spring 2012 and being greeted with the surprised comment, "James, you're back!" As more time passed, the artists regularly asked me variations of the same question: "So, when are you going to write something?" I am not sure I ever fully convinced the team members what anthropology was about, but I am confident they no longer considered me a journalist.

My first full day of fieldwork ended with Tyler driving me to a nearby airport hotel, where I stayed overnight before a flight the next day. It was a generous gesture on his part, and it gave us both the chance to ask a few more questions. Tyler was curious about a range of things, from the courses I taught to whether I was married. I asked him about the team meeting that day and some details of his life (e.g., where he lived in the area, where he went to church). Among other things, Tyler noted that the team members had been very "polite" to each other because of my presence; normally, he continued, they were a bit more "aggressive." From their galvanized critique of the Ark trailer to artistic clashes, the team did not persist with this overly polite presentation of self. I secured a fieldwork presence in which their creative labor proceeded in quite candid ways.

## MORE OBSERVER THAN PARTICIPANT

In *Advertising Diversity*, anthropologist Shalini Shankar examines processes of cultural production at several Asian American advertising agencies.[3] Shankar described her fieldwork as pragmatically difficult, demanding different strategies than traditional ethnography. For example, she adjusted expectations around participant observation, a hallmark of the traditional model. Consistent with other "studying up" projects, the same was true for my work with the Ark team.[4]

The only way I could truly participate with the team was during brainstorming sessions. For example, in May 2012 the team members had been tasked with developing ideas for a free gift to accompany attendance at an upcoming fund-raising event. Roger called everyone together, asked for initial concept proposals, and invited me to contribute. I offered a few possibilities that came directly to mind: A pen? An iPod case? A bumper sticker? A year's free subscription to *Answers* magazine? Roger was not enthusiastic about any of my ideas, though his responses to a few were instructive. "It's not bumper sticker time yet," he said, providing a clue to how they manage advertising. He complimented the free subscription idea but noted that they were trying not to make overt connections with the broader ministry. I found these comments revealing for reasons of publicity and in the context of Ark Encounter's legal controversies.

My fieldwork days were dominated by one particular form of research labor: sitting next to the artists in their cubicles while they worked. On average, I spent four to five hours at the studio on each visit. A great deal of this time was spent waiting: for the right moment to ask questions, for private meetings to finish so I could follow up, for artists to return from running errands. I took seriously the condition that I was not to disturb the creative process, knowing that my continued access hinged on not being perceived as a nuisance.

Selecting the right opportunity to ask about the creative labor happening in the moment was a difficult skill that I never perfected. I did find that useful openings appeared when the artists were waiting for large print jobs to finish or, even better, waiting for large computer files to back up. A bit of good news for me was that there was never an absence of work to discuss. Every piece of art—whether hanging on a wall or still in progress on a computer screen—could serve as an elicitation tool, a culturally meaningful artifact that I could use to learn about the production of religious publicity.

In his ethnography of Japanese anime designers, Ian Condry reflects on his initial impression of a studio space: "I was surprised by the piles and piles of paper, the intensity of hand-drawn work, and the sheer amount of labor required. I was also impressed by the workers' focus, energy, and commitment to working together on an enormous project."[5] I would say the same thing about the Ark Encounter creative team. My time at the studio was full of awed impressions and insightful surprises; I had never worked with professional artists before, and everything about designing a theme park (creationist or otherwise) was new to me. There was a certain excitement to this, but it was always tempered by the realities of budgets, deadlines, team and ministry hierarchies, and the accumulated effect of a stressful working environment.

The truth is that my fieldwork at the studio involved significant amounts of boredom. When not actively engaging the team members in talk about their art, I took a lot of pictures, browsed bookshelves, and read any materials they were able and willing to share (e.g., art books they were consulting for a project, preliminary scripts for an exhibit). Still, substantial time was left for me to wait, and the space for waiting was confined to a few spots in the studio. Eventually, I decided boredom was an unavoidable experience. I never liked it, sometimes dreaded it on the hour-long drive to the studio, bemoaned it on the hour-long drive home, and frequently felt awkward in the midst of it, but I learned to accept it.

This part of the fieldwork experience did resemble more traditional forms. Bronislaw Malinowski's diary and countless other volumes report "long periods of boredom occasionally punctuated by events that broke the monotony."[6] However, unlike some other accounts of ethnographic boredom, the waiting I experienced was not a by-product of everyday life or an instrumental component of ritual action.[7] It was a necessary form of action, a dull discipline that I dedicated myself to so that my status would not flirt with what I wanted most to avoid: being a distraction.

## AS IF

The nature of my fieldwork with the team meant that I would often go several weeks without spending time at the studio. To remain in an engaged research mode, I maintained several productive practices.

First, I signed up for a Google News alert for the phrase "Ark Encounter." This relieved me from having to regularly search for new stories and enabled me to see which media outlets were covering the ark and how the project was being reported. Second, I subscribed to e-mail updates from Ark Encounter, Answers in Genesis, and the Creation Museum. These kept me informed about ministry events and how Ark Encounter was being publicized to subscribers and provided a sampling of the ministry's weekly stream of discourse. Third, and most useful, I closely monitored the Ark Encounter blog. Blog posts offered numerous kinds of data, from creationist theological details to backstage "sneak peeks" at the creative team's work. One valuable use I found for these posts was as the basis for informal interviewing with the team, yet another strategy for elicitation.

Another supplemental research practice I maintained throughout the fieldwork period was what I called an "if I were a creationist diary." This separate set of notes, which consisted of observations I made throughout day-to-day life, enabled me to operate in an as-if mode, recording public moments that were incongruent with a creationist worldview.

For example, when browsing kiosks in supermarkets and airports, I regularly noted how popular magazine covers (e.g., *Scientific American*, *Newsweek*) operated in a pro-evolutionary science register. Once when traveling I had a connecting flight through Chicago's O'Hare airport. Walking from gate to gate, I came upon a huge dinosaur fossil display, an exhibit on loan from the Field Museum. It informed the flying public that this fossil was from the Jurassic period and was nearly 200 million years old. On another occasion, as I was waiting to cross the street in my hometown of Oxford, Ohio, a U-Haul van drove by. On the side it advertised a tourist site in the American West, which included geologic features dating to 300 million years ago. On November 24, 2015, I went to the Google home page to enter a search term. There, to commemorate the forty-first anniversary of the Lucy fossil discovery in Ethiopia, was a "Google Doodle" that depicted Lucy's transitional place in the human evolutionary lineage.

These moments are a small sampling of the kinds of observations that filled my as-if diary. This exercise helped me to further appreciate the everyday ways in which the fundamentalist disposition of feeling "embattled" could be internalized.[8]

CALLING IT QUITS

A sense of anxious anticipation persisted throughout my time with the team members. I never stopped wondering when they might decide to sever the generous access they had granted. This anxiety dissipated a bit in late fall 2013 following a frank conversation with Roger. The ministry's latest fund-raising strategy (the investment bond described in the introduction) was in full swing, and everyone seemed hopeful that it would deliver the needed funds. After an interview in his office, Roger informed me that my fieldwork could not continue in the same form after the funding was secured. The team would be too busy, and even minor distractions could disturb the creative process. We outlined an agreement for how the fieldwork might continue, primarily shifting the focus from cubicle creative labor to collective team meetings. I left his office feeling assured.

Then, in June 2014, it happened. I suspected as much from the e-mail exchange leading up to the visit. The reply from the administrative assistant came within a few hours, which was rare. It read only: "Monday June 30 at 2:00 will work for us. You will be meeting with Roger. If you have any questions just let me know." My suspicions were confirmed when I arrived. In his office, Roger stood to welcome me, then closed the door. He had never done that before.

After a few pleasantries, Roger moved swiftly to his purpose: "We have to call it quits." His words were certain, even stern. Before I could respond, he added that this extended even to team meetings. I reminded him of our discussion a few months prior and asked what had changed. He didn't really acknowledge the previous agreement, just continued saying that it was too much effort to involve "an outside person," and that the meetings were "private." The decision was clearly final. We talked for nearly another hour, with Roger updating me on their progress since my last visit and their plans moving forward. It was difficult to concentrate. I was upset and even a bit embarrassed. Something about the experience was akin to being dumped by a romantic partner without any chance to argue your case. When we were finished, he walked me to the outside door and wished me well, another first in forty-three months.

The drive home was an emotional jumble. In subsequent days, I realized I was wrestling with at least four distinct feelings. I was angry with Roger for dismissing our earlier agreement. I was disappointed; my research design of following the team's work from beginning to end was cut short. Strangely, I was also relieved. The fieldwork had become cumbersome, with last-minute cancellations; arriving at the studio only to find most of the team gone for the day; the tedium, awkwardness, and boredom of sitting in cubicles. Difficulties I had learned to accept were taken away, and it was freeing. Tagging along with the relief, however, was guilt. I had dedicated hundreds of hours to this project; feeling relieved felt a bit shameful. In any case, the other shoe had finally dropped, and my time with the team was over.

CONSUMPTION

When my access to the creative team ended, I spent the next month seeking the wisdom of colleagues and assessing how to continue the project.[9] The decision I settled on was to add a research phase focusing on how committed creationists interact with Ark Encounter. Cultural production, after all, is only part of a broader process that includes cultural consumption. My plan was to locate a pro-creationist congregation, seek permission to work with members from the church leadership, interview a sample of people intending to visit the park, go with them after the park opened, and interview them again about their experience at the park.

While this plan was partially successful, it was not able to be fully realized. Much like my experience with the creative team, there are lessons here for other fieldworkers regarding research design and improvisation.

I started with churches in Oxford, Ohio. A campus pastor and personal acquaintance had his finger on the pulse of the local congregational landscape. He pointed me to several churches that were in formal theological agreement with Answers in Genesis. I e-mailed pastors and requested a coffee meeting to discuss my research proposal.

I met with two pastors, who listened earnestly, if a bit cautiously. Ultimately, both declined, citing vague conversations with church members who were not interested in participating. Already, though, this added phase proved surprising. For example, one pastor, "a big supporter" of AiG who regularly takes out-of-town guests to the Creation Museum, also frequently takes his family to "regular" museums, such as the Cincinnati Museum Center (which includes exclusively evolutionary exhibits in its natural history and science wing). Immediately, I was fascinated by the possible questions to ask around practices of museum consumption. What other kinds of educational attractions do Creation Museum and Ark Encounter supporters visit? And how do they integrate these experiences? Still, finding a congregation in Oxford looked to be a dead end. What next?

Answers in Genesis is not organized with member churches or any such equivalent. However, the ministry does publicize where staff members travel for speaking engagements. I examined the upcoming itineraries for fall 2014 on the AiG website, identifying churches within a two-hour drive of my home. After one such search, I had a substantial list of congregations. After a round of e-mail inquiries, I received several polite but uninterested replies. Then, I received the following from a pastor north of Dayton, Ohio:

> Greetings James,
> Would love to get together sometime. As you have deduced, I am a supporter of the Creation Museum and look forward to the ARK encounter [sic] when it opens. Please let me know a date that will work for you. Any day but Wednesdays is good for me. We can meet in Dayton or you are welcome to join me in the "metropolis" that is Sydney. I would love to

ask you questions also since you would be the first anthropologist I have met. I would be delighted to answers any questions and be of any help. Blessings

I was encouraged. The pastor's enthusiastic response, brimming with good humor, was a breath of fresh air compared with the series of nonstarter e-mails, coffee meetings, and, of course, the cumbersome challenges of working with the creative team.

Pastor Harry and I met for lunch in October 2014, and he was even more gracious in person. He peppered me with curious and lively questions about my faith background, my life as a teacher, my previous research projects, and more. His church is affiliated with the Assemblies of God, though he joked that some congregants call their style "Bapticostal" due to Harry's theological influences (fundamentalist celebrities like John Piper and Al Mohler Jr.). Harry had been at the church for twelve years and described it as "spiritually, numerically, financially" stronger than it had ever been. The congregation was currently in the process of planting a new church in a nearby small town. He joked self-effacingly that it must be "the spirit of God" at work, since he is a non-charismatic person with "a voice like a cartoon character." We laughed. I found him endearing, and we closed the meeting with an agreement that I could present my research proposal one Sunday morning during the weekly announcements.

I visited the church in December 2014 and spoke to the crowd of 100 or so people in attendance at the worship service. Harry kindly arranged an informal luncheon following the service, inviting anyone who wanted to hear more to join us for fried chicken and assorted side dishes. It was informal and enjoyable and offered a few surprising moments. For example, I spoke at length with Pastor Jaime, who was leading the new church plant. Like Harry, he was full of intellectual curiosity and asked engaging questions about my stance in the creation-evolution debate. At one point, he asked if I had ever read Christopher Hitchens's writings on "deistic evolution." I told him that I had, and admitted that I did not enjoy New Atheist figures like Hitchens, neither their positions nor their manner of performing them. Jaime agreed but said that he really appreciated Hitchens's talent as a writer. He had read numerous essays multiple times and admired the author's rhetorical acumen. A creation-ist fan of Hitchens: this was a first for me.

I walked away from the luncheon with e-mail addresses of ten individuals to contact for interviews. From early 2015 through spring 2016, I conducted interviews with church members, including Harry and Jamie. The interviews were semistructured, organized into three sections of questions. The first was a short spiritual life history, in which participants narrated their religious journey from childhood to the present. The second focused on practices and preferences in visiting museums, zoos, and other educational attractions. This included questions about visiting the Creation Museum. Finally, I used Ark Encounter publicity materials as elicitation tools. After viewing promotional videos (e.g., the ark trailer for which the creative team had designed the set), we shared an open-ended discussion about the participants' reactions to each video's content and style.

These interviews were very productive and informed the arguments presented in chapter 6. Unfortunately, however, scheduling conflicts throughout the late summer and fall of 2016 prevented me from visiting Ark Encounter with any of the interviewees. Between August 2016 and September 2017, I spent four full days at the ark, separated by several months. I took more than 700 photographs altogether and made extensive field notes on each visit. These notes focused on the pedagogical style and content of exhibits; the aesthetic experiences afforded by exhibits; observations of visitor engagements with the space; comparisons with the Creation Museum and other attractions that materialize the Bible; and reflections on how the finalized version being consumed by the public compared with the creative team's vision. After my first visit to the park, I sent an e-mail to the creative team detailing some of these reflections, including honest observations about which exhibits I found most memorable. As I review the final copyedits of this book manuscript, I have not received a reply from any of the team members.

MATERIALIZING THE BIBLE

When I initiated this project in spring 2011, I knew the Creation Museum and Ark Encounter were not the only attractions of their kind, but I was clueless about the extent of the phenomenon. Expanding the project to more systematically analyze other attractions began to flourish in spring

2015 with the research assistance of an undergraduate student at Miami University, Amanda White.

I had received a small grant from the university's Humanities Center to employ two undergraduate assistants to help with ongoing research. Part of Amanda's work was to turn an informal listing of biblical attractions I had accumulated into a more systematic catalog. She did more than this, however, doubling the collection's size and discovering sites I didn't know existed. In May 2015, Amanda accepted an offer to extend her research appointment and help create a digital scholarship project.

In July 2015, we launched Materializing the Bible, an online, interactive curation of this collection. This project was the basis for chapter 2, and our work building it has provided a wealth of materials from and about different attractions around the world (e.g., site maps, emic histories, publicity videos, mission statements, guiding materials). This project also inspired me to visit as many of the attractions as possible. Altogether, I made firsthand observations at thirty-eight sites (Table A.1), and I enjoyed visiting select sites with family, friends, and colleagues. I want to thank the following people who accompanied me to attractions, both for their time and for their keen insight: Judith Bielo, Sara Williams, Dave Williams, Mary Ann Williams, Jackie Feldman, Yemima Cohen, Joe Webster, Steve Watkins, David Morgan, Larissa Carneiro, Jeb Card, Dana Miller, Omri Elisha, and Michael Walker.

For each site, I recorded extensive field notes and photographs, took public guided tours whenever possible, and collected tour brochures, detailed guidebooks, and any other materials that were available. On several occasions, I conducted informal interviews with site guides and caretakers. These attractions were extremely valuable for analyzing the religious publicity of Ark Encounter. A central focus was on how different sites perform the immersive imperative (with particular attention to how they choreographed aesthetic experiences) and how they mixed different experiential registers: devotion, religious pedagogy, evangelism, and fun.

CODA

When I reflect on the research undergirding this book, a few lessons shine through: the challenges and rewards of studying up; the need for diligence and creativity in doing anthropology; and the significant payoff

TABLE A.1. Materializing the Bible Attractions Visited by the Author, Arranged by Date of Visit

| Attraction | Location | Subgenre | Visit Date |
|---|---|---|---|
| Creation Museum | Petersburg, Kentucky | Creation museum | July 2009–December 2016 |
| Billy Graham Center Museum | Wheaton, Illinois | Bible history museum | January 2014, April 2015 |
| Holy Land Experience | Orlando, Florida | Re-creation | March 2014 |
| Living Bible Museum | Mansfield, Ohio | Re-creation | April 2014 |
| Temple Institute | Jerusalem, Israel | Re-creation | June 2014 |
| Akron Fossils and Science Center | Akron, Ohio | Creation museum | September 2014 |
| Franciscan Monastery of the Holy Land in America | Washington, DC | Re-creation | December 2014 |
| Wyatt Archaeological Museum | Cornersville, Tennessee | Creation museum | March 2015 |
| Creation and Earth History Museum | Santee, California | Creation museum | April 2015 |
| Treasuring the Word Rare Book and Bible Museum | Sevierville, Tennessee | Bible history museum | May 2015 |
| Biblical History Center | La Grange, Georgia | Re-creation | May 2015 |
| Fields of the Wood Bible Park | Murphy, North Carolina | Re-creation | May 2015 |
| Camp Sunrise Museum | Fairmount, Georgia | Creation museum | May 2015 |
| The Bible Museum | Goodyear, Arizona | Bible history museum | May 2015 |
| Agritopia Biblical Garden | Gilbert, Arizona | Biblical garden | May 2015 |
| Holy Land, USA | Waterbury, Connecticut | Re-creation | December 2015 |
| Garden of Hope | Covington, Kentucky | Re-creation | March 2016 |
| Trinity Lutheran Church | Centerville, Ohio | Biblical garden | April 2016 |
| Warsaw Biblical Gardens | Warsaw, Indiana | Biblical garden | April 2016 |
| Paradise Valley United Methodist Church | Paradise Valley, Arizona | Biblical garden | April 2016 |
| Congregation Beth Israel | Scottsdale, Arizona | Biblical garden | April 2016 |
| Redeemer Lutheran Church | Jackson, Michigan | Biblical garden | May 2016 |
| Congregation Beth Ahm | West Bloomfield, Michigan | Biblical garden | May 2016 |
| Shrine of Our Lady of Stomoria | Kastel Novi, Croatia | Biblical garden | June 2016 |
| St. George's College | Jerusalem, Israel | Biblical garden | July 2016 |
| Neot Kedumim | Lod, Israel | Biblical garden | July 2016 |
| Biblical Village | Yad Hashmona, Israel | Re-creation | July 2016 |

Table A.1. Materializing the Bible Attractions Visited by the Author, Arranged by Date of Visit (*continued*)

| Attraction | Location | Subgenre | Visit Date |
|---|---|---|---|
| Jerusalem Botanical Gardens | Jerusalem, Israel | Biblical garden | July 2016 |
| St. John the Divine Cathedral | New York, New York | Biblical garden | August 2016 |
| Ark Encounter | Williamstown, Kentucky | Re-creation | August–December 2016 |
| The Shrine of Christ's Passion | St. John, Indiana | Re-creation | August 2016 |
| Lutheran Church of the Ascension | Citrus Heights, California | Biblical garden | January 2017 |
| St. Paul's United Methodist Church | Manteca, California | Biblical garden | January 2017 |
| Fountain Hills Presbyterian Church | Fountain Hills, Arizona | Biblical garden | January 2017 |
| St. Francis of Assisi Episcopal Church | Simi Valley, California | Biblical garden | January 2017 |
| Ojai Presbyterian Church | Ojai, California | Biblical garden | January 2017 |
| Naugatuck Valley Community College | Waterbury, Connecticut | Biblical garden | April 2017 |
| National Shrine of Divine Mercy | Stockbridge, Massachusetts | Re-creation | April 2017 |

of working comparatively. The fieldwork with Ark Encounter's creative team was revelatory, difficult, and frustrating in equal parts. I found adapting, improvising, making the most of the data you have, waiting, and persistence to be invaluable skills. As part of the fieldworker's craft, perfection eludes, but these skills are distinctly worth the labor of constant honing. The collaborative work with students on Materializing the Bible breathed new life into this project and thoroughly demonstrated how ethnography is enhanced by historical, comparative data. This appendix is intended to instill these reflections, offering methodological transparency for other scholars drawn to the promise of tracking processes of cultural production.

# NOTES

INTRODUCTION

1 Twain 1995 [1905]: 120.
2 Brown 2003: 111; see Cohn 1996 on the earliest representations.
3 Cohn 1996.
4 Brown 2003: 116.
5 Numbers 1992.
6 John Prine, "Sweet Revenge" (1973); Pharoahe Monch (featuring Talib Kweli), "D.R.E.A.M." (2014).
7 Montgomery 2012; Finkel 2014.
8 Eskridge 1999.
9 Christina Ng, "Baywatch Alum Determined to Continue Search for Noah's Ark," *ABC News*, www.abcnews.go.com (accessed April 4, 2017).
10 Numbers 1992.
11 Trollinger and Trollinger 2016.
12 Numbers 1992; Eve and Harrold 1991: 21.
13 Larson 1997; cf. Harding 1991.
14 "News Release: Ark Encounter," Answers in Genesis, www.answersingenesis.org (accessed April 4, 2017).
15 Numbers 1992; Toumey 1994; Watkins 2014; Carneiro 2016.
16 Scott 1997.
17 Ammerman 1987; Harding 2000.
18 Crapanzano 2000; Malley 2004; Bielo 2009.
19 Toumey 1994; Butler 2010.
20 Coleman 2015.
21 Morgan 2012: 147.
22 It is important to note that the creationist movement is composed of transnational networks (Coleman and Carlin 2004).
23 Frank Newport, "In U.S., 46% Hold Creationist View of Human Origins," Gallup, www.gallup.com (accessed April 4, 2017).
24 Hill 2014.
25 Ibid.
26 Numbers 1992.
27 Eve and Harrold 1991: 26.
28 Gilbert 1997; Hendershot 2004: 145–175.
29 Eve and Harrold 1991: 28.

30 Gilbert 1997: 5, 7.

31 The Museum of Creation and Earth History is still in operation, having expanded under new ownership since the ICR's relocation to Dallas in 2007.

32 Interview with the author, August 31, 2011.

33 "History," Answers in Genesis, www.answersingenesis.org (accessed April 4, 2017).

34 "News Release: Ark Encounter," Answers in Genesis, www.answersingenesis.org (accessed April 4, 2017).

35 See chapter 5 for analysis of the Nye-Ham debate.

CHAPTER 1. THE POWER OF ENTERTAINMENT

1 View the trailer at "Noah," YouTube video, 1:00, posted by Ark Encounter, February 26, 2014, www.youtube.com/watch?v=gMUmuK42a3w&list=PLn_fa5Im3js_ytfMUcKKri3h_nX8hsvLl&index=49 (accessed: October 19, 2017).

2 Throughout the book, I use pseudonyms for all creative team members.

3 Author's transcription.

4 Morgan 2007: 160.

5 Hendershot 2004.

6 Moore 1994.

7 Ibid., 3.

8 Ibid., 10.

9 Ibid.; Blanton 2015; Lofton 2011.

10 Messenger 1999: 5, 26.

11 Ketchell 2007; cf. Bremer 2014.

12 Toumey 1994: 82; cf. Harding 2000.

13 Laycock 2015.

14 Hendershot 2004.

15 Stromberg 2009: 2–3.

16 Ibid., 3.

17 Bryman 1999.

18 Chidester 2005: 146.

19 Stromberg 2009: 8.

20 Hannigan 1998; Grazian 2008: 29–62.

21 Wallace 1996: 65.

22 Magelssen 2014.

23 Linenthal 1995: 88.

24 Ibid., 102, 116, 167, 171, 189.

25 This description is based on the author's visit in July 2015.

26 Publicity materials, Center for Civil and Human Rights, www.civilandhumanrights.org (accessed April 4, 2017).

27 Magelssen (2014) and Auslander (2014) address the political and ethical complexities of white bodies reenacting traumatic events in the African American experience.

28  Rutherford 2016.
29  Pellegrini 2007: 912.
30  Agnew 2007: 301.
31  Meyer 2015.
32  Droogers 2014.
33  Huizinga 1955.
34  Ibid., 13.
35  Bado-Fralick and Norris 2010: 1.
36  Ibid., 1, 7.
37  Ibid., 110.
38  Luhrmann 2012: 372.
39  Ibid.
40  Bado-Fralick and Norris 2010: 113; cf. Coleman and Elsner (2004) on the way play invites sincerity and irony among pilgrims to Walsingham, a Marian apparition shrine in England.
41  Casanova 1994.
42  For example, Dochuk 2011; Elisha 2011; Walton 2009; Weiner 2014.
43  Engelke 2013: xv.
44  Ibid., xiv.
45  Warner 2002.
46  Wagner 1990; Kunzman 2009; cf. *The Revisionaries* (2012), a documentary film about creationist challenges to public education in the state of Texas.
47  Warner 2002: 56.
48  Ibid., 118.
49  Hill 2014.
50  Bourdieu 1977.
51  Lincoln 1994: 8.

## CHAPTER 2. MATERIALIZING THE BIBLE

1  Morgan 2007: 164.
2  Ibid.
3  Bowen 1992.
4  Harding 2000.
5  Boyarin 1989.
6  Malley 2004; Bielo 2009; cf. Wimbush 2008.
7  Engelke 2010.
8  Morgan 2010.
9  Blanton 2015.
10  McDannell 1995.
11  Lindquist 2014.
12  Janes 2016.
13  Gundaker 2000.
14  Long 2003; Messenger 1999.

15 Shamir 2012; Beal 2005; Wharton 2006.

16 Bialecki 2012.

17 Conkin 1997: 1.

18 For a curated list of global sites, see the digital scholarship project Materializing the Bible, www.materializingthebible.com (accessed April 4, 2017).

19 Rowan 2004.

20 Wharton 2006.

21 Lukens-Bull and Fafard 2007.

22 Long 2003.

23 Stevenson 2013.

24 Beal 2005.

25 Patterson 2016.

26 Salvation Mountain is a staple feature in publications like Bishop, Oesterie, and Marinacci (2009).

27 This account is based on the author's visit in May 2015. Cf. Beal 2005: 102–116.

28 "The Biblical Garden," Paradise Valley United Methodist Church, www.pvumc. org (accessed April 4, 2017).

29 Blanton 2015.

30 "Biblical Gardens," Trinity Lutheran Church, www.trinitylutherancville.org (accessed April 20, 2017).

31 "Groups and Activities," Germantown Jewish Centre, www.germantownjewish centre.org (accessed April 4, 2017). I include Jewish gardens in this analysis to illustrate the comparative purchase of the argument presented. Devotionally and pedagogically, Christian and Jewish gardens promise nearly identical experiences. The primary difference is that Jewish gardens will often connect planting seasons with the Jewish calendar and align certain botanical varieties with ritual actions.

32 Rogers 2011: 32; cf. Kaell 2014: 32.

33 Rodef Shalom Biblical Botanical Garden, www.biblicalgardenpittsburgh.org (accessed April 4, 2017).

34 The following is based on the author's visit to the site in September 2014.

35 Dodwell 1993: 85.

36 "Badé Museum of Biblical Archaeology," Pacific School of Religion, www.psr.edu (accessed April 4, 2017).

37 Museum of the Bible, www.museumofthebible.org (accessed April 4, 2017).

38 Wharton 2006: 126–130.

39 Long 2003: 30.

40 Holy Land Waterbury, www.holylandwaterbury.com (accessed April 4, 2017).

41 The following is based on the author's visit to the site in March 2014.

42 Feldman 2007.

43 Beal 2005; Patterson 2016.

44 Kaell 2014: 32–33.

45 Peirce 1934; cf. Keane 2003.

46 Keane 2003: 415.

47 "Biblical Tabernacle Reproduction," Mennonite Information Center, www.men noniteinfoctr.org (accessed April 4, 2017).

48 "The Journey through the Tabernacle," Tabernacle Experience, www.tabernacle experience.com (accessed April 4, 2017).

49 Palestine Gardens, www.palestinegardens.org (accessed April 4, 2017).

50 Messenger 1999.

51 Ibid., 106.

52 Ibid., 111–112.

53 "About the Blue Army Shrine," World Apostolate of Fatima, USA, www.wafusa .org (accessed April 4, 2017).

54 Kaell 2014.

55 The Coming King Foundation, "The Coming King Sculpture Prayer Gardens," www.thecomingkingfoundation.org (accessed April 4, 2017).

56 Beal 2005: 45–46.

57 Patterson 2016; cf. Coleman 2004.

58 "History," Noank Baptist Church, www.noankbaptistchurch.org (accessed April 4, 2017).

59 Gundaker 2015: 126.

60 Keane 2003.

61 King 1941: xi–xii.

62 Ron and Timothy 2013: 242.

63 Gaden 1976.

64 Morgan 2012: 36.

65 Ron and Feldman 2009: 208; Kaell 2014: 33.

66 Keane 2003: 419.

67 See Bielo 2009 on textual ideology; Ron and Feldman 2009 on the Protestant gaze.

68 Beal 2010.

69 Malley 2004.

70 Wolf 2012: 267.

CHAPTER 3. CULTURAL PRODUCERS

1 Laura Entis, "The Open-Office Concept Is Dead," *Fortune*, www.fortune.com (accessed April 5, 2017).

2 Lofton 2014: 149.

3 Mahon 2000.

4 For example, Powdermaker 1950; Dornfield 1998; Condry 2013; Shankar 2015.

5 Nader 1969: 284.

6 Pype 2012: 14; cf. Meyer 2015.

7 Bakhtin 1981.

8 "Statement of Faith," Answers in Genesis, www.answersingenesis.org (accessed April 5, 2017).

9 See Gonzalez (2014) on how evangelical video games foster a different immersive experience.

10 N. D. Wilson, "Our Love-Hate Relationship with Christian Art," *Christianity Today*, www.christianitytoday.com (accessed April 5, 2017).

11 Harding 2000.

12 Bado-Fralick and Norris 2010: 69.

13 An example of this critique can be read in this blog post: Ken Ham, "'Bathtub Arks' Are Dangerous," Answers in Genesis, www.answersingenesis.org (accessed April 5, 2017). Cf. Butler 2010 on how the Creation Museum mobilizes conspiracy discourse in its teaching exhibits.

14 Appleby 2011.

15 Kunda 2006.

16 Robbins 2012.

17 None of these ideas had materialized in Ark Encounter's first six months of operation. Still, note that the strategy of distributing a card to visitors borrows from other successful museum experiences—such as the U.S. Holocaust Memorial Museum in Washington, DC (Linenthal 1995).

18 Answers in Genesis has actually argued against Giglio's theologizing of laminin. One of AiG's "research scientists," Dr. Georgia Purdom, who holds a PhD in molecular genetics from Ohio State University, posted a sympathetic critique on the AiG website: "The main problem with this type of argument is that it appears that something outside of Scripture (in this case, laminin) is vital to know the truthfulness of a biblical truth. . . . What we observe in the world can certainly be used to confirm God's Word (and it does), but our finite observations are not in a position to evaluate the infinite things of God." Georgia Purdom, "Laminin and the Cross," Answers in Genesis, www.answersingenesis.org (accessed April 5, 2017).

19 Smith 1998: 89.

20 Tannen 1989.

21 The Defenders Study Bible is an edition of the Bible with creationist commentary written by Henry Morris, co-author of *The Genesis Flood* (1961) and founder of the Institute for Creation Research.

CHAPTER 4. CONVERSION AS PLAY

1 All quotations in this section come from a field note recording of an interview with Roger on June 30, 2014.

2 These four audiences are composites based on my fieldwork with the team. At no point did I observe the team explicitly outlining these particular audiences.

3 Stromberg 2009.

4 Eskridge 1999: 256.

5 Robbins 2004; Gross 2012; Meyer 2015.

6 Pellegrini 2007.

7 Jones 2012.

8 Wolf 2012.

9 Ibid., 17.

10 Ibid., 155.
11 Saler 2012: 67.
12 Genesis 6:13 (NIV).
13 I have shown Figure 4.2 in multiple professional conference and classroom presentations, and audiences have instantly made the association with maps of Middle Earth.
14 Wilensky-Lanford 2011.
15 Pellegrini 2007: 924.
16 For example, see A. A. Gill, "Roll Over, Charles Darwin!," *Vanity Fair*, www.vanityfair.com (accessed April 5, 2017).
17 Numbers 1992.
18 See chapter 6 for an extended discussion of how the historical conditions of taste judgment contextualize the production and consumption of Ark Encounter.
19 Individual team members are named in the credits for their contributions, so they did remain involved as consultants for the production of "The Noah Interview."
20 Meyer 2015.
21 Agnew 2007; Magelssen 2014.
22 Stromberg 2009.
23 Turner 1974.
24 Feldman 2007; Kaell 2014.
25 Coleman and Elsner 2004: 281.
26 Bado-Fralick and Norris 2010.
27 Ibid., 113.
28 Luhrmann 2012.
29 Ibid., 372.
30 Ibid.
31 Harding 2000; Luhrmann 2004.

CHAPTER 5. THE PAST IS NOT HISTORY
1 Harding 2000: 232.
2 I attended the debate with Dr. Steve Watkins, whose dissertation (2014) explores the museum's language and politics.
3 "Two Kinds of Science?," Answers in Genesis, www.answersingenesis.org (accessed April 5, 2017).
4 Author's transcription. View the full debate at "Bill Nye Debates Ken Ham," YouTube video, 2:45:32, posted by Answers in Genesis, February 4, 2014, www.youtube.com/watch?v=z6kgvhG3AkI (accessed April 5, 2017).
5 Williams 1956 [1925].
6 Hirsch and Stewart 2005: 262.
7 Wallace 1996: 24.
8 Handler and Gable 1997: 224.
9 Coleman and Carlin 2004: 6.
10 Asma 2011: 162.

11 Samuel 1994: 8.
12 "What Is a Dragon?", Answers in Genesis, www.creationmuseum.org (accessed April 5, 2017).
13 Job 40:15–18 (NIV).
14 Job 41:18–21 (NIV).
15 Asma 2011: 142.
16 Numbers and Willey 2015.
17 Butler 2010: 236.
18 Dodwell 1993: 85.
19 Hirsch and Stewart 2005: 262.
20 Ibid., 266.
21 Author's transcription.
22 Author's transcription. For the full video, see "Bill Nye: Creationism Is Not Appropriate for Children," YouTube video, 2:31, posted by Big Think, August 23, 2012, www.youtube.com/watch?v=gHbYJfwFgOU (accessed April 5, 2017).
23 Author's transcription.
24 Author's transcription. For video of the Gish-Doolittle debate, see "Gish-Doolittle Debate, Part 1," YouTube video, 30:11, posted by Paul Humber, January 19, 2014, www.youtube.com/watch?v=aOfenEX_808 (accessed April 5, 2017).
25 Bourdieu 1991: 246.
26 Bourdieu 1977: 159.
27 Ibid., 169.
28 Ross 1997: 38.
29 Wallace 1996: x.
30 Agnew 2007.
31 Stromberg 2009: 8.
32 Handler and Gable 1997; Asma 2001.

## CHAPTER 6. A WALKING POETICS OF FAITH

1 Morgan 2012: 69.
2 Ibid., 69–70.
3 Harding 2000: 88.
4 It is worth noting that evolution museums make a similar appeal. Stephen Asma writes in his history of science and natural history museums: "You must oscillate between knowing that it's a man-made construction and suspending your disbelief to enter into a play-along relationship with the display" (2001: 38).
5 Harding 2000: 231–234.
6 Robbins 2012: 46; Butler 2010.
7 Butler 2010: 237.
8 For further rhetorical analysis of the Creation Museum's Lucy, see Carneiro (2016).
9 Bryan 1924: 124.
10 Morgan 2012: xvii.

11  Trollinger and Trollinger 2016: 41, 119.

12  Morgan 2012; Blanton 2015.

13  Oppenheimer 1968: 206; cf. Trollinger and Trollinger 2016: 25; Barry 1998.

14  This section is based on the author's visit to the Holy Land Experience in March 2014. An earlier version was published as part of Anderson Blanton's digital scholarship project, *The Materiality of Prayer*, in May 2014. This strategy of materializing prayer through writing can also be found at other attractions, including Fields of the Wood Bible Park in Murphy, North Carolina, and the Coming King Sculpture Prayer Gardens in Kerrville, Texas.

15  Kaell 2014; Feldman 2007.

16  Coleman and Elsner 2004: 283.

17  Phelps (2016) is published open access online: www.ncse.com (accessed April 5, 2017).

18  McDannell 1995.

19  Ibid., 163, 167.

20  Harding 2000: 62.

21  Smout 1995.

22  Ibid., 60.

## CONCLUSION

1  This description is based on publicity materials from the Institute for Creation Research: "ICR Discovery Center for Science and Earth History," www.icr.org (accessed April 5, 2017).

2  This description is based on publicity materials from the proposed museum: "About Us," Northwest Science Museum, www.northwestsciencemuseum.com (accessed April 5, 2017).

3  This description is based on news stories about the proposed park from the United States, Canada, and China.

4  This description is based on publicity materials from Genesis Land: "The Idea," www.genesis-land.ch (accessed April 5, 2017).

5  Of course, materializing scripture is not an exclusively Christian phenomenon. As is evident from chapter 2, Jewish communities foster a parallel tradition. In addition, Muslim and Hindu communities have extensive traditions of materializing scripture (e.g., McDermott 2011).

6  Davis 1996: 399.

7  Ibid., 401–402.

8  Ibid., 407.

9  Young 2002: 4.

10  Lowenthal 2002: 15.

11  Davis 1996: 403.

12  Harding 1991.

13  Ibid., 377.

14  Ibid., 391.

15  Harding 2000.
16  Harding 1991: 374.
17  Stromberg 2009: 8.
18  Asma 2001: 15.
19  Gould 1993.

APPENDIX: THE ARK AND THE ANTHROPOLOGIST

1  Toumey 1994.
2  Engelke 2013: 108.
3  Shankar 2015.
4  Nader 1969: 306.
5  Condry 2013: 7.
6  Chung 2009: 65.
7  Sjorlsev 2013.
8  Smith 1998.
9  I owe a special thanks to colleagues who discussed this methodological fork in the road with me: Eric Hoenes del Pinal, Rebekka King, Tim Langille, Brian Howell, and Jennifer Hammer.

# BIBLIOGRAPHY

Agnew, Vanessa. 2007. "History's Affective Turn: Historical Reenactment and Its Work in the Present." *Rethinking History* 11 (3): 299–312.

Ammerman, Nancy. 1987. *Bible Believers: Fundamentalists in the Modern World*. New Brunswick, NJ: Rutgers University Press.

Appleby, R. Scott. 2011. "Rethinking Fundamentalism in a Secular Age." In *Rethinking Secularism*, edited by Craig Calhoun, Mark Juergensmeyer, and Jonathan VanAntwerpen, 225–247. Oxford: Oxford University Press.

Asma, Stephen T. 2001. *Stuffed Animals and Pickled Heads: The Culture and Evolution of Natural History Museums*. New York: Oxford University Press.

———. 2011. "Risen Apes and Fallen Angels: The New Museology of Human Origins." *Curator* 54 (2): 141–163.

Auslander, Mark. 2014. " 'Give Me Back My Children!': Traumatic Reenactment and Tenuous Democratic Public Spheres." *North American Dialogue* 17 (1): 1–12.

Bado-Fralick, Nikki, and Rebecca Sachs Norris. 2010. *Toying with God: The World of Religious Games and Dolls*. Waco, TX: Baylor University Press.

Bakhtin, M. M. 1981. *The Dialogic Imagination*. Translated by C. Emerson and M. Holquist. Austin: University of Texas Press.

Barry, Andrew. 1998. "On Interactivity: Consumers, Citizens, and Culture." In *The Politics of Display: Museums, Science, Culture*, edited by Sharon Macdonald, 85–102. New York: Routledge.

Beal, Timothy K. 2005. *Roadside Religion: In Search of the Sacred, the Strange, and the Substance of Faith*. Boston: Beacon Press.

———. 2010. *The Rise and Fall of the Bible: The Unexpected History of an Accidental Book*. New York: Harcourt Brace.

Bialecki, Jon. 2012. "Virtual Christianity in an Age of Nominalist Anthropology." *Anthropological Theory* 12 (3): 295–319.

Bielo, James S. 2009. *Words upon the Word: An Ethnography of Evangelical Group Bible Study*. New York: NYU Press.

Bishop, Greg, Joe Oesterie, and Mike Marinacci 2009. *Weird California: Your Travel Guide to California's Local Legends and Best Kept Secrets*. New York: Sterling.

Blanton, Anderson. 2015. *Hittin' the Prayer Bones: Materiality of Spirit in the Pentecostal South*. Chapel Hill: University of North Carolina Press.

Bourdieu, Pierre. 1977. *Outline of a Theory of Practice*. Cambridge: Cambridge University Press.

———. 1991. *Language and Symbolic Power*. Cambridge, MA: Harvard University Press.

Bowen, John. 1992. "Elaborating Scriptures: Cain and Abel in Gayo Society." *Man* 27 (3): 495–516.

Boyarin, Jonathan. 1989. "Voices around the Text: The Ethnography of Reading at Mesivta Tifereth Jerusalem." *Cultural Anthropology* 4 (4): 399–421.

Bremer, Thomas S. 2014. "A Touristic Angle of Vision: Tourist Studies as a Methodological Approach for the Study of Religions." *Religion Compass* 8 (12): 371–379.

Brown, Janet. 2003. "Noah's Flood, the Ark, and the Shaping of Early Modern Natural History." In *When Science and Christianity Meet*, edited by David C. Lindberg and Ronald L. Numbers, 111–138. Chicago: University of Chicago Press.

Bryan, William Jennings. 1924. *Seven Questions in Dispute*. New York: Fleming H. Revell.

Bryman, Alan. 1999. "The Disneyization of Society." *Sociological Review* 47 (1): 25–47.

Butler, Ella. 2010. "God Is in the Data: Epistemologies of Knowledge at the Creation Museum." *Ethnos* 75 (3): 229–251.

Carneiro, Larissa Soares. 2016. "Divine Technology: How God Created Dinosaurs and People." PhD diss., North Carolina State University.

Casanova, Jose. 1994. *Public Religions in the Modern World*. Chicago: University of Chicago Press.

Chidester, David. 2005. *Authentic Fakes: Religion and American Popular Culture*. Berkeley: University of California Press.

Chung, Jae A. 2009. "Ethnographic Remnants: Range and Limits of the Social Method." In *Fieldwork Is Not What It Used to Be: Learning Anthropology's Method in a Time of Transition*, edited by James D. Faubion and George E. Marcus, 52–72. Ithaca, NY: Cornell University Press.

Cohn, Norman. 1996. *Noah's Flood: The Genesis Story in Western Thought*. New Haven, CT: Yale University Press.

Coleman, Simon. 2004. "From England's Nazareth to Sweden's Jerusalem: Movement, (Virtual) Landscapes, and Pilgrimage." In *Reframing Pilgrimage: Cultures in Motion*, edited by Simon Coleman and John Eade, 45–68. London: Routledge.

———. 2015. "The Social Life of Concepts: Public and Private 'Knowledge' of Scientific Creationism." In *Religion and Science as Forms of Life: Anthropological Insights into Reason and Unreason*, edited by Carles Salazar and Joan Bestard, 104–119. New York: Berghahn.

Coleman, Simon, and Leslie Carlin. 2004. "The Cultures of Creationism: Shifting Boundaries of Belief, Knowledge, and Nationhood." In *The Cultures of Creationism: Anti-evolutionism in English-Speaking Countries*, edited by Simon Coleman and Leslie Carlin, 1–28. London: Ashgate.

Coleman, Simon, and John Elsner. 2004. "Tradition as Play: Pilgrimage to 'England's Nazareth.'" *History and Anthropology* 15 (3): 273–288.

Condry, Ian. 2013. *The Soul of Anime: Collaborative Creativity and Japan's Media Success Story*. Durham, NC: Duke University Press.

Conkin, Paul. 1997. *American Originals: Homemade Varieties of Christianity*. Chapel Hill: University of North Carolina Press.

Crapanzano, Vincent. 2000. *Serving the Word: Literalism in America from the Pulpit to the Bench*. New York: New Press.

Davis, Susan G. 1996. "The Theme Park: Global Industry and Cultural Form." *Media, Culture, and Society* 18 (3): 399–422.

Dochuk, Darren. 2011. *From Bible Belt to Sunbelt: Plain-Folk Religion, Grassroots Politics, and the Rise of Evangelical Conservatism*. New York: Norton.

Dodwell, Charles R. 1993. *Pictorial Arts of the West, 800–1200*. New Haven, CT: Yale University Press.

Dornfield, Barry. 1998. *Producing Public Television, Producing Public Culture*. Princeton, NJ: Princeton University Press.

Droogers, Andre. 2014. *Religion at Play: A Manifesto*. Eugene, OR: Cascade.

Elisha, Omri. 2011. *Moral Ambition: Mobilization and Social Outreach in Evangelical Megachurches*. Berkeley: University of California Press.

Engelke, Matthew. 2010. "Religion and the Media Turn: A Review Essay." *American Ethnologist* 37 (2): 371–379.

———. 2013. *God's Agents: Biblical Publicity in Contemporary England*. Berkeley: University of California Press.

Eskridge, Larry. 1999. "A Sign for an Unbelieving Age: Evangelicals and the Search for Noah's Ark." In *Evangelicals and Science in Historical Perspective*, edited by David N. Livingstone, D. G. Hart, and Mark A. Noll, 244–263. Oxford: Oxford University Press.

Eve, Raymond A., and Francis B. Harrold. 1991. *The Creationist Movement in Modern America*. Boston: G. K. Hall.

Feldman, Jackie. 2007. "Constructing a Shared Bible Land: Jewish Israeli Guiding Performances for Protestant Pilgrims." *American Ethnologist* 34 (2): 351–374.

Finkel, Irving. 2014. *The Ark before Noah: Decoding the Story of the Flood*. New York: Anchor Books.

Gaden, Eileen. 1976. *Biblical Garden Cookery*. Chappaqua, NY: Christian Herald Books.

Gilbert, James. 1997. *Redeeming Culture: American Religion in an Age of Science*. Chicago: University of Chicago Press.

Gonzalez, Vincent. 2014. "Born-Again Digital: Exploring Evangelical Video Game Worlds." PhD diss., University of North Carolina at Chapel Hill.

Gould, Stephen Jay. 1993. "Dinomania." *New York Review of Books, August 12*, 51–56.

Grazian, David. 2008. *On the Make: The Hustle of Urban Nightlife*. Chicago: University of Chicago Press.

Gross, Toomas. 2012. "Changing Faith: The Social Costs of Protestant Conversion in Rural Oaxaca." *Ethnos* 77 (3): 344–371.

Gundaker, Grey. 2000. "The Bible *as* and *at* a Threshold: Reading, Performance, and Blessed Space." In *African Americans and the Bible: Sacred Texts and Social Textures*, edited by Vincent L. Wimbush, 754–772. New York: Continuum.

———. 2015. "Cast Out of the Garden: Edenic Scripturalization, Flowers, and Fallen Africa." In *Scripturalizing the Human: The Written as the Political*, edited by Vincent L. Wimbush, 121–149. New York: Routledge.

Handler, Richard, and Eric Gable. 1997. *The New History in an Old Museum: Creating the Past at Colonial Williamsburg*. Durham, NC: Duke University Press.

Hannigan, John. 1998. *Fantasy City: Pleasure and Profit in the Postmodern Metropolis*. London: Routledge.

Harding, Susan. 1991. "Representing Fundamentalism: The Problem of the Repugnant Cultural Other." *Social Research* 58 (2): 373–393.

———. 2000. *The Book of Jerry Falwell: Fundamentalist Language and Politics*. Princeton, NJ: Princeton University Press.

Hendershot, Heather. 2004. *Shaking the World for Jesus: Media and Conservative Evangelical Culture*. Chicago: University of Chicago Press.

Hill, Jonathan P. 2014. "National Study of Religion and Human Origins." BioLogos.

Hirsch, Eric, and Charles Stewart. 2005. "Introduction: Ethnographies of Historicity." *History and Anthropology* 16 (3): 261–274.

Huizinga, Johan. 1955. *Homo Ludens: A Study of the Play Element in Culture*. Boston: Beacon Press.

Janes, Dominic. 2016. "The Wordless Book: The Visual and Material Culture of Evangelism in Victorian Britain." *Material Religion* 12 (1): 26–49.

Jones, Graham. 2012. "Magic with a Message: The Poetics of Christian Conjuring." *Cultural Anthropology* 27 (2): 193–214.

Kaell, Hillary. 2014. *Walking Where Jesus Walked: American Christians and Holy Land Pilgrimage*. New York: NYU Press.

Keane, Webb. 2003. "Semiotics and the Social Analysis of Material Things." *Language and Communication* 23 (2–3): 409–425.

Ketchell, Aaron. 2007. *Holy Hills of the Ozarks: Religion and Tourism in Branson, Missouri*. Baltimore: Johns Hopkins University Press.

King, Eleanor Anthony. 1941. *Bible Plants for American Gardens*. New York: Dover.

Kunda, Gideon. 2006. *Engineering Culture: Control and Commitment in a High-Tech Corporation*. Philadelphia: Temple University Press.

Kunzman, Robert. 2009. *Write These Laws on Your Children: Inside the World of Conservative Christian Homeschooling*. Boston: Beacon Press.

Larson, Edward J. 1997. *Summer for the Gods: The Scopes Trial and America's Continuing Debate over Science and Religion*. New York: Basic Books.

Laycock, Joseph P. 2015. *Dangerous Games: What the Moral Panic over Role-Playing Games Says about Play, Religion, and Imagined Worlds*. Berkeley: University of California Press.

Lincoln, Bruce. 1994. *Authority: Construction and Corrosion*. Chicago: University of Chicago Press.

Lindquist, Benjamin. 2014. "Mutable Materiality: Illustrations in Kenneth Taylor's Children's Bibles." *Material Religion* 10 (3): 316–345.

Linenthal, Edward. 1995. *Preserving Memory: The Struggle to Create America's Holocaust Museum*. New York: Columbia University Press.

Lofton, Kathryn. 2011. *Oprah: The Gospel of an Icon*. Berkeley: University of California Press.

———. 2014. "The Spirit in the Cubicle: A Religious History of the American Office." In *Sensational Religion: Sensory Cultures in Material Practice*, edited by Sally M. Promey, 135–158. New Haven, CT: Yale University Press.

Long, Burke O. 2003. *Imagining the Holy Land: Maps, Models, and Fantasy Travels*. Bloomington: Indiana University Press.

Lowenthal, David. 2002. "The Past as a Theme Park." In *Theme Park Landscapes: Antecedents and Variations*, edited by Terence G. Young and Robert B. Riley, 11–23. Washington, DC: Dumbarton Oaks.

Loxton, Daniel, and Donald R. Prothero. 2013. *Abominable Science: Origins of the Yeti, Nessie, and Other Famous Cryptids*. New York: Columbia University Press.

Luhrmann, Tanya. 2004. "Metakinesis: How God Becomes Intimate in Contemporary U.S. Christianity." *American Anthropologist* 106 (3): 518–528.

———. 2012. "A Hyper-real God and Modern Belief: Toward an Anthropological Theory of Mind." *Current Anthropology* 53 (4): 371–395.

Lukens-Bull, Ronald, and Mark Fafard. 2007. "Next Year in Orlando: (Re)creating Israel in Christian Zionism." *Journal of Religion and Society* 9:1–20.

Magelssen, Scott. 2014. *Simming: Participatory Performance and the Making of Meaning*. Ann Arbor: University of Michigan Press.

Mahon, Maureen. 2000. "The Visible Evidence of Cultural Producers." *Annual Review of Anthropology* 29:467–492.

Malley, Brian. 2004. *How the Bible Works: An Anthropological Study of Evangelical Biblicism*. Walnut Creek, CA: AltaMira Press.

McDannell, Colleen. 1995. *Material Christianity: Religion and Popular Culture in America*. New Haven, CT: Yale University Press.

McDermott, Rachel F. 2011. *Revelry, Rivalry, and Longing for the Goddesses of Bengal: The Fortunes of Hindu Festivals*. New York: Columbia University Press.

Messenger, Troy. 1999. *Holy Leisure: Recreation and Religion in God's Square Mile*. Philadelphia: Temple University Press.

Meyer, Birgit. 2015. *Sensational Movies: Video, Vision, and Christianity in Ghana*. Berkeley: University of California Press.

Montgomery, David R. 2012. *The Rocks Don't Lie: A Geologist Investigates Noah's Flood*. New York: Norton.

Moore, R. Laurence. 1994. *Selling God: American Religion in the Marketplace of Culture*. Oxford: Oxford University Press.

Morgan, David. 2007. *The Lure of Images: A History of Religion and Visual Media in America*. New York: Routledge.

———, ed. 2010. *Religion and Material Culture: The Matter of Belief*. New York: Routledge.

———. 2012. *The Embodied Eye: Religious Visual Culture and the Social Life of Feeling*. Berkeley: University of California Press.

Nader, Laura. 1969. "Up the Anthropologist—Perspectives Gained from Studying Up." In *Reinventing Anthropology*, edited by Dell Hymes, 284–311. New York: Vintage.

Numbers, Ronald. 1992. *The Creationists: The Evolution of Scientific Creationism*. Berkeley: University of California Press.

Numbers, Ronald L., and T. Joe Willey. 2015. "Baptizing Dinosaurs: How Once-Suspect Evidence of Evolution Came to Support the Biblical Narrative." *Spectrum* 43 (1): 57–68.

Oppenheimer, Frank. 1968. "Rationale for a Science Museum." *Curator: The Museum Journal* 1 (3): 206–209.

Patterson, Sara M. 2016. *Middle of Nowhere: Religion, Art, and Pop Culture at Salvation Mountain*. Albuquerque: University of New Mexico Press.

Peirce, Charles S. 1934. *Collected Papers of Charles Sanders Peirce*. Vol. 5. Edited by Charles Hartshorne and Paul Weiss. Cambridge, MA: Harvard University Press.

Pellegrini, Ann. 2007. " 'Signaling through the Flames': Hell House Performance and Structures of Religious Feeling." *American Quarterly* 59 (3): 911–935.

Phelps, Dan. 2016. "Kentucky Gets an Ark-Shaped Second Creation 'Museum.' " Oakland, CA: National Center for Science Education.

Powdermaker, Hortense. 1950. *Hollywood: The Dream Factory*. New York: Little, Brown.

Pype, Katrien. 2012. *The Making of the Pentecostal Melodrama: Religion, Media, and Gender in Kinshasha*. New York: Berghahn.

*The Revisionaries*. 2012. Directed by Scott Thurman. New York: Silver Lining Film Group. DVD.

Robbins, Joel. 2004. *Becoming Sinners: Christianity and Moral Torment in a Papua New Guinea Society*. Berkeley: University of California Press.

———. 2012. "On Enchanting Science and Disenchanting Nature: Spiritual Warfare in North America and Papua New Guinea." In *Nature, Science, and Religion: Intersections Shaping Society and the Environment*, edited by Catherine M. Tucker, 45–64. Santa Fe, NM: School for Advanced Research Press.

Rogers, Stephanie Stidham. 2011. *Inventing the Holy Land: American Protestant Pilgrimage to Palestine, 1865–1941*. Lanham, MD: Lexington Books.

Ron, Amos S., and Jackie Feldman. 2009. "From Spots to Themed Sites—the Evolution of the Protestant Holy Land." *Journal of Heritage Tourism* 4 (3): 201–216.

Ron, Amos S., and Dallen J. Timothy. 2013. "The Land of Milk and Honey: Biblical Foods, Heritage, and Holy Land Tourism." *Journal of Heritage Tourism* 8 (2–3): 234–247.

Ross, Andrew. 1997. *The Celebration Chronicles*. New York: Ballantine.

Rowan, Y. 2004. "Repacking the Pilgrimage: Visiting the Holy Land in Orlando." In *Marketing Heritage: Archaeology and the Consumption of the Past*, edited by Y. Rowan and U. Baram, 249–266. Walnut Creek, CA: AltaMira Press.

Rutherford, Danilyn. 2016. "Affect Theory." *Annual Review of Anthropology* 45:285–300.

Saler, Michael. 2012. *As If: Modern Enchantment and the Literary Prehistory of Virtual Reality*. Oxford: Oxford University Press.

Samuel, Raphael. 1994. *Theatres of Memory*. Vol. 1, *Past and Present in Contemporary Culture*. New York: Verso.

Scott, Eugenie C. 1997. "Antievolution and Creationism in the United States." *Annual Review of Anthropology* 26:263–289.

Shamir, Milette. 2012. "Back to the Future: The Jerusalem Exhibit at the 1904 St. Louis World's Fair." *Journal of Levantine Studies* 2 (1): 93–113.

Shankar, Shalini. 2015. *Advertising Diversity: Ad Agencies and the Creation of Asian American Consumers*. Durham, NC: Duke University Press.

Sjorlsev, Inger. 2013. "Boredom, Rhythm, and the Temporality of Ritual: Recurring Fieldwork in the Brazilian Candomble." *Social Analysis* 57 (1): 95–109.

Smith, Christian. 1998. *American Evangelicalism: Embattled and Thriving*. Chicago: University of Chicago Press.

Smout, Kary D. 1995. "Attacking (Southern) Creationists." In *Religion in the Contemporary South*, edited by O. Kendall White Jr. and Daryl White, 59–66. Athens: University of Georgia Press.

Stevenson, Jill. 2013. *Sensational Devotion: Evangelical Performance in 21$^{st}$ Century America*. Ann Arbor: University of Michigan Press.

Stromberg, Peter. 2009. *Caught in Play: How Entertainment Works on You*. Stanford, CA: Stanford University Press.

Tannen, Deborah. 1989. *Talking Voices: Repetition, Dialogue, and Imagery in Conversational Discourse*. Cambridge: Cambridge University Press.

Toumey, Christopher. 1994. *God's Own Scientists: Creationists in a Secular World*. New Brunswick, NJ: Rutgers University Press.

Trollinger, Susan L., and William V. Trollinger Jr. 2016. *Righting America at the Creation Museum*. Baltimore: Johns Hopkins University Press.

Turner, Victor. 1974. "Liminal to Liminoid." In *Play, Flow, and Ritual: An Essay in Comparative Symbology*. Rice Institute Pamphlet, Rice University Studies 60 (3): 53–92.

Twain, Mark. 1995 [1905]. "Adam's Soliloquy." In *The Bible according to Mark Twain*, edited by Howard G. Baetzhold and Joseph B. McCullough, 117–125. New York: Touchstone.

Wagner, Melinda Bollar. 1990. *God's Schools: Choice and Compromise in American Society*. New Brunswick, NJ: Rutgers University Press.

Wallace, Mike. 1996. *Mickey Mouse History and Other Essays on American Memory*. Philadelphia: Temple University Press.

Walton, Jonathan L. 2009. *Watch This! The Ethics and Aesthetics of Black Televangelism*. New York: NYU Press.

Warner, Michael. 2002. *Publics and Counterpublics*. New York: Zone Books.

Watkins, Steve. 2014. "An Analysis of the Creation Museum: Hermeneutics, Language, and Information Theory." PhD diss., University of Louisville.

Weiner, Isaac. 2014. *Religion Out Loud: Religious Sound, Public Space, and American Pluralism*. New York: NYU Press.

Wharton, Annabel Jane. 2006. *Selling Jerusalem: Relics, Replicas, Theme Parks*. Chicago: University of Chicago Press.

Whitcomb, John C., and Henry M. Morris. 1961. *The Genesis Flood: The Biblical Record and Its Scientific Implications*. Phillipsburg, NJ: Presbyterian and Reformed Publishing.

Wilensky-Lanford, Brook. 2011. *Paradise Lust: Searching for the Garden of Eden*. New York: Grove Press.

Williams, William Carlos. 1956 [1925]. *In the American Grain*. New York: New Directions.

Wimbush, Vincent. 2008. "Introduction: TEXTureS, Gestures, Power: Orientations to Radical Excavation." In *Theorizing Scriptures: New Critical Orientations to a Cultural Phenomenon*, edited by Vincent Wimbush, 1–22. New Brunswick, NJ: Rutgers University Press.

Wolf, Mark J. P. 2012. *Building Imaginary Worlds: The Theory and History of Subcreation*. London: Routledge.

Young, Terence. 2002. "Grounding the Myth: Theme Park Landscapes in an Era of Commerce and Nationalism." In *Theme Park Landscapes: Antecedents and Variations*, edited by Terence G. Young and Robert B. Riley, 1–10. Washington, DC: Dumbarton Oaks.

# INDEX

U.S. Supreme Court, 8
Ussher, James, 7

Virtuality, 36

Walsingham shrine, 107–108, 166,
  203n40
Warner, Michael, 28
Whitcomb, John, 8

White, Ellen, 7
Whitefield, George, 21
Wilderness Tabernacle replicas, 45–46,
  50–51, 174
Williams, William Carlos, 114
Winfrey, Oprah, 21
Witnessing, 20, 89, 169, 197
Wolf, Mark J. P., 58, 98
Wyatt Archaeological Museum, 2, 3

## ABOUT THE AUTHOR

James S. Bielo is Assistant Professor in the Department of Anthropology at Miami University in Oxford, Ohio.